A COMPANY'S RIGH·
NON-PECUN......

Applying appropriate legal rules to companies with as much consistency and as little consternation as possible remains a challenge for legal systems. One area causing concern is the availability of damages for non-pecuniary loss to companies, a disquiet that is rooted in the very nature of such damages and of companies themselves. In this book Vanessa Wilcox presents a detailed examination of the extent to which damages for non-pecuniary loss can properly be awarded to companies. The book focusses on the jurisprudence of the European Court of Human Rights and English law, with a chapter also dedicated to comparative treatment. While the law must be adaptable, considerations of coherency, certainty and ultimately justice dictate that the resulting rules should conform to certain core legal principles. This book lays the foundation for further comparative research into this topic and will be of interest to both the tort law and broader legal community.

VANESSA WILCOX is a senior legal researcher at the Austrian Academy of Sciences' Institute for European Tort Law, Vienna (ETL, Vienna). She is also a Fellow of the European Centre of Tort and Insurance Law (ECTIL, Vienna) and an Honorary Professor at the Law School of Yantai University (China). Vanessa has lectured at a number of Universities in Austria and in Italy. She spent several months working for the European Court of Human Rights and conducting research on this study in 2009, for which she was awarded the Dr Maria Schaumayer-Stiftung Prize (in 2015) and the Austrian Bankers' Association Prize (in 2016).

A COMPANY'S RIGHT TO DAMAGES FOR NON-PECUNIARY LOSS

VANESSA WILCOX

CAMBRIDGE
UNIVERSITY PRESS

CAMBRIDGE
UNIVERSITY PRESS

University Printing House, Cambridge CB2 8BS, United Kingdom

One Liberty Plaza, 20th Floor, New York, NY 10006, USA

477 Williamstown Road, Port Melbourne, VIC 3207, Australia

314-321, 3rd Floor, Plot 3, Splendor Forum, Jasola District Centre, New Delhi - 110025, India

79 Anson Road, #06-04/06, Singapore 079906

Cambridge University Press is part of the University of Cambridge.

It furthers the University's mission by disseminating knowledge in the pursuit of education, learning and research at the highest international levels of excellence.

www.cambridge.org
Information on this title: www.cambridge.org/9781316504970

First published 2016
First paperback edition 2018

A catalogue record for this publication is available from the British Library

ISBN 978-1-107-13927-5 Hardback
ISBN 978-1-316-50497-0 Paperback

Cambridge University Press has no responsibility for the persistence or accuracy of URLs for external or third-party internet websites referred to in this publication, and does not guarantee that any content on such websites is, or will remain, accurate or appropriate.

To My Mother and Father

CONTENTS

PREFACE

The history of the law is a history of new and unexpected instances. To be effective, therefore, the law must evolve. As a living thing, a growing organism, it must be adaptable to the changing needs of time. Such adaptability, however, must be achieved by balancing sets of competing interests and, most importantly, the resulting principles must operate in a coherent and consistent manner. Failing this, the law exposes itself to scrutiny and possible ridicule. One such area that is causing disquiet is that on the availability of damages for non-pecuniary loss to business entities, in particular companies. This book seeks to present a detailed examination on the extent to which such damages can properly be awarded in favour of such persons. This research seems expedient in light of the current debates brought about by the expansion of the protection of corporate interests in new and diversified fields. It also seems expedient in light of reform campaigns and careful studies that question the historical applications of the law to these legal subjects. Regrettably, the amount of time at my disposal only permitted detailed coverage of two jurisdictions – the European Court of Human Rights and England. The study has been personally rewarding, and it is hoped that the value to its readers is somewhat proportional to the effort invested here. It is also hoped that this research will induce others to add to what has been a subject of great interest for me: a more comprehensive comparative study on this topic would encourage informed discourse in an area that would benefit from it. To that extent, this publication has been designed to capture the attention of a diverse European readership.

I am of course deeply indebted to someone recently described as the *God*father – not *Grand*father as was once put in jest – of tort law, Univ-Prof iR Dr DDr hc Helmut Koziol (em). His readiness to look through multiple drafts of this research, quite often during his few moments of leisure, and his stimulating guidance and encouragement are what every researcher dreams of but will very rarely experience. I would equally like to express my most grateful acknowledgement to Univ-Prof Dr iur Christiane

Wendehorst, LLM (Cantab), for her patience and constructive criticism and wish to also record my obligations to Prof Ken Oliphant, BA, BCL (Oxon), whose exactness prevented me from publishing this text with several errors. I incorporated his suggestions almost without exception. Last, but by no means least, it is to Univ-Prof Mag Dr Bernhard A Koch, LLM, that I owe profound thanks to for bringing me to Vienna and for suggesting the topic that forms the subject of this book.

I note the contribution of the ever-cheerful Donna Stockenhuber, MA for taking on the task of proofreading the manuscript. This has materially lightened my load.

Like many before me, I publish this book in the knowledge that I remain 'strictly' liable for any remaining errors. I hope, however, that those familiar with the intricacies of law will pardon me for them.

TABLE OF CASES

England

European Union

Germany

International Centre for Settlement of Investment Disputes

Italy

New Zealand

Russia

Scotland

South Africa

Switzerland

United States

TABLE OF LEGISLATION

England: Statutes

England: Bills and Secondary Legislation

Ireland

New Zealand

Poland

Portugal

Principles of European Tort Law (PETL)

PART I

Background

1

Introduction

I The Four Premises

1/1   This book explores the propriety of awarding damages for non-pecuniary loss to legal entities. It concludes that: (a) damages for non-pecuniary loss should be available only for interference in the bodily, mental or emotional spheres on the one hand and/or interference with the personality sphere on the other; (b) a corporation, not being a physical person, cannot suffer interferences in the bodily, mental or emotional spheres; (c) notwithstanding the foregoing, a principle of 'equality' demands that, since a company can be directly liable for the acts of its organs, it should in principle also be entitled to sue for damages for *some* non-pecuniary harm experienced by them; (d) a company has a 'personality' which is not merely an interest of a proprietary character (e.g. the property a company has in its 'goodwill') and should therefore be entitled to damages for non-pecuniary loss for interference with the non-proprietary aspects of its personality.

II The Propriety of Awarding Damages for Non-Pecuniary Loss to Corporations

1/2   As Spelling observed in his work on Corporations, the great and ever-increasing number of companies assuming the functions of individuals has created a tendency for the law to assimilate the rights of companies to the rights of natural persons,[1] the corollary being the granting of remedies to companies some of which in fact warrant closer scrutiny; for just as natural persons have distinctive features which cannot be ignored, so too, companies have attributes or a lack thereof which sit uneasily

---

[1] T. C. Spelling, *A Treatise on the Law of Private Corporations*, 2 vols. (New York: L. K. Strouse & Co. Law Publishers, 1892), vol. 2, p. 1058.

with recompense traditionally awarded to individuals. This is particularly the case with respect to damages for non-pecuniary loss – an expression synonymous with so-called 'non-pecuniary damages', 'immaterial damages', 'non-material damages', 'non-' or 'extra-patrimonial damages', 'non-economic damages' and 'moral damages'. The English refer to them as 'general damages', a term which denotes losses 'which are not capable of precise quantification in monetary terms'.[2] The latter are not exclusively non-pecuniary losses, however. For this reason, reference to 'general damages' will be avoided, except where that broad meaning is intended. Damages for non-pecuniary loss remedy a wide range of losses, some heads of which, when awarded to corporations, raise fewer brows than others. In the succeeding chapters, the extent to which such damages can properly be awarded in favour of a company will be examined in light of their particular features.

III   Jurisdictions Covered

A   The EctHR and England

1/3   Conscious of the enormity of the potential scope of research such as this, prominence has been given to the jurisprudence of two key jurisdictions: the *European Court of Human Rights* (EctHR) and *England*; the former because it is a case of that Court – *Comingersoll SA v. Portugal*[3] – that first drew the author's attention to the topic at hand and the latter for reasons explained shortly.

1/4   Colourful superlatives have been lavished on the Strasbourg Court, whose jurisdiction is directly accessible to over 800 million citizens. Among others, it has been described as the most active, prominent and authoritative rights protecting court in the world. The price of its popularity, however, 'must be a closer scrutiny of the consistency and legitimacy of its activities.'[4] Regrettably, a recurring theme of studies which have done so, at least insofar as the Strasbourg Court's application of art. 41 of the European Convention on Human Rights (ECHR)[5] (on just satisfaction) is concerned, has been that the Court adopts a notoriously flexible

---

[2] A. Tettenborn, *Halsbury's Laws Commentary on Damages* (London: LexisNexis Butterworths, 2014), vol. 29, para. 317.

[3] 06.04.2000, no. 35382/97.

[4] C. A. Gearty, 'European Court of Human Rights and the Protection of Civil Liberties: An Overview', *Cambridge Law Journal*, 52(1) (1993), 89–127, 93.

[5] Adopted 4 November 1950, entered into force 3 September 1953, ETS 5; 213 UNTS 221.

and seemingly unprincipled basis in awarding compensation.[6] This book adds to those concerns.

1/5 An analysis of the law in key Council of Europe Member States reveals noteworthy inconsistencies between them and the Strasbourg Court's approach to the topic under consideration. Indeed, it seems right to have regard to such domestic practices since the Court itself has stated that 'it may decide to take guidance from domestic standards'[7] in making an award under art. 41 ECHR and also in light of the fact that the Court's decisions affect national approaches. Attention will therefore be given to the jurisprudence of some parties to the Convention in assessing the propriety of the Court's jurisprudence. More consideration is given to English law,[8] however, for a number of reasons.

1/6 First, it can safely be said that among the various Council of Europe Member States, the UK (or England to be precise) has a developed corpus of jurisprudence in the area of damages for non-pecuniary loss which has a long, continuous and historical underpinning. When one inquires into what might have facilitated this generous disposition, the history of the common law, its procedural aspects included, seems a persuasive starting point. Damages for non-pecuniary loss of sorts can be traced back to the first extant Saxon laws committed to writing: *Leges Æthelberht* – the laws of Anglo-Saxonian King Ethelbert of Kent. The purpose of *Leges Æthelberht* was to lay down a tariff system for wrongs through the payment of a fixed sum – a *weregild* (or *were, wergild, weregildum, wergeld, weregeld*) – to make *bót*.[9] Although criminal and civil redress ran into each other at the time, the *weregild* is not to be confused with the *wíte* – satisfaction to

---

[6] See among others, The Law Commission and the Scottish Law Commission, *Damages under the Human Rights Act 1998*, Law Com 266/Scot Law Com 180 (2000), para. 3.4. W. V. H. Rogers, 'Comparative Report' in W. V. Horton Rogers (ed.), *Damages for Non-Pecuniary Loss in Comparative Perspective* (Wien/New York: Springer, 2001), no. 68; A. P. Lester and D. Pannick (eds.), *Human Rights Law and Practice*, 3rd edn (London: LexisNexis Butterworths, 2009), para. 2.8.4; See also K. Reid, 'European Court of Human Rights: Practice and Procedure' in J. Simor and B. Emmerson (eds.), *Human Rights Practice* (London: Sweet & Maxwell, looseleaf), para. 19.063; D. Shelton, *Remedies in International Human Rights Law*, 3rd edn (Oxford University Press, 2015), p. 2; R. Clayton and H. Tomlinson, *The Law of Human Rights*, 2nd edn, 2 vols. (Oxford University Press, 2009), vol. 1, para. 21.30; the various contributions in A. Fenyves, E. Karner, H. Koziol and E. Steiner (eds.), *Tort Law in the Jurisprudence of the European Court of Human Rights* (Berlin/Boston: De Gruyter, 2011).
[7] *Practice Direction on Just Satisfaction Claims* (2016), para. 3.
[8] Developments in other common law countries will feature where appropriate.
[9] Bosworth-Toller's Anglo-Saxon Dictionary Online defines 'bót' as 'amends, reparation, compensation for injury'.

be rendered to the King or community for the public wrong which had been committed (i.e. to buy back the peace) – as the *were* was paid to the injured person or his family for the private injury. The loss of an eye or a leg, among other injuries, demanded the highest *bót* – fifty shillings.[10] Lower down the tariff was loss of liberty: 'If any one bind a freeman, let him make "bót" with xx shillings.'[11] These and other passages reveal how, as early as the first part of the seventh century, English law was concerned with the remedy of losses of what modern lawyers consider analogous to damages for non-pecuniary loss.[12] There were subtle differences, however: first, the amount of the award then was largely dependent on the social rank of the victim; second, it was the responsibility of the wrong-doer's kinsmen to intercede if the former was unable to make *bót*; and third, unlike most modern awards of damages for non-pecuniary loss, the *bót* mostly compensated the injury itself (e.g. loss of a leg) as opposed to its consequences (e.g. pain and suffering). Pecuniary 'dooms' were also laid down.

1/7   It was not until the twelfth century, however, that damages as we know them today supplemented the old system of *bót* payments and it was also at this time that juries were used as fact finders; by 1773 juries were awarding damages for non-pecuniary loss, inter alia, for pain and loss of honour.[13] Despite the large awards made by juries, who were observed to have been often 'roused to indignation by partisan advocacy',[14] courts held themselves incompetent to review their verdicts except in the case of mayhem or where the latter were mistaken or had misbehaved themselves.[15] Juries – composed of butchers, bakers and candlestick-makers – were considered better able to gauge human pain and suffering; better able to understand, appreciate and estimate the nature and extent of such damages than the most learned and eminent judge of appellate courts, particularly as juries saw and heard the witnesses, while courts (on appeal

---

[10] S. Turner, *The History of the Anglo-Saxons from the Earliest Period to the Norman Conquest*, 7th edn, 3 vols. (London: Longman, Brown, Green and Longmans, 1852), vol. 2, p. 445.

[11] F. W. Maitland and F. C. Montague, *A Sketch of English Legal History* (New York and London: Putnam, 1915), p. 195.

[12] See how similar damage is assessed today in The Judicial Studies Board, *Guidelines for the Assessment of General Damages in Personal Injury Cases*, 13th edn (Oxford University Press, 2015).

[13] J. O'Connell and K. Carpenter, 'Payment for Pain and Suffering through History', *Insurance Counsel Journal*, 50(3) (1983), 411–417, 412.

[14] *Broome* v. *Cassell & Co. Ltd (No. 1)* [1972] AC 1027, 1128 per Lord Diplock.

[15] M. Lobban, 'Tort' in W. Cornish et al. (eds.), *The Oxford History of the Laws of England*, 13 vols. (Oxford University Press, 2010), vol. 12, pp. 899–902.

at least) got their impressions from printed transcripts which often lose much by transposition.[16] This state of affairs was compounded by the vague and uncertain principles of compensation for personal suffering at the time.[17] Thus, the systemic chaos of the common law in times past as a result of the role of juries – accompanied by the reluctance of English judges to interfere, despite their competence and security via tenure – may well have contributed to the broad acceptance of damages for non-pecuniary loss in England today. Similar recognition is due independently to the common law itself which, in contrast to some civil systems, encouraged judges to shape and develop the law in a pragmatic fashion. It may well be that other factors also played decisive roles. What is certain, however, is that damages for non-pecuniary loss continue to be a well-established feature of English law today and their development is singular. As early as 1893, the Court of Appeal in *South Hetton Coal Company Ltd* v. *North-Eastern News Association Ltd*[18] unanimously rejected the argument that a trading company could not recover such damages. While there are obvious differences between individuals and companies, this did not justify the denial of a remedy to companies. It is this receptive feature of damages for non-pecuniary loss that qualifies English law as a favourable comparator for the purpose of this research.

1/8   That said, a glance at recent reforms in England will at once correct any misconceived sense of flawlessness of English law with respect to this head of damages. Like statutory laws embarked upon as and when the need arises, the common law is a heterogeneous mass of rulings, some of which becomes inadequate especially in light of careful historical studies. This fuelled a call for the legislature to abandon archaic rules on the one hand and a plea for caution against expanding awards of damages for non-pecuniary loss to companies in an unprincipled manner on the other. Such reforms are thus another reason for the focus on English law.

B   *Discounting other Council of Europe Member States*

1/9   Arguably, the laws on damages for non-pecuniary loss in Continental jurisdictions are equally highly developed and systematically applied. However, the influence of fundamental legal ideas or ideas of justice in the first place and several social, economic and political forces in

---

[16] F. A. Taell, 'Right of Court to Interfere with the Determination of the Amount of Damages Fixed by a Jury', *Central Law Journal*, 61 (1905), 286–289, 286.

[17] *Huckle* v. *Money* (1763) 2 Wilson KB 205, 206 per Pratt CJ.   [18] [1894] 1 QB 133.

the second directed Continental lawmakers to adopt restrictive attitudes towards such damages generally.

1/10   In his report on damages for non-pecuniary loss in civil law countries, Stoll begins with a historical background on such damages. Unlike in England, where 'public and private aspects of injurious acts were pretty clearly distinguished by the Anglo-Saxon terms',[19] it was only in eighteenth century Germany that composite sums were done away with. The peculiarity of non-pecuniary loss – i.e. that it was incapable of calculation in money – was therefore irrelevant, 'as long as the payment of reparation to the injured person was based not only on the extent of the injury, but also on a punishment to the wrongdoer and appeasement of the injured person's desire for retribution.'[20] In connection with the abolition of private law penalties, the view came to prevail that every payment of damages exceeding actual financial loss was a penalty, which civil courts were not permitted to impose.[21]

1/11   The feeling towards damages for non-pecuniary loss was, as Mugdan wrote in 1888, that they run counter to 'the modern German sense of justice and morality'.[22] Such an award, when eventually admitted, was reserved for the peasantry and common bourgeois class, not those of higher standing.[23] Local legislation deemed it 'unworthy of a free individual to permit his honor to be appraised in an estimatory action for damages or his emotions to be assessed as an object of commerce'.[24] The anxiety was that recognition would open the gates to a deluge of litigious pleadings motivated by sheer greed. A further apprehension was, as Magnus tells us, that 'compensation of non-pecuniary loss in money . . . might lead to a great amount of judicial discretion, enhancing the influence of trial judges far beyond their traditional role in German civil procedure and rendering control on appeal unnecessarily difficult'.[25] Continental

---

[19] F. Pollock and F. W. Maitland, *The History of English Law before the Time of Edward I*, 2 vols. (Cambridge University Press, 1898), vol. 1, p. 48.

[20] H. Stoll, 'General Report on the Civil Law Countries' in Council of Europe (ed.), *Colloquy on European Law: Redress for Non-Material Damage* (1970), p. 24.

[21] Stoll, 'General Report on the Civil Law Countries', p. 24.

[22] Referred to in H. Stoll, 'Consequences of Liability: Remedies' in A. Tunc (ed.), *International Encyclopedia of Comparative Law*, 17 vols. (Mohr Siebeck, 1983), vol. 11(2), para. 8-36, fn 254.

[23] 'In the case of persons of a higher class, the wrongfully inflicted pain could only be taken into account in determining the proper statutory punishment': Stoll, 'General Report on the Civil Law Countries', p. 24.

[24] See Stoll, 'Consequences of Liability: Remedies', para. 8-36 for specific references.

[25] U. Magnus and J. Fedke, 'Germany' in W. V. Horton Rogers (ed.), *Damages for Non-Pecuniary Loss in Comparative Perspective* (Wien/New York: Springer, 2001), no. 8.

legislators thus sought completeness, coherence and clarity in the drafting of codes or other laws. This also protected against the impairment of certainty – a principle accorded paramount status. The desire to thwart judicial subjectivity also explains why case law was not accepted as a formal source of law: *stare decisis* or the doctrine of precedent was not the norm.[26] Of relevance to us, however, is that primary significance attached to numerically calculable losses as a means to control judicial autonomy. Nevertheless, with the introduction of the Civil Code (*Bürgerliches Gesetzbuch*, BGB), which entered into effect on 1 January 1900, came a general acceptance of damages for non-pecuniary loss for injury to body, health, freedom or sexual self-determination: § 253(2). Such damages were also available where statute so stipulated. However, rather 'few provisions'[27] did so. Indeed, it was not until 1958 – when the *Bundesgerichtshof* (Federal Court of Justice of Germany, BGH) ruled, having controversially interpreted art. 1, para. 1 and art. 2 of the (then) West German Constitution – that damages for non-pecuniary loss were available for injury to personality in civil actions.[28] Moreover, before the Second Act on the Amendment of Provisions Pertaining to the Law of Damages took effect in April 2002,[29] damages for non-pecuniary loss were not generally available for statutory provisions which operated on a strict liability basis.

1/12   While these developments support observations of declining legislative authority and confirm that the traditional image of the German judge is waning, it would be inaccurate to assume that decisions of the German judiciary necessarily exhibit a significant drift away from their traditional mooring. Thus, although the BGH has in the past accepted that a religious community is capable of suffering non-pecuniary loss,[30]

---

[26] J. H. Merryman and R. Pérez-Perdomo, *The Civil Law Tradition: An Introduction to the Legal Systems of Europe and Latin America*, 3rd edn (Stanford University Press, 2007), p. 36.

[27] Magnus and Fedke, 'Germany', no. 1.

[28] See the *Herrenreiter* decision: BGH, 14 February 1958, BGHZ 26, 349. As in a number of civil systems, redress was available under criminal law and in addition damage of a non-pecuniary nature could be alleviated by restitution in kind, e.g. the publication of a judgment was considered capable of vindicating a claimant's reputation in whole or in part and the defendant could be made to retract a defamatory statement if its continued publication affected another's honour: Stoll, 'General Report on the Civil Law Countries', pp. 36–37. G. Wagner, 'Germany' in H. Koziol and K. Warzilek (eds.), *The Protection of Personality Rights against Invasions by Mass Media* (Wien/New York: Springer, 2005).

[29] *Zweites Gesetz zur Änderung schadensersatzrechtlicher Vorschriften*, BGBl 2002 I 2674.

[30] BGH, 23 September 1980, BGHZ 78, 274. See also S. Martens and R. Zimmermann, 'Germany' in B. Winiger, H. Koziol, B. A. Koch and R. Zimmermann (eds.), *Digest of European Tort Law*, 2 vols. (Berlin/Boston: De Gruyter, 2011), vol. 2, 24/2 nos. 1–3 and

this was quickly followed by a statement by the *Oberlandesgericht* (Higher Regional Court, OLG) that the BGH's decision was exceptional and could therefore not serve as precedent for 'legal persons' in general, and companies in particular.[31]

1/13   In Austria the approach to damages for non-pecuniary loss was and, save for a brief spell, continues to be more liberal than is the case with its northern neighbour, Germany. In the nineteenth century, the *Oberste Gerichtshof* (OGH), the highest court in civil and criminal matters, took a broad approach to such damages. By the turn of that century, however, it had 'changed its established practices, probably under the influence of § 253'[32] of the German Civil Code which had just entered into force. Thus, in 1908, the OGH ruled by way of plenary decision that damages for non-pecuniary loss would be restricted to instances expressly provided for by statute.[33] Predictably, the drawback was that the OGH's approach eventually led to the 'arbitrary, inconsistent accumulation' of instances in which damages for non-pecuniary loss were awardable under statutes 'created by historical and political coincidences'.[34] Later Austrian commentators, in an attempt to correct this position, convinced themselves and eventually others of the existence of a general rule on compensation for non-pecuniary loss so that today – as was the position before the change in 1908 – the prevailing opinion is that such a norm does exist by virtue of §§ 1323 and 1324 of the Austrian Civil Code 1811 (*Allgemeines Bürgerliches Gesetzbuch*, ABGB). That said, damages for non-pecuniary loss are only awardable under these provisions in the case of gross negligence or intent (cf personal injury under § 1325 ABGB).[35] Of relevance for our present purposes is that, pursuant to § 26(2) ABGB, 'legal persons are capable of having rights; they have the same rights and duties as natural persons, insofar as the law concerned does not require a natural person due to its intrinsic nature.'[36] Consequently, in cases of unfair competition and tenancy, the Austrian Supreme Court has ruled that legal entities are

---

J. Oster, 'The Criticism of Trading Corporations and their Right to Sue for Defamation', *Journal of European Tort Law*, 2 (2011), 255–279, 257–258.

[31] OLG München, 28 May 2003, 21 U 1529/03.

[32] E. Karner and H. Koziol, 'Austria' in W. V. Horton Rogers (ed.), *Damages for Non-Pecuniary Loss in Comparative Perspective* (Wien/New York: Springer, 2001), no. 1.

[33] OGH in G1U Neue Folge (G1U New Series, G1UNF), no. 4185. See Karner and Koziol, 'Austria', no. 1.

[34] Karner and Koziol, 'Austria', no. 3.   [35] Karner and Koziol, 'Austria', no. 4.

[36] See E. Karner, 'Austria' in B. Winiger, H. Koziol, B. A. Koch and R. Zimmermann (eds.), *Digest of European Tort Law*, 2 vols. (Berlin/Boston: De Gruyter, 2011), vol. 2, 24/3 no. 3.

entitled to damages for non-pecuniary loss.[37] The laws in Austria will thus be examined where relevant.

1/14 As in the above systems, a number of other jurisdictions originally limited damages for non-pecuniary loss to instances specifically enumerated by statute – among them, Italy and the Scandinavian countries,[38] where the reference to statute was narrowly taken to refer exclusively to criminal laws. Such an interpretation 'survived more or less intact until recent times'.[39] Since 2003, however, a more liberal stance has been adopted in Italy[40] and indeed, the jurisprudence of the Strasbourg Court on awards of damages for non-pecuniary loss to corporations has been particularly influential there (no. 8/12). In Scandinavia, damages for non-pecuniary loss are also more generously awarded today.

1/15 Moving east, as Ollier and Le Gall inform us, monetary compensation for non-pecuniary harm was also criticised as an aspect of bourgeois mentality in socialist society where the only legitimate source of income was work.[41] The constraints placed by the Communist regime meant that such damages were entirely barred in Hungary, for example, though attempts were made to conceal losses of a non-pecuniary nature in other awards.[42] Promoted by the fall of the Soviet Union and its dissolution in 1991, several post-Soviet States and former Soviet occupied Eastern Bloc countries gradually recognised non-pecuniary losses. In Romania, for example, where compensation for non-pecuniary loss was 'forbidden during the Communist era for almost 40 years', the first Supreme Court decision to be rendered on the subject was delivered in 2002.[43] Indeed, if that is the position with respect to damages for non-pecuniary losses

---

[37] H. Koziol, *Basic Questions of Tort Law from a Germanic Perspective* (Wien: Sramek Verlag, 2012), no. 5/21. See also Karner and Koziol, 'Austria', no. 101.

[38] Stoll, 'Consequences of Liability: Remedies', para. 8-41.

[39] B. Markesinis, M. Coester, G. Alpa and A. Ulistein, *Compensation for Personal Injury in English, German and Italian Law: A Comparative Outline* (Cambridge University Press, 2005), p. 6.

[40] Markesinis et al., *Compensation for Personal Injury in English, German and Italian Law*, pp. 6–7.

[41] P. D. Ollier and J. P. Le Gall, 'Various Damages' in A. Tunc (ed.), *International Encyclopedia of Comparative Law*, 17 vols. (Mohr Siebeck, 1983), vol. 11(2), para. 10–75.

[42] Stoll, 'Consequences of Liability: Remedies', paras. 8–17, 8–38. See A. Menyhárd, 'Hungary' in H. Koziol (ed.), *Basic Questions of Tort Law from a Comparative Perspective* (Wien: Sramek Verlag, 2015), no. 4/71.

[43] M. Józon, 'Romania' in B. Winiger, H. Koziol, B. A. Koch and R. Zimmermann (eds.), *Digest of European Tort Law*, 2 vols. (Berlin/Boston: De Gruyter, 2011), vol. 2, 1/26 no. 5 and 11/26 no. 5.

generally, one begins to appreciate the paucity of jurisprudence in some of these countries in the case of such damages for companies.

1/16   While France is one of few jurisdictions that historically placed pecuniary and non-pecuniary harm on an equal footing,[44] the overtly vague nature of art. 1382 of the *Code Civil* and the particularly liberal approach of French law inclined the author away from a detailed account of the position there. It is astounding, given the encompassing reach of its provisions, that the French *Code Civil* 'was envisioned as a kind of popular book that could be put on the shelf next to the family Bible, or perhaps in place of it.'[45] French customs aside, what is certain is that the law of torts, which rests on a mere five articles, 'is almost entirely the product of judicial decisions',[46] which are invariably brief.

1/17   To stop at that would, however, be an excuse. Admittedly, the author also lacked the command of a number of European languages to give full weight and proper construction to jurisprudence on awards of damages for non-pecuniary loss to corporate entitles on an in-depth comparative basis. However, some references are made to reliable sources in English and to some extent non-English literature on the topic in Council of Europe jurisdictions, though the lack of depth here will be apparent. There are fewer hurdles to overcome in the case of developments in other common law countries where reciprocal references have been made with English law for decades and these will feature where appropriate.

IV   Structure

1/18   A few words will explain the general plan of this book. Chapter 2 defines the three main institutions or ideas on which the study is focused: companies, damage (in particular non-pecuniary loss) and damages for non-pecuniary loss. The first element introduces the key idea of the company's separate legal personality – a company, as are its rights and obligations, is distinct from the individuals who own and control it; the second that non-pecuniary loss of necessity, give or take some overlap,

---

[44] Stoll, 'Consequences of Liability: Remedies', paras. 8–17, 8–41; P. Brun and C. Quézel-Ambrunaz, 'French Tort Law Facing Reform', *Journal of European Tort Law*, 4(1) (2013), 78–94, 84.

[45] J. H. Merryman and R. Pérez-Perdomo, *The Civil Law Tradition: An Introduction to the Legal Systems of Europe and Latin America*, 3rd edn (Stanford University Press, 2007), p. 29.

[46] Merryman and Pérez-Perdomo, *The Civil Law Tradition*, p. 83.

involves interference with a person's bodily, mental, emotional and/or personality spheres and the third that damages for non-pecuniary loss seek to compensate loss other than a diminution of money, property or wealth.

1/19   Part II is dedicated to the practices of the European Court of Human Rights. After a preliminary discussion of the Court's canons of interpretation and the interpretive aids it employs, Chapter 3 turns to the 'victim status' and settles the question of corporate standing under the Convention. There follows an article-by-article account of the Convention rights that companies enjoy and those that are not open for them to pursue. Where the EctHR is yet to determine an issue, Chapter 3 speculates on its likely ruling, with particular attention being paid to the right to private life under art. 8 ECHR. The final substantive Section of the Chapter introduces the concept of 'just satisfaction' under art. 41 of the Convention, leaving it to Chapter 4 to elaborate on the Strasbourg Court's ruling in *Comingersoll* and developments subsequent to it. Chapter 4 also explores the true meaning behind the labels 'objective' and 'subjective' damages for non-pecuniary loss and tries to discern the Court's theory behind its findings of violations as just satisfaction.

1/20   Since the Strasbourg Court may be assisted by comparative insights, Part III looks to English law. Chapter 5 opens with the common law's conceptualisation of corporations, as conceived by academics and as evidenced in the law reports. In the absence of English case law on the implementation of the EctHR's jurisprudence in this field, the focus lies beyond the Human Rights Act 1998. A tort-by-tort analysis is undertaken of the wrongs that can be committed against companies in England and the availability or likely availability of damages for non-pecuniary loss to them. The Chapter highlights the correlation between the nature of the tort and remedy on the one hand and legal subject on the other as determinative of the extent of protection afforded to the latter, a correlation only partially reflected in the EctHR's case law. Having highlighted the torts that entitle claimants to a head of damages peculiar to the common law – 'aggravated damages' – in the preceding Chapter, Chapter 6 explains the nature of such damages and explores their suitability for companies.

1/21   Chapter 7 focuses on the premise that since a company can be directly liable for the acts of its organs, it should also be entitled to sue for damages for some of the non-pecuniary harm experienced by them. It sets out the extent of a company's liability for others and the possible candidates whose injured feelings, etc., might be rightly attributed to it – directors, managers and shareholders/members – before examining the soundness of the attribution theory and the prospects of its importation into England. A brief comparative survey of the issues addressed earlier is attempted in Part IV, Chapter 8 and Chapter 9 concludes the study, among other things, with a call for judicial dialogue.

2

Corporations, Damage and Damages

I The Corporation

2/1   The purposes for which businesses are formed are multifarious and it is often their objects, along with other principal considerations (among them, formal requirements, liability, capital needs, tax implications, etc.), that determine the appropriate business medium. Indeed, several types of business structures are available to entrepreneurs. Though they may differ from jurisdiction to jurisdiction, approximate equivalents can be identified. Sole proprietorships, partnerships and companies rank among the most common forms of business entities. Of these, however, it is the company that dominates economic activities and it is the company that this study concerns itself with. It is beyond the scope of this book to trace the origins of companies. Yet it is expedient to begin by exploring those privileges that formal incorporation brings with it.

A Definition and Terminology

2/2   Neither the European Convention on Human Rights nor its Court has elaborated on the concept of a 'company', which tends to be regarded as a product of national law. Colloquially, the term is sometimes applied to both partnerships and incorporated entities. In modern legal parlance, however, a company is treated as different from a partnership. Whereas English law regulates the former under the Partnership Act 1890, the latter is mainly regulated under the Companies Act 2006, which sets out a circular definition of 'company' in its s. 1.[1] Throughout this study, reference to 'company' is used in the narrow sense to denote an entity incorporated to conduct business or some other activity that has a distinct legal personality. This encompasses private companies (whether limited or unlimited),

---

[1] 'In the Companies Acts, unless the context otherwise requires "company" means a company formed and registered under this Act'.

public companies (whether trading publicly or otherwise) and for profit (trading) as well as not-for-profit (non-trading) companies, regardless of their form of incorporation. Private limited companies incorporated by registration under the Companies Act 2006 (and its predecessors) are by far the most commonly established legal entities in England.[2] As such, this research focuses primarily on them. The study also touches on the limited liability partnership (LLP), an entity regulated under the Limited Liability Partnerships Act 2000. Like the company, the LLP is a 'body corporate (with personality separate from that of its members)'[3] and as its name suggests, its partners have limited liability. Although a hybrid legal vehicle, the LLP is so similar to the company that its title is rightly said to be misleading. The law relating to partnerships does not generally apply to LLPs.[4] Rather, such firms are governed by tailored company law principles although their members remain subject to the laws on the taxation of partnerships. LLPs have members (or partners) but no directors or shareholders. Given their nature, LLPs fall within the scope of this research and will be referred to as 'companies'.

2/3   A few other terminological points to note: first, the word 'company' is used interchangeably with 'corporation' in this work. The second point relates to the term 'legal person'. While a corporation is a 'legal person',[5] a 'legal person' need not necessarily be limited to a corporation. The phrase is understood differently under different legal systems[6] and may be used to signify a natural person or other businesses capable of legal rights and duties.[7] The term 'entity' is necessarily a business, but its application is not restricted to companies.

B   Attributes of a Corporation

2/4   In earlier times, one fundamental difference between companies and partnerships was size. Section 716(1) Companies Act 1985, re-enacting earlier legislation, prohibited the formation of an association with more

---

[2] Companies House, Statistical Release, Companies Register Activities 2014/15.

[3] Limited Liability Partnerships Act 2002, s. 1(2).

[4] Limited Liability Partnerships Act 2002, s. 1(5).

[5] *Re Sheffield and South Yorkshire Permanent Building Society* (1889) 22 QBD 470, 476 per Cave J.

[6] J. F. Avery Jones et al., 'Characterisation of Other States' Partnerships for Income Tax', *British Tax Review*, 5 (2002), 375–436, 392. In Scotland, for example, a partnership is a 'legal person distinct from the partners of whom it is composed': s. 4(2) Partnership Act 1890.

[7] *Re Sheffield and South Yorkshire Permanent Building Society* (1889) 22 QBD 470, 476 per Cave J.

than twenty members unless registered as a company. Partnerships were thus capped at twenty persons. Like size, gainsome trade is not a defining character of companies. While some such entities conduct business for profitable reasons, some do not. For those who choose to incorporate, limited liability is overwhelmingly preferred as shareholders' liability is restricted to the amount of investment they have paid or undertaken to pay in respect of the shares held by them.[8] As with size and trade, limited liability is not coterminous with company. Limited partnerships (LPs) have existed since the enactment of the Limited Partnerships Act 1907. While similar to a general partnership, in addition to one or more general partners, LPs have one or more limited partners: s. 4(2). English law, in contrast to Scots law, does not recognise such entities as companies. Just as limited liability is not bound to companies, companies are not bound to limited liability. Unlimited companies exist, at least under English law.[9]

2/5   This leads us finally to *the* fundamental attribute of a corporation from which all the other attributes flow: i.e. its separate legal personality. No other business structures boast this. In England, the doctrine of corporate personality was firmly upheld in respect of a private company by the (then) House of Lords in its seminal decision of *Salomon* v. *Salomon & Co. Ltd* in 1896. In Lord Halsbury LC's words, once a company is 'legally incorporated it must be treated like any other independent person with its rights and liabilities appropriate to itself'.[10] This is the case even though, as Lord MacNaughten observed, 'it may be that after incorporation the business is precisely the same as it was before, and the same persons as managers, and the same hands receive the profits'.[11] Once registered, the company is given a certificate of incorporation as conclusive evidence that the requirements of the Companies Act 2006 or the Limited Liability Partnerships Act 2000 as to registration have been complied with.[12] It is at this stage that the company is born.

2/6   Attention is also called to EU legislation which allows for the creation of two companies: the European Economic Interest Grouping (EEIG) and the European Company (*Societas Europaea*, SE). The interest in European companies highlights the varieties of corporate structures available and in

---

[8] Companies Act 2006, s. 3.   [9] Companies Act 2006, s. 3(4).

[10] *Salomon* v. *Salomon & Co. Ltd* [1897] AC 22, 30. Recently confirmed in *Petrodel Resources Ltd* v. *Prest* [2013] 2 AC 415. As L. S. Sealy and S. Worthington explain in *Cases and Materials in Company Law*, 8th edn (Oxford University Press, 2007), p. 52, fn 25, the doctrine of separate personality was recognised long before Salomon's case. The true significance of that case lies in its application to private (very small) companies.

[11] *Salomon* v. *Salomon & Co. Ltd* [1897] AC 22, 51.

[12] Companies Act 2006, s. 15(4); s. 3(4) Limited Liability Partnerships Act 2000.

turn the complexities these cause in the formation of general rules in the area under consideration. The SE has legal personality.[13] EU regulations bestow full legal capacity on the EEIG[14] but leave it to Member States to determine whether or not groupings registered at their registries have legal personality.[15] In Great Britain reg. 3 European Economic Interest Grouping Regulations (SI 1989/638), as amended by SI 2009/2399, confers this.

2/7   A final word should be mentioned as regards the concept of separate personality: although the starting point, there will be times when the courts are prepared to impute to the corporation the wrongful deeds of a particular individual or class of individuals and conversely to attribute acts executed by the company that are detrimental to the interests of others, to a particular individual or class thereof. As will be shown in Chapter 7, the laws, inter alia, on vicarious, statutory and criminal liability, frequently engage the responsibility of the company for the acts or omissions of its organs, agents or employees.

2/8   Unlike other business entities, a further essential characteristic of a corporation is that it is capable of continuous, even perpetual, existence, facilitating the transferability of shares. Without this, and in the absence of an agreement to the contrary, the corporation would cease to exist upon the death or change of any member or shareholder.[16] In addition, a corporation can acquire, possess and sell property in its own name. Although its individual members may derive benefit from the increase or suffer loss from the destruction of the company's property, in no legal sense do they own it.[17] The corporation thus has rights and obligations: it can sue to vindicate the former, usually through its organs, and can be sued in respect of the latter.

2/9   That said, whatever attributes a company has depends upon the granting of the State. The attributes outlined earlier are inherent in the company. In addition, the company's constitution (in particular, its articles of association) may expressly give it additional powers (except such as

---

[13] Council Regulation (EC) No. 2157/2001 of 8 October 2001 on the Statute for a European Company, OJ 2001 No. L294, 10 November 2001, p. 1, art. 16(1).

[14] Council Regulation (EEC) No. 2137/85 of 25 July 1985 on the European Economic Interest Grouping, OJ 1985 No. L199, 31 July 1985, p. 9, art. 1(2).

[15] Council Regulation (EEC) No. 2137/85 of 25 July 1985 on the European Economic Interest Grouping, OJ 1985 No. L199, 31 July 1985, p. 9, art. 1(3).

[16] Partnership Act 1890, s. 33(1) reads: 'Subject to any agreement between the partners, every partnership is dissolved as regards all the partners by the death or bankruptcy of any partner'.

[17] See *Macaura* v. *Northern Assurance Co. Ltd* [1925] AC 619, 633 per Lord Wrenbury among other authorities.

Table 1 'The Composition of Companies'

Company type	Directors	Managers[a]	Partners	Members	Shareholders
Private Company	×	×		×	×[b]
Public Limited Company	×	×		×	×
European Economic Interest Grouping (EEIG)		×		×	
Societas Europaea (SE)	×	×		×	×
Limited Liability Partnership (LLP)		×	×	×	

[a] There is no insistence on the existence of managers, except in the case of EEIGs. All members can participate in the management of LLPs although designated members tend to have extra responsibilities.
[b] There are no shareholders in the case of a company limited by guarantee (companies suited to not-for-profit activities).

are already regulated by Parliament and except insofar as they are not forbidden by law). Finally, from time to time the law may add other rights or powers. However, this is in respect only of those which are reasonably necessary and proper for the company to possess to enable it to carry into effect its existing inherent or express powers.[18]

C   The Corporate Structure: Separation of Ownership and Control

2/10   A few words should be said about the individuals within the company. While in strict legal contemplation the company is separate from the individuals that form or manage it, it is manifest that a corporation cannot exist without them. Moreover, the increasing separation of ownership and control means that it is not always investors who control the company's activities.[19] Rather, this responsibility may be surrendered to a unified cadre of individuals (directors, managers, etc). The significance of the individuals within the company – that is, their various roles and responsibilities – is a matter that is given particular attention in this study (Chapter 7). Different compositions exist depending on the corporate structure in question, as indicated in Table 1 above.

[18] W. M. Fletcher, *The Law of Private Corporations* (Chicago: National Cyclopedia Publishing Co., 1913), pp. 101–104.
[19] A. Berle and G. Means, *The Modern Corporation and Private Property* (New Jersey: Transaction Publishers, 1932).

D   Conclusion

2/11   As mentioned earlier, the law has implied the ability for companies –
entities with separate personalities from the individuals within them – to
be capable of suffering damage and to sue in respect of the same. Where
liability is found for damage caused to the company, the law of damages
is engaged and it is at this point that the central inquiry of this study is
stimulated: that is, if and the extent to which damages for non-pecuniary
loss can properly be awarded in favour of a company. To answer this
question it is expedient to examine the terms damage and damages.

II   Damage

2/12   Despite the relative ease with which the term damage (which usually implies actionable damage) can be defined in its natural sense, a
legal description is seldom attempted. This is the case under the European Convention on Human Rights and English tort law also knows
of 'no general concept of "damage"'.[20] Given the absence of a general
definition of damage – synonymous with 'loss', 'harm', etc. – in both
jurisdictions under consideration, we turn to other sources for assistance.
Of the few Continental European civil codes that lay down a meaning of the expression, the Austrian Civil Code in its § 1293 defines it
broadly as every *detriment* inflicted upon the property, rights or person of
another.[21]

2/13   Such language resonates with two of the major drivers of future har-
monisation of the law of tort in Europe: the Draft Common Frame of
Reference (DCFR)[22] and the Principles of European Tort Law (PETL).[23]
The DCFR defines damage even more generally as 'any type of detrimental

---

[20] For the position under the Convention see K. Oliphant and K. Ludwichowska, 'Damage'
in A. Fenyves, E. Karner, H. Koziol and E. Steiner (eds.), *Tort Law in the Jurisprudence of
the European Court of Human Rights* (Berlin/Boston: De Gruyter, 2011), no. 6/1. For the
position in England and Wales see K. Oliphant, in B. Winiger, H. Koziol, B. A. Koch and
R. Zimmermann (eds.), *Digest of European Tort Law*, 2 vols. (Berlin/Boston: De Gruyter,
2011), vol. 2, 1/12 no. 1.

[21] See also U. Magnus, 'Comparative Report on the Law of Damages' in U. Magnus (ed.),
Unification of Tort Law: Damages (Hague/London/New York: Kluwer Law International,
2001), no. 33. H. Koziol, 'Austria' in U. Magnus (ed.), *Unification of Tort Law: Damages*
(Hague/London/New York: Kluwer Law International, 2001), no. 16.

[22] By the Study Group on a European Civil Code and the Research Group on EC Private Law
(Acquis Group).

[23] The brainchild of the European Group on Tort Law (EGTL).

effect'.[24] Although refraining from setting forth the meaning of the term, the PETL states that damage requires *material* or *immaterial* harm to a legally protected interest.[25] We will return to the term 'legally protected interest' in due course (no. 3/20). For now, it is sufficient to note the above two categories of damage – i.e. 'material' and 'immaterial' or 'pecuniary' and 'non-pecuniary'. These are well-known in all European tort systems.[26] Etymologically, the word 'pecuniary' finds its roots in the Latin *pecuniarius*. The suffix 'ary' or its Latin equivalent 'arius' means 'pertaining to' and *pecunia* means 'money, property, wealth'. Pecuniary damage is thus a detriment that involves a diminution of the victim's money, property or wealth: e.g. loss of income or profit. It refers to past or future losses whether or not these are precisely calculable.

2/14   Relevant to this study, non-pecuniary loss is a detriment of a sort which is not pecuniary: that is, loss which does not involve a diminution of the victim's money, property or wealth. The deciding criterion is not the 'immaterial' nature of the injured interest (hence the preference here for non-pecuniary as opposed to immaterial damage); nor is it the difficulties in quantifying the extent of such damage *per se* as some pecuniary damage cannot be measured exactly in money either (these would be recoverable as 'general damages' under English law). Rather, an analysis of such damage under English law reveals that the core criterion of non-pecuniary loss is *interference with a person's bodily, mental, emotional* and/or *personality spheres* (nos. 5/60–5/69) resulting in loss other than money, property or wealth. This finding is also consistent with the position in Continental[27] and indeed global systems, although some recognise such damage in a wider range of cases than others (Chapter 8). Moreover, it ought to be emphasised that a single interference may impact several spheres.

2/15   The first italicised set of words includes bodily injury, damage to general health, psychological and emotional harm and physical inconvenience and discomfort. Such harm may entail physical impact. It may also arise indirectly. The extent to which non-pecuniary loss is recognised in the

---

[24] C. von Bar and E. Clive (eds.), *Principles, Definitions and Model Rules of European Private Law: Draft Common Frame of Reference*, 6 vols. (Munich: Sellier, 2009), vol. 1, p. 68.

[25] PETL, art. 2:101.

[26] U. Magnus, 'Damages' in European Group on Tort Law (ed.), *Principles of European Tort Law: Text and Commentary* (Wien/New York: Springer, 2005), no. 1, p. 186. See also *Practice Direction on Just Satisfaction Claims* (2016), para. 6.

[27] Rogers, 'Comparative Report' in W. V. Horton Rogers (ed.), *Damages for Non-Pecuniary Loss in Comparative Perspective* (Wien/New York: Springer, 2001). V. V. Palmer (ed.), *The Recovery of Non-Pecuniary Loss in European Contract Law* (Cambridge University Press, 2015).

latter case largely rests on the extent of the injury in question. Where damage is on the emotional side (e.g. mental distress or anxiety) or amounts to merely inconvenience or discomfort, such injury is more common and more difficult to verify, so the law is more inclined to let the loss lie where it falls. That is not to say, however, that it is never compensated.

2/16   Stoll, to whom the second italicised phrase is attributed, fails to define 'personality sphere' and indeed, no universally accepted definition exists. Personality can be seen as rights in respect of 'non-physical aspects of the persona'.[28] According to one source, autonomy, privacy, dignity and reputation rank among the core attributes of personality.[29] Another includes honour[30] and another liberty.[31]

2/17   The taxonomy in nos. 14–16 above also accords with most European jurisdictions.[32] Additionally, it is in harmony with art. 10:301 PETL which endorses an award of damages for non-pecuniary loss, 'in particular where the victim has suffered personal injury; or injury to human dignity, liberty, or other personality rights.' The article goes on to provide that such damages can also be the 'subject of compensation for persons having a close relationship with a victim suffering a fatal or very serious non-fatal injury', i.e. relational emotional harm. The absence of physical damage to the secondary victim or their property explains why such losses are regulated under statute in England (no. 5/67).[33]

2/18   In this context, Brüggemeier rightly reminds us that the language of 'rights' expands beyond merely private law rights, including personality

---

[28] G. Brüggemeier, 'Protection of Personality Rights in the Law of Delict/Torts in Europe: Mapping out Paradigms' in G. Brüggemeier, A. Colombi Ciacchi and P. O'Callaghan (eds.), *Personality Rights in European Tort Law* (Cambridge University Press, 2010), p. 6.

[29] Brüggemeier, 'Protection of Personality Rights in the Law of Delict/Torts in Europe', p. 6.

[30] G. Brüggemeier, A. Colombi Ciacchi and P. O'Callaghan, 'A Common Core of Personality Protection' in G. Brüggemeier, A. Colombi Ciacchi and P. O'Callaghan (eds.), *Personality Rights in European Tort Law* (Cambridge University Press, 2010), p. 567.

[31] PETL, art. 10:301. See also A. Warzilek, 'Comparative Report' in H. Koziol and K. Warzilek (eds.), *The Protection of Personality Rights against Invasions by Mass Media* (Wien/New York: Springer, 2005), nos. 18–52 who also refers, inter alia, to the right to one's image, the right to a name, the protection of one's own words and voice, the protection of the presumption of innocence and the protection of various anonymity interests.

[32] See Magnus (ed.), *Unification of Tort Law* and Winiger et al. (eds.), *Digest of European Tort Law*, vol. 2.

[33] Relatives were allowed to recover damages for pecuniary loss by statute from 1846, but damages for their non-pecuniary loss were not allowed until 1976 when the Fatal Accidents Act was passed.

rights, into public law fundamental rights designed to safeguard citizens against the actions or inactions of public authorities.[34] The European Convention on Human Rights thus elevated existing intrusions of an individual and a company's private sphere into the realm of supranational law in addition to recognising new and legitimate types of such intrusions. Since state liability is built on the framework of tort and other national disciplines,[35] parallels can and indeed should be drawn.

III Damages

2/19   Actionable damage gives rise to a legal right to recompense, and the principal, though not the exclusive, form of redress open to a victim of an actionable wrong is an award of damages: i.e. a monetary payment. In Continental jurisdictions, however, compensation in kind takes first priority so that financial recompense is only an option if the former is impossible or impracticable. This is specifically stipulated in § 1323 of the Austrian Civil Code, for example.[36] Compensation in kind is indeed a form of recompense which the Strasbourg Court resorts to. This redress mechanism will thus be considered further below (nos. 3/60–3/62, 4/4– 4/5, 4/9 and 4/37–4/38).

2/20   Turning back to pecuniary recompense awarded for pecuniary and non-pecuniary loss, most jurisdictions, including the Strasbourg system and English law, formally categorise damages as redress for pecuniary (remedying loss arising from a diminution of the victim's money, property or wealth) and non-pecuniary (remedying loss of a sort not arising from a diminution of the victim's money, property or wealth) losses. The chief *aim* of an award of damages is to restore the victim, so far as money can, to the position he would have been in if the wrong complained of had not been committed.[37] In reality, however, the notion that damages are commensurate to the injury has been said to attribute to the law 'a degree

---

[34] Brüggemeier, 'Protection of Personality Rights in the Law of Delict/Torts in Europe', pp. 5–6.

[35] D. Shelton, *Remedies in International Human Rights Law*, 3rd edn (Oxford University Press, 2015), p. 91.

[36] 'In order to compensate for damage caused, everything must be returned to its previous state, or, if this is inappropriate, the estimated value must be reimbursed.': B. C. Steininger, 'Austria' in K. Oliphant and B. C. Steininger (eds.), *European Tort Law: Basic Texts* (Wien: Sramek Verlag, 2011), p. 7.

[37] As to the Convention, see *Practice Direction on Just Satisfaction Claims* (2016), paras. 9 and 10. This has been established by a line of English authorities, among them *Livingstone v. Rawyards Coal Co.* (1880) 5 App Cas 25, 39 per Lord Blackburn.

of perfection which it is very far from possessing.'[38] This deficiency is especially marked in the case of 'non-pecuniary damages' or 'damages for non-pecuniary loss' as is preferred here (since all damages must in the nature of things be pecuniary, i.e. in money) where it has been recognised that while money can be used to ameliorate the victim's loss, it can never restore the victim of such damage to their original position.[39] Most legal systems also accept the notion of deterrence as an aim of damages in general and damages for non-pecuniary loss in particular, albeit as a secondary one.[40]

2/21   By definition no true arithmetical calculation can establish the exact amount of damages for non-pecuniary loss due.[41] The law has, however, evolved ways to ensure even-handed justice to all litigants: a conventional figure derived from experience and from awards in comparable cases. Such evaluation is preferred to depending on idiosyncrasies of the assessor.[42] Moreover, this is usually the only appropriate redress open as generally neither the Strasbourg courts nor English law will elicit an apology[43] from the wrongdoer or sanction a retraction; nor for obvious reasons will any legal system force the latter to provide physical or other care.

2/22   It is worth recording at this stage that damages for non-pecuniary loss are not to be confused with punitive or exemplary damages – a controversial head of damages which many consider a blot on private law. Such damages are rooted in the common law which is not intolerant of anomaly. We need not enter into long academic arguments for or against such damages here. While considered an important safeguard of individual liberty in most common law jurisdictions, such awards are extra-compensatory – and do not seek to remedy non-pecuniary loss – and to that extent they do not largely impact upon this research. In any case,

---

[38] T. Sedgwick, *A Treatise on the Measure of Damages: Or an Inquiry into the Principles which Govern the Amount of Compensation Awarded by Courts of Justice*, 9th edn, 4 vols. (New York: Baker, Voorhis & Co., 1912), vol. 1, § 38.

[39] *Fletcher* v. *Autocar and Transporters Ltd* [1968] 2 QB 322, 339 per Diplock LJ. H. McGregor, *McGregor on Damages*, 19th edn (London: Sweet & Maxwell, 2014), para. 38–057. Compare the aim of awards in respect of non-pecuniary damage in para. 13 of the *Practice Direction on Just Satisfaction Claims* (2016) to that in para. 10 on awards for pecuniary damage. No mention of restoration is made in the former case.

[40] Rogers, 'Comparative Report', no. 69. For the deterrent effect of tort law in general see, Lord Bingham, 'The Uses of Tort', *Journal of European Tort Law*, 1 (2010), 3–15, 4 and fn 2 for further references.

[41] *Owners of the Steamship Mediana* v. *Owners of the Lightship Comet* [1900] AC 113, 116–117 per the Earl of Halsbury LC.

[42] *Wright* v. *British Railways Board* [1983] 2 AC 773, 777 per Lord Diplock.

[43] Cf s. 9 Defamation Act 1996. See also ss. 12 and 13 of the Defamation Act 2013.

they do not feature in Strasbourg jurisprudence; at least not formally.[44] Aggravated damages, another head of damages peculiar to the common law, seek to remedy non-pecuniary losses and will thus be fully examined (Chapter 6).

IV Conclusion

2/23   Despite the fact that corporations have existed for centuries, the law relating to them is nevertheless still developing, rapidly in certain quarters. This is so as in conceiving corporations the law only endowed them with the very minimum of attributes necessary for them to function. Other powers and rights continue to be worked out gradually. The law has developed to entitle corporations to receive damages for non-pecuniary loss; whether and the extent to which this is appropriate is open to debate. In adapting itself to meet the demands of its subjects, it is crucial that the resulting laws conform to certain core legal principles. Such consideration is in the interest of coherency, certainty and ultimately justice. As such, a presumption exists against constructions that mar the coherence of specific practice areas (mainly tort and company law here) or the overarching legal system. To address the question of this research, recourse must therefore be had to the rules governing and principles underpinning the above fields.

2/24   From company law, we derive the key attributes of corporations. As has been illustrated, companies have separate legal personality and as such cannot be treated as one and the same as the individuals who own or manage them. There will be instances, however, when the law will be prepared to treat the acts of those within the company as its acts and vice versa (Chapter 7).

2/25   We turn to tort, as the law governing non-contractual damage and damages. It is easy to accept that incorporated entities, many of which seek to conduct trade or business for profit, may suffer damage that involves a diminution of their money, property or wealth. Even non-trading companies can conceivably suffer such losses. On the other hand, the idea that corporate entities can also suffer a broad range of losses

---

[44] *Practice Direction on Just Satisfaction Claims* (2016), para. 9. See also V. Wilcox, 'Punitive and Nominal Damages' in A. Fenyves, E. Karner, H. Koziol and E. Steiner (eds.), *Tort Law in the Jurisprudence of the European Court of Human Rights* (Berlin/Boston: De Gruyter, 2011). Cf concurring opinion of Judge Pinto de Albuquerque, joined by Judge Vučinić in *Cyprus* v. *Turkey* [GC], 12.05.2014, no. 25781/94.

which do not involve a diminution of their money, property or wealth may surprise and even vex some. This is especially so when coupled with the defining criteria of non-pecuniary loss; in particular that it necessarily involves interference with one's bodily, mental, emotional and/or personality spheres.

2/26   Ultimately, therefore, the extent to which a corporation can suffer losses which are so closely associated with corporeal persons must be consistent with the nature of the corporation (as regulated by company law at both domestic and increasingly, at EU level) and the nature of non-pecuniary losses and damages for such losses (as fashioned by tort law).

2/27   Equally, the recognition of remedial rights or the extent thereof at Convention level ought to be grounded in coherency, not only within the Convention system but also in parallel to fundamental tort and company law principles of the majority of Signatory States to the Council of Europe, except where a departure is justified in the circumstances. Accepting domestic authority on corresponding rights as persuasive preserves long-standing and settled practice that accords with general legal schemes. To examine whether this is indeed the case, we now turn to the jurisprudence of the Strasbourg Court and the texts upon which it is based.

PART II

The European Court of Human Rights

3

Corporate Rights under the ECHR

I Introduction

3/1   On 8 May 1945 the curtains of the stage of the European theatre fell. Germany had unconditionally surrendered to the Allied Powers, and peace was on the agenda for the victorious camp. At this juncture of triumph, ten principal countries of Western Europe met to form an alliance, not against race or nation but tyranny in all forms.[1] On 5 May 1949, the Treaty of London establishing the Council of Europe was signed, and a new European conscience came into being. Europe had taken its first practical step to recreating a regional fabric of peace, safety and freedom. With salutary impatience, the European Convention on Human Rights (ECHR), formally the Convention for the Protection of Human Rights and Fundamental Freedoms, was opened for signature and 3 September 1953 marked its entry into force. Since then, thirty-seven other States have joined the Council of Europe and necessarily, the Convention. Despite the Convention's post-war origins, in reality, the jurisdiction of the European Court of Human Rights, established in 1959, is a relatively recent one and its key authorities are still comparatively new: in the first five years of its youth, the Court dealt with no more than two substantive cases and after a further ten years it had only delivered a total of ten judgments on substantive issues. Today, the Court's judgments number nearly 19,000. In the course of issuing these, the Strasbourg bench has been confronted with cases that have required it to define and redefine the Convention's boundaries. This was the case in 2000 in *Comingersoll SA v. Portugal*,[2] for example, where for the first time in its history, the Court awarded monetary compensation for non-pecuniary loss alleged by a juristic person. Given its growing body of jurisprudence, it is now both legitimate and desirable to analyse the judgments of this Court.

---

[1] Speech by W. S. Churchill, 12 August 1949, Strasbourg.   [2] 06.04.2000, no. 35382/97.

3/2   To appreciate the Court's rulings, generally and in respect of the topic
under consideration in particular, it is useful to first discuss the various
canons of interpretation that have served it, and the Commission before it,
for it is these very rules that have guided Strasbourg's adjudicative body
in the work of the Convention. Before turning to these, a preliminary
point is worth noting: while the Convention primarily concerns itself
with infractions of Contracting States and their agents, acquiescence or
connivance by the latter in acts of private individuals which violate the
Convention rights of other individuals within a State's jurisdiction may
engage State responsibility under the Convention. Protection under the
ECHR is thus broad. A different conclusion would be at variance with the
obligation contained in art. 1 of the Convention.[3]

II   Principles of Interpretation

3/3   Like most treaties, the Convention does not 'convey the fullness of its
legal effect.'[4] Rather in accordance with art. 32 ECHR, jurisdiction in matters concerning interpretation is given to the main agency for supervising
and enforcing the Convention, the Court. While this practice leaves room
for controversy, it is to be remembered that the primary intention of the
ECHR's proponents was to set down an irreducible *minimum* in terms
of guarantees. A degree of generality was thus unavoidable in light of the
temporal context, the tight timeframe given to the drafters to achieve their
mandate and the need for consensus among Council of Europe Signatories. It was in 1975 in *Golder v. the United Kingdom* that the Court, referring to arts. 31 to 33 of the Vienna Convention on the Law of Treaties 1969,[5]
stated that it was prepared to consider that it should be guided by
them.[6] Like the Commission, the Court justified itself by observing
that the provisions of the Convention on the Law of Treaties 'enunciate

---

[3] *Cyprus v. Turkey* [GC], 10.05.2001, no. 25781/94, § 81.
[4] L. G. Loukaidēs, *The European Convention on Human Rights: Collected Essays* (Leiden: Martinus Nijhoff Publishers, 2007), p. 1. See generally G. Lestas, 'Strasbourg's Interpretive Ethic: Lessons for the International Lawyer', *European Journal of International Law*, 21(3) (2010), 509–542 and W. Karl, '"Just Satisfaction" in Art 41 ECHR and Public Interna- tional Law – Issues of Interpretation and Review of International Materials' in A. Fenyves, E. Karner, H. Koziol and E. Steiner (eds.), *Tort Law in the Jurisprudence of the European Court of Human Rights* (Berlin/Boston: De Gruyter, 2011).
[5] Adopted 23 May 1969, entered into force 27 January 1980, 1155 UNTS 331.
[6] This was despite the fact that the Vienna Convention had not yet entered into force at the time. Moreover, its art. 4 states that it does not operate retroactively.

in essence generally accepted principles of international law'[7] recognised by nations, including the Contracting Parties to the Convention. The following tools have been systematically endorsed in Strasbourg case law.

A Canons of Interpretation

3/4   In line with art. 31(1) of the Vienna Convention, as the primary rule, the interpretation of the Human Rights Convention must be in accordance with the natural or ordinary meaning of the provision in question. Such *textual interpretation* only serves as a point of departure, however, and, as the Court ruled in *Golder*, it is the context in which words occur that convey meaning, legal or otherwise.[8] Art. 31(2) and (3) Convention on the Law of Treaties elaborates on this in providing, inter alia, that the preamble to a treaty forms an integral part of an exercise in *contextual interpretation*. The Court in the *Golder* case also considered the Convention's Preamble as authoritative for *purposive interpretation*. Such interpretation calls for a textual reading that seeks to determine the Convention's object and purpose.[9] In order to achieve the Convention's object and realise its purpose, both the Commission and the Court have favoured an expansive approach, not one which would restrict the obligations undertaken by the Contracting Parties to the greatest possible degree.[10]

3/5   The Court has at times given special meaning to terms as foreseen by art. 31(4) of the Vienna Convention.[11] Such *autonomous interpretation*, which entails the Court giving its own construction to a text, in the light of the Convention's object and purpose, may necessitate a departure from interpretation solely by reference to the ordinary meaning or a reading independent of an identical term in domestic or international law. This interpretative ethic has understandably laid the Court open to criticism for showing minimal deference to the intentions of the Convention's progenitors and exposing sovereign States to obligations they did not explicitly undertake.[12] The concept of 'damage' is one of several terms

---

[7]   *Golder* v. *the United Kingdom*, 21.02.1975, no. 4451/70, § 29. See also *Golder* v. *the United Kingdom* (decision), 01.06.1973, no. 4451/70, § 44.

[8]   *Golder* v. *the United Kingdom*, 21.02.1975, no. 4451/70, § 34.

[9]   *Golder* v. *the United Kingdom*, 21.02.1975, no. 4451/70, § 34.

[10] *Golder* v. *the United Kingdom* (decision), 01.06.1973, no. 4451/70, § 44; *Wemhoff* v. *Germany*, 27.06.1968, no. 2122/64, § 8.

[11] See *Engel* v. *the Netherlands*, 08.06.1976, no. 5100/71; 5101/71; 5102/71; 5354/72; 5370/72, § 81, for example.

[12] J. G. Merrills, *The Development of International Law by the European Court of Human Rights*, 2nd edn (Manchester University Press, 1995), p. 66. See the opinions of Judge

that has acquired such autonomous meaning.[13] It is worth noting that, as regards the 'general rule' in art. 31 of the Vienna Convention, the 'process of interpretation of a treaty is a unity, a single combined operation; this rule, closely integrated, places on the same footing the various elements enumerated in the four paragraphs of the Article.'[14]

3/6   Apart from the Vienna Convention canons, the Court relies on interpretive methods it has developed independently over the years. Among them is the notion that, as a 'living instrument', the Convention 'must be interpreted in the light of present-day conditions': *Tyrer* v. *the United Kingdom*.[15] Thus, variable and changing conditions prevailing at the time of the Court's deliberations (that is, developments in society, in public opinion, etc.) are relevant. The *living instrument doctrine* or *evolutive interpretation* has provoked the question of where the Convention ends and where judicial revision or amendment of it begins.[16] That said, the Court has specifically acknowledged that there are limits to evolutive interpretation. In *Johnston* v. *Ireland*, for example, it stated that it 'cannot, by means of an evolutive interpretation, derive from [the Convention and its Protocols] a right that was not included therein at the outset. This is particularly so . . . where the omission was deliberate.'[17] Evolutive interpretation has been used to legitimise the grant of rights under the Convention to companies.[18]

3/7   Since its decision in *Airey* v. *Ireland*, the Court has stated on a number of occasions that the 'Convention is intended to guarantee not rights that are theoretical or illusory but rights that are practical and effective.'[19] This *effectiveness principle* has featured prominently in the area of awards of damages for non-pecuniary loss to companies.[20] The approach is consistent with the living instrument doctrine and the views of the Commission

---

Matscher in *König* v. *Germany*, 28.06.1978, no. 6232/73 and *Öztürk* v. *Germany*, 21.02.1984, no. 8544/79.

[13] K. Oliphant and K. Ludwichowska, 'Damage' in A. Fenyves, E. Karner, H. Koziol and E. Steiner (eds.), *Tort Law in the Jurisprudence of the European Court of Human Rights* (Berlin/Boston: De Gruyter, 2011), no. 6/1.

[14] *Golder* v. *the United Kingdom*, 21.02.1975, no. 4451/70, § 30.

[15] 25.04.1978, no. 5856/72, § 31.

[16] P. van Dijk and G. J. H. van Hoof, *Theory and Practice of the European Convention on Human Rights*, 3rd edn (Leiden: Martinus Nijhoff Publishers, 1998), p. 79. See also M. Forowicz, *The Reception of International Law in the European Court of Human Rights* (Oxford University Press, 2010), p. 12.

[17] 18.12.1986, no. 9697/82, § 53.

[18] For example, *Société Colas Est* v. *France*, 16.04.2002, no. 37971/97, § 41.

[19] 09.10.1979, no. 6289/73, § 24.

[20] *Comingersoll SA* v. *Portugal* [GC], 06.04.2000, no. 35382/97, § 35.

and the Court that the Convention should not be interpreted restrictively so as to prevent its aims and objectives from being achieved.

B   Aids to Interpretation

3/8   In the course of interpretation, recourse can be and is naturally also had to aids that are external to a Convention. In line with art. 31(3)(c) of the Vienna Convention, the Court can consult *relevant international instruments* 'and the interpretation of such elements by competent organs.'[21] By observing these, where appropriate, the Court avoids according inconsistent meanings to similar guarantees in texts that the Convention's Signatories may be party to. It can also have recourse to the *French text* of the Convention which the ECHR and art. 33 Vienna Convention recognise as equally authentic and equally authoritative respectively to the English one. In addition, recourse to the *legislative history* of the Convention, namely the *travaux préparatoires*,[22] can be had to confirm the ordinary meaning of a clause. It can also be had if the attempt to interpret a provision 'leaves the meaning ambiguous or obscure' or if it 'leads to a result which is manifestly absurd or unreasonable': art. 32 of the Convention on the Law of Treaties. It is not uncommon for the Court to have regard to the *domestic law and practice* of its Contracting Parties in a bid to deduce the nature and extent of a particular right or freedom guaranteed by the Convention.[23] Such practice originates from the Preamble.[24] To determine the common denominator, a comparative analysis of the domestic laws of (some) Contracting States is conducted and no doubt the Court's multinational composition helps here. Recourse to domestic law is a legitimate exercise since it is valid to suppose – in the absence of a conclusive reading of the Convention itself – that the eventual reading of the text should not be at total variance with the majority of the legal systems of the State concerned. That said, concrete consensus is not a necessity nor is the Court bound by such an assessment. In *Comingersoll*, for example, although 'difficult to identify a precise rule common to all the member states', the Court concluded, on the basis of the practice of

---

[21] *Bayatyan* v. *Armenia* [GC], 07.07.2011, no. 23459/03, § 102.

[22] *Handyside* v. *the United Kingdom*, 07.12.1976, no. 5493/72, § 62.

[23] *Practice Direction on Just Satisfaction Claims* (2016), para. 3.

[24] This reads: 'Being resolved, as the governments of European countries which are likeminded and have a *common heritage of* political traditions, ideals, freedom and *the rule of law*, to take the first steps for the collective enforcement of certain of the rights stated in the Universal Declaration'. Emphasis added.

the Member States of the Council of Europe, that the possibility that 'a juristic person may be awarded compensation for non-pecuniary damage could not be ruled out'.[25] The other aids have also been instrumental in the expansion of corporate rights.

C   Conclusion

3/9   In sum, the diverse techniques on the interpretation of treaties under the Vienna Convention are invoked by the Court as a guiding rod, subject to the consideration of the special nature of the Convention. The above normative propositions are by no means exhaustive; nor are they mutually exclusive. The Court will often have recourse to a number of such canons and aids at any given time with the aim of rendering a fair reading of the Convention. In practice, however, the Court has been observed to be less inclined to theories which tie interpretation back to the time when the Convention was enacted. Rather its interpretive ethic is to honour the substance or spirit and intendment of the right at issue with the aim of developing rights for victims – whether procedural, substantive or remedial – in a manner that best serves the purpose of the human rights regime. To achieve this, the Court frequently resorts to its doctrines of autonomous and evolutive interpretation and the effectiveness principle. The extent to which these pervasive approaches have influenced the topic under investigation will thus be treated in further detail below.

III   Corporations and the Victim Status

A   Direct Actions

3/10   Reference to awards of damages for non-pecuniary loss to corporations by the Strasbourg bench has pre-emptively answered the question of the standing of companies under the Convention. Art. 34 ECHR confers the right of individual petition. The provision reads: 'The Court may receive applications from any person, nongovernmental organisation or group of individuals claiming to be victims of a violation by one of the High Contracting States.' The term 'victim' is one of several terms given autonomous meaning so that it is interpreted independently of concepts of domestic law concerning such matters.[26] In particular, the

---

[25] *Comingersoll SA v. Portugal* [GC], 06.04.2000, no. 35382/97, § 34.
[26] *Middelburg, van der Zee and Het Parool BV v. the Netherlands* (decision), 21.10.1998, no. 28202/95, § 1.

Court has ruled that 'victim' denotes 'the person *directly affected* by the act or omission which is in issue'.[27]

3/11   That the European Convention on Human Rights also bestows rights to non-natural victims, and corporations in particular, is indisputable. This is so notwithstanding the absence of express reference to such persons in the Statute of the Council of Europe, which speaks broadly of the enjoyment of *all persons* of rights and fundamental freedoms in its art. 3 ECHR.[28] Reference to corporations is absent from the Preamble of the European Convention, and in a similarly ambiguous vein, the Convention itself requires its High Contracting Parties under art. 1 ECHR to secure to *everyone* within their jurisdiction the rights and freedoms enshrined in section I. In its ordinary sense, 'everyone' carries a connotation of 'every natural person' as is supported by the title of the Convention.[29] Reference to *toute personne physique* (literally translated as 'any physical person') in art. 34 ECHR of the French text of the Convention (no. 3/8) as opposed to just 'any person', as is the case with the English text, shows that the Convention's drafters possibly did not intend 'person' to include non-natural persons. However, 'although in a less technical sense than in civil or public law doctrine',[30] the phrase 'non-governmental organisations' also encompasses corporations. One need only consult the *travaux préparatoires* (no. 3/8) to confirm unequivocally the intentions of the ECHR drafters.

3/12   Indeed, the very first initiative undertaken by the European Movement, an unofficial body which later created the Council of Europe, envisaged petitions by corporate persons. At the Inaugural Meeting of the International Council of the European Movement in Brussels on 25–28 February 1949, a number of conclusions and recommendations were adopted. Recommendation 1(c) read that: 'The Governments of the Member States, as well as all natural or *corporate persons* . . . shall have the right to appear

---

[27]   *De Wilde, Ooms and Versyp (Vagrancy)* v. *Belgium* (Article 50), 10.03.1972, no. 2832/66; 2835/66; 2899/66, § 23. Emphasis added.

[28]   Signed 5 May 1949, entered into force 3 August 1949, ETS No. 001.

[29]   A. J. Dignam and D. Allen, *Company Law and the Human Rights Act 1998* (London/Dublin/Edinburgh: Butterworths, 2000), p. 150, fn 5 contrasts the title of the Convention and its reference to 'human rights' with other instruments where the preference is for a more accommodating phrase, e.g. 'basic rights'. As to potential objections to corporate standing see M. Emberland, *The Human Rights of Companies: Exploring the Structure of ECHR Protection* (Oxford University Press, 2006), pp. 26–32.

[30]   C. Schwaighofer, 'Legal Persons, Organisations, Shareholders and Applicants' in M. de Salvia and M. E. Villiger (eds.), *The Birth of European Human Rights Law* (Baden-Baden: Nomos Verlagsgesellschaft, 1998), p. 321.

before the Court'.[31] That corporate persons in the territory of Contracting States should be granted *locus standi* was also carried through to the draft European Convention on Human Rights prepared by the European Movement – more specifically, its International Juridical Section under the chairmanship of Pierre-Henri Teitgen with Sir David Maxwell-Fyfe and Professor Fernand Dehousse as joint *rapporteurs*. Today, Teitgen and Maxwell-Fyfe are rightly considered the founding fathers of the Convention.

3/13   On 12 July 1949, the European Movement's draft was submitted to the Council of Europe, which had been established just two months prior.[32] From there, the Consultative Assembly of the Council of Europe took over, charging its Committee on Legal and Administrative Questions to examine further the issue of the collective guarantee of human rights. Maxwell-Fyfe was now Chairman of the Assembly's Committee and Teitgen its *rapporteur*. In the 8th sitting of the Consultative Assembly on 19 August 1949, Teitgen made it known that freedom encompassed not only 'freedom of the person, of work and of conscience' but also 'economic liberalism, free enterprise, freedom of competition, of profit and of money.'[33] Consequently, Teitgen, in his report of 5 September 1949, on behalf of the Committee on Legal and Administrative Questions, foresaw corporate bodies as potential victims of violations under the Convention.[34] While the Consultative Assembly went on to adopt the report and recommended (in Recommendation 38[35]) the Committee of Ministers prepare a draft convention of collective guarantees, to the regret

---

[31] www.cvce.eu/content/publication/2008/4/9/85c16975-ad28-48fc-bb27-f86a54dc1228/ publishable_en.pdf. Emphasis added.

[32] Art. 7(a) of the draft reads: 'Any State a party to this Convention and any natural or *corporate person* in the territory of any such State, shall have the right to petition the Council of Europe in respect of any infringement of Part I of this Convention'. Emphasis added. Council of Europe, *Collected Edition of the 'Travaux Préparatoires' of the European Convention*, 8 vols. (Leiden: Martinus Nijhoff Publishers, 1975), vol. 1, p. 298.

[33] Council of Europe, *Collected Edition of the 'Travaux Préparatoires' of the European Convention*, vol. 1, p. 40.

[34] Para. 20 states: 'All persons or *corporate bodies*, who are victims of a violation of the Convention, may petition the Commission . . .'. Emphasis added. See also art. 12 of the draft text which reads: 'After all other means of redress within a State have been tried, any person, or *corporate body*, which claims to have been victim of a violation of the Convention by one of the signatory States, may lay the matter before the Commission in a petition presented through legal channels.' Emphasis added. Council of Europe, *Collected Edition of the 'Travaux Préparatoires' of the European Convention*, vol. 1, pp. 224, 232.

[35] Adopted 8 September 1949. See Council of Europe, *Collected Edition of the 'Travaux Préparatoires' of the European Convention*, vol. 2, pp. 274–287.

of many, the Committee of Ministers did not give its approval in principle to the draft convention but proposed the convening of a Committee of Experts, which was given a mandate to undertake the draft *ab initio*.[36] Nonetheless, the Committee of Experts, which sat between 2–8 February and 6–10 March 1950, used the Consultative Assembly's recommendation as a template in its drafting efforts. It was in the course of these meetings that reference to corporate bodies was replaced with *nongovernmental organisation*. Predictably, the question of the precise ambit of the italicised phrase arose. As will be shown in nos. 3/14–3/16, the interpreting bodies of the Convention imposed only a modest restriction on themselves in this respect and rightly so as the intention of the Committee of Experts in employing the term was to enable 'a *wider definition* of those bodies, other than individual persons, who would be qualified to petition the Commission in order not to exclude any person or group of persons from the right of access to the Commission'.[37]

3/14   When in 1975 in *Times Newspaper[s] Ltd, The Sunday Times, Evans* v. *the United Kingdom*, the Commission was called for the first time to decide on the admissibility of an application lodged by the Times Newspapers Ltd, The Sunday Times (a group of journalists) and the editor of The Sunday Times, the Commission affirmed emphatically that each of the applicants was clearly an 'injured party' or 'victim' for the purposes of former art. 25 (now art. 34) ECHR and had standing to be heard. In particular, the Commission ruled that:

> As regards the first applicant it is clear that both conditions [one of which included the victim requirement under art. 25] are satisfied, and this is not in dispute between the parties. Times Newspapers Ltd. is a legal person under English law, a company with corporate capacity and limited liability, created by registration under the relevant statute. As such it falls clearly within one of the categories of petitioners set out in Art. 25 of the Convention as a "non-governmental organisation".[38]

3/15   Sixteen years after its establishment and in its 26th decision, the Court on 26 April 1979 tacitly upheld the Commission's reasoning and in so doing put to rest any ambiguity as to whether Convention rights were

---

[36] See the text of the Standing Committee of the Consultative Assembly of November 1949. Available in Council of Europe, *Collected Edition of the 'Travaux Préparatoires' of the European Convention*, vol. 2, pp. 298–301.

[37] Council of Europe, *Collected Edition of the 'Travaux Préparatoires' of the European Convention*, vol. 4, p. 38. Emphasis added.

[38] 21.03.1975, no. 6538/74, § 1.

conferrable to corporations.[39] This also served to indicate the intended reach the Court had in view for the Convention.

3/16   In any case, despite scant reference to companies in the body of the Convention, a lengthy look at it unambiguously attests to the drafter's vision that, in order for the Court to conduct its tasks effectively, access to it was to be available to corporate entities too. In particular, art. 10(1) ECHR sets limitations on *enterprises'* right to freedom of expression. Further, art. 1 of Protocol 1 expressly provides that every 'natural or *legal person*' is entitled to the peaceful enjoyment of his or its possessions.[40]

3/17   That said, it is not all companies that come within the purview of the Convention's protection but only those which are 'distinct from the State, of which they are completely independent.'[41] The Commission has stated that 'the public or private law nature of a corporation, although an important indication, is not decisive for the determination of the government or non-governmental character of an organisation under the Convention.'[42] The key question is thus whether the entity exercises public functions.[43]

B   Indirect Actions

3/18   While 'victim' under art. 34 denotes the person directly affected by the act or omission which is in issue, this is only the starting point. The Commission and Court have ruled specifically in the case of corporate litigants that not only substantive rights under section I of the Convention or its Protocols but also provisions which confer a right of a procedural nature such as art. 25 (now art. 34 under section II of the Convention) ECHR must be interpreted as guaranteeing rights which are practical and effective as opposed to theoretical and illusory.[44] An excessively formalistic interpretation of the 'victim' concept would therefore make protection

---

[39] *Sunday Times* v. *the United Kingdom (No. 1)*, 26.04.1979, no. 6538/74. See also *Sunday Times* v. *the United Kingdom* (Article 50), 06.11.1980, no. 6538/74, § 13: 'Each of the applicants is clearly an "injured party" – a phrase synonymous with the term "victim" as used in Article 25 (art. 25) – in the sense that they were persons directly affected by the decision held by the Court in its judgment of 26 April 1979 to be in conflict with the obligations arising from the Convention'.

[40] Emphasis added.

[41] *The Holy Monasteries* v. *Greece*, 09.12.1994, no. 13092/87; 13984/88, § 49.

[42] *The Holy Monasteries* v. *Greece* (unpublished), 05.06.1990, no. 13092/87; 13984/88.

[43] *Gemeinde Rothenthurm* v. *Switzerland* (decision), 14.12.1988, no. 13252/87.

[44] *Agrotexim Hellas SA, Biotex SA, Hymofix Hellas SA, Kykladiki SA, Mepex SA and Texema SA* v. *Greece* (decision), 12.02.1992, no. 14807/89.

of the rights guaranteed by the Convention ineffectual.[45] The Court has accordingly held that the questions on the status of victims are closely linked to the merits of the case.[46] It accepts that where there is a personal and specific link between the direct victim and the applicant, a claim by the latter – an indirect victim – is permissible. Of relevance here is that while the general rule is that a company's shareholders cannot claim to be victims of a violation of their company's rights,[47] there are exceptions.

IV   Corporate Rights under the ECHR

3/19   While corporations have standing under the Convention, it is not every provision that is open for them to pursue. The following is an article-by-article examination of each right enshrined in the Covenant. It covers all but the final three articles (16 ECHR to 18 ECHR) of section I. Art. 16 ECHR merely allows restrictions on certain rights of 'aliens' under section I; a term which is not taken to include companies (see no. 3/48). Although yet to be successfully litigated by companies, arts. 17 and 18 ECHR are applicable to them provided they are in respect of recognised corporate rights under the Convention (discussed below). Section II (arts. 19 to 51 ECHR) deals with the set-up of the Court and its rules of operation and section III (arts. 52 to 59 ECHR), miscellaneous provisions. Only arts. 34 and 41 ECHR will therefore be considered, as will the Protocols to the Convention.

3/20   Returning to the Principles of European Tort Law (PETL), damage is said to require harm to a *legally protected interest*: art. 2:101.[48] This introduces a phrase that does not form part of the parlance of the Human Rights Court. That said, the line taken by the Principles has considerable practical merit as a means to approach the concept of 'damage' structurally. The first step is to enquire into whether a legally protected interest has been infringed. Whether and the extent to which an interest is legally protected is said to be ascertainable on the basis of the legal system as a whole.[49] To assist in this exercise, the Principles list several guiding factors to be taken into consideration. This depends, inter alia, on its nature: 'the higher its value, the precision of its definition and its obviousness,

---

[45] *Gorraiz Lizarraga* v. *Spain*, 27.04.2004, no. 62543/00, § 38.
[46] *Siliadin* v. *France*, 26.07.2005, no. 73316/01, § 63.
[47] *Agrotexim* v. *Greece*, 24.10.1995, no. 14807/89, §§ 62–65.
[48] See Oliphant and Ludwichowska, 'Damage', no. 6/2.
[49] H. Koziol, 'Damage' in European Group on Tort Law (ed.), *Principles of European Tort Law: Text and Commentary* (Wien/New York: Springer, 2005), no. 1, p. 34.

the more extensive is its protection'.[50] According to art. 2:102(2) PETL the most extensive protection is accorded to the following interests: life, bodily or mental integrity, human dignity and liberty. This is broadly consistent with the Strasbourg approach.

A   Art. 2 ECHR

3/21   Whether *all* the rights and freedoms enumerated in the Convention can be logically ordered in a meaningful hierarchy is debatable. What is certain, however, is that the Court has acknowledged the relative prepotency of such rights and freedoms by expressly stating that art. 2 ECHR (which safeguards the right to life) 'forms the supreme value in the hierarchy of human rights'.[51] So fundamental is it that, except in respect of deaths resulting from lawful acts of war, art. 2 ECHR is non-derogable in time of emergency under art. 15 ECHR. The former Commission on Human Rights and the Court have ruled, however, that certain rights guaranteed under certain Convention provisions are 'by their very nature not susceptible of being exercised by a legal person'.[52] While 'the great majority of them apply directly to such persons as autonomous legal entities deserving the protection of the Convention',[53] States cannot be said to be under a duty to abide by others because companies cannot claim to have suffered any violation or legally recognisable damage in respect of them. Notably, this is the case as regards the foremost rights, including art. 2 ECHR. Although insolvency marks the end or 'death' of a company, the Court, sitting in Grand Chamber, has ruled that the right to life is 'an inalienable attribute of *human beings*'.[54]

B   Art. 3 ECHR

3/22   Similarly, art. 3 ECHR (which protects the right to physical, personal and psychic integrity) has been held as 'one of the fundamental values of the democratic societies making up the Council of Europe'.[55] So

---

[50] PETL, art. 2:102(1).

[51] *K-HW* v. *Germany* [GC], 22.03.2001, no. 37201/97, § 96. Elsewhere it has stated that it is 'one of the most fundamental provisions in the Convention': *McCann* v. *the United Kingdom* [GC], 27.09.1995, no. 18984/91, § 147.

[52] *Verein Kontakt-Information-Therapie (KIT) and Hagen* v. *Austria* (decision), 12.10.1988, no. 11921/86, § 1.

[53] Concurring opinion of Judge Rozakis joined by Judges Sir Nicolas Bratza, Caflisch and Vajić in *Comingersoll SA* v. *Portugal* [GC], 06.04.2000, no. 35382/97.

[54] *K-HW* v. *Germany* [GC], 22.03.2001, no. 37201/97, § 96. Emphasis added.

[55] *Mubilanzila Mayeka and Kaniki Mitunga* v. *Belgium*, 12.10.2006, no. 13178/03, § 48.

fundamental is this provision that, unlike most of the substantive clauses of the Convention – including art. 2 ECHR – art. 3 ECHR makes no provision for exceptions. Like art. 2 ECHR, art. 3 ECHR is also non-derogable in time of emergency under art. 15 ECHR. Yet the Commission has said that 'the right not to be subjected to degrading treatment or punishment (Article 3) (Art. 3), [is] by [its] very nature *not susceptible of being exercised by a legal person*'.[56]

C Art. 4 ECHR

3/23   No derogation from art. 4(1) ECHR (prohibition of slavery or servitude) is permitted under art. 15 ECHR. To the author's knowledge, the Court is yet to decide on the applicability of art. 4(1) ECHR to companies. Given its interpretations of arts. 2 and 3 ECHR, it would seem doubtful that legal persons can bring a successful action under the provision. That said, the possibility for a corporation to claim they have been subjected to forced or compulsory labour (art. 4(2) ECHR) has not been excluded.[57]

D Art. 5 ECHR

3/24   As seen above, PETL also regards liberty as warranting extensive protection. There is no doubt that personal liberty is a fundamental value especially since its deprivation is likely to have an adverse impact upon other rights. Despite the presumption in favour of liberty under art. 5(1) ECHR (on the right to liberty and security), the provision is not absolute. Moreover, art. 5 ECHR is one of several permissive derogations under art. 15 ECHR. As to corporate claims, Strasbourg judges have held, taking their decision in plenary session, that the 'right to liberty' under art. 5(1) ECHR contemplates '*individual liberty* in its classic sense, that is to say the *physical liberty of the person*'.[58] Thus, a corporate petition under art. 5(1) ECHR would not be entertained; by analogy, nor is one likely to be considered in respect of other subsections of art. 5 ECHR.

---

[56] *Verein Kontakt-Information-Therapie (KIT) and Hagen* v. *Austria* (decision), 12.10.1988, no. 11921/86. Emphasis added.
[57] See *Four Companies* v. *Austria* (decision), 27.09.1976, no. 7427/76, § 1 where the court was prepared to assume that the concept of forced labour was applicable to corporate bodies. No violation was found on the facts.
[58] *Engel* v. *the Netherlands*, 08.06.1976, no. 5100/71; 5101/71; 5102/71; 5354/72; 5370/72, § 58. Emphasis added.

E   Art. 6 ECHR

3/25   Companies have standing following infringements of their due process rights (whether civil or criminal) under art. 6(1) ECHR (right to
a fair trial).[59] Indeed, as with natural persons, art. 6(1) ECHR is, by
an appreciable distance, the most frequently litigated provision by corporate applicants. This is not to say, however, that corporations have
parallel rights as natural persons under the article. In *Granos Organicos
Nacionales SA* v. *Germany*,[60] for example, the Court ruled – in light of
the fact that the law of a substantial number of States (no. 3/8) does not
provide any form of legal aid to legal persons – that limitations imposed
on the applicant company's right of access to a court were proportionate
to the aims pursued. Art. 6(3) ECHR (on the presumption of innocence
in respect of a criminal offence) is also open for legal persons to pursue,[61]
and on that basis, so probably is art. 6(2) ECHR (on the rights of persons
charged with a criminal offence) although a successful case is yet to be
heard.

F   Art. 7 ECHR

3/26   Since the law recognises a company as a potential perpetrator of criminal offences, understandably, it is also open for them to pursue an action
under art. 7 ECHR (no punishment without law).[62] This is significant
given that art. 7 ECHR is one of a handful of non-derogable provisions
under the Convention: art. 15 ECHR.

G   Art. 8 ECHR

3/27   As to the right to respect for private and family life, the Commission
at one point was of the view that 'unlike Article 9, Article 8 of the Convention has more an individual than a collective character, the essential
object of Article 8 of the Convention being to protect the individual
against arbitrary action by the public authorities'.[63] However, the Court's

---

[59] See *Comingersoll SA* v. *Portugal* [GC], 06.04.2000, no. 35382/97 and *Marpa Zeeland BV and
Metal Welding BV* v. *the Netherlands*, 09.11.2004, no. 46300/99 among other authorities.

[60] 22.03.2012, no. 19508/07, § 53.

[61] *OAO Neftyanaya Kompaniya Yukos* v. *Russia*, 20.09.2011, no. 14902/04.

[62] See *Sud Fondi Srl* v. *Italy*, 20.01.2009, no. 75909/01, § 118.

[63] *Church of Scientology of Paris* v. *France* (decision), 09.01.1995, no. 19509/92, § 2.

subsequent case law on art. 8 ECHR eventually developed in a more expansive light. The article states that *everyone* has the right to respect for his:

(a) *private* and *family* life;
(b) *home*; and
(c) *correspondence*.

1 Home

3/28 The case law of the Strasbourg Court with respect to home and correspondence is fairly settled. As regards the former, the Court extends the notion of 'home' to a company's business premises. *Société Colas Est v. France*[64] was an application lodged by three construction companies which alleged a violation of their right to respect for their *home*. The petition was in respect of a large-scale investigation by government authorities into the conduct of public works contractors, resulting in raids and in the seizure of the applicants' documents allegedly containing evidence of unlawful dealings. Now the Court had already ruled in *Chappell v. the United Kingdom*[65] that a search conducted at *a private individual's home*, which was also the registered office of a company run by him, had amounted to an interference with his right to respect for his home within the meaning of art. 8 of the Convention. It expanded its interpretation further in *Niemietz v. Germany*,[66] an action brought by an individual, Mr Niemietz, a lawyer, alleging that a search of *a law office* belonging to him and his colleague and subsequent seizures had violated, inter alia, *his* right to respect for *his* home and correspondence. The respondent government in *Niemietz* had sought to draw a distinction between private life and home on the one hand, to which the Convention sought to afford protection, and professional and business life and premises on the other. In arriving at its decision, the Court had regard both to municipal law on the subject (no. 3/8) and to the equally authentic French version of the Convention (no. 3/8). In particular, it observed that certain Contracting States, notably Germany, extended the concept of 'home' to business premises. Such an interpretation, it felt, was fully consonant with the French text of the Convention, since the word 'domicile' has a broader

---

[64] 16.04.2002, no. 37971/97.
[65] 30.03.1989, no. 10461/83, § 51. No violation was found on the facts, however.
[66] 16.12.1992, no. 13710/88. See also *Buck* v. *Germany*, 28.04.2005, no. 41604/98, § 32 and *Sallinen* v. *Finland*, 27.09.2005, no. 50882/99, § 71.

connotation than the word 'home' and may extend, for example, to a professional person's office. The Court thus concluded by expanding the notion of 'home' to incorporate professional activities and premises so that a violation was found. At the same time, the Court felt that such an interpretation would not unduly hamper Contracting States, for they would retain their entitlement to 'interfere' to the extent permitted by art. 8(2) ECHR. That entitlement, the Court acknowledged, might well be more far-reaching where professional or business activities or premises were involved than would otherwise be the case.

3/29   In *Société Colas Est* v. *France* the Court began by reiterating that the Convention is a living instrument which must be interpreted in the light of present-day conditions (no. 3/6). Building on its dynamic interpretation of the Convention in *Comingersoll* (as to which see nos. 4/10–4/19), it considered that the time had come to hold that in certain circumstances the rights guaranteed by art. 8 ECHR may be construed as including the right to respect for a company's registered office, branches or other business premises. The decision is a pragmatic one which ran contrary to some speculations.[67] The Court continued that even supposing that the entitlement to interfere may be more far-reaching where the business premises of a juristic person are concerned, the operations must be strictly proportionate to the legitimate aims pursued.[68]

2   Correspondence

3/30   The protection of companies under art. 8 ECHR was extended further in *Wieser and Bicos Beteiligungen GmbH* v. *Austria*. The application was brought by an Austrian national who was the owner and general manager of the second applicant, a holding company which was, inter alia, the sole owner of the limited liability company, Novamed. Upon a request for legal assistance by the Naples Public Prosecutor's Office, a court in Austria issued a warrant to search the seat of the applicant company and Novamed.

---

[67] See the ECJ's ruling in Joined cases 46/87 and 227/88 *Hoechst AG* v. *Commission of the European Communities* [1989] ECR 2859, para. 18 predating the above decisions: 'The protective scope of that article [i.e. art. 8 ECHR] is concerned with the development of man's personal freedom and may not therefore be extended to business premises.' See also D. J. Harris, M. O'Boyle and C. Warbrick (eds.), *Law of the European Convention on Human Rights* (London/Dublin/Edinburgh: Butterworths, 1995), pp. 318–319 who had opined in respect of art. 8 ECHR that 'some interferences with wholly work premises might be protected against by relying on private life but surely not as an aspect of the right to respect for one's home.'

[68] *Société Colas Est* v. *France*, 16.04.2002, no. 37971/97, § 49. *Société Colas* was recently applied in *Saint-Paul Luxembourg SA* v. *Luxembourg*, 18.04.2013, no. 26419/10. Cf *Bernh Larsen Holding AS* v. *Norway*, 14.03.2013, no. 24117/08, § 174.

Both companies had their seats at the first applicant's law office. The only complaint was in respect of the search and seizure of electronic data. The Court concluded that this constituted an interference with the applicants' right to respect for their correspondence within the meaning of art. 8 ECHR. Having regard to its above-cited case law extending the notion of 'home' to a company's business premises, the Court saw 'no reason to distinguish between the first applicant, a natural person, and the second applicant, a legal person, as regards the notion of "correspondence"'.[69]

3   Family Life

3/31   No company has petitioned the Court on this ground as yet. While 'family life' has been held to exist where there is no blood ties or legal nexus of marriage or adoption and in everyday parlance terms such as 'sister company' or 'parent company' are used, out of all four aspects under art. 8 ECHR, the concept of 'family life' is considered least applicable to corporations.[70]

4   Private Life

3/32   As the Court has ruled, the concept of 'private life' is broad and not susceptible to exhaustive definition.[71] The Commission has repeatedly stated, however, that the right is not only limited to privacy but also encompasses, to a certain extent, the right to establish and develop relationships with other human beings, *especially in the emotional field*.[72] 'Through this decision', Loukaides observes, 'the concept of "personality" is accepted for the first time as the basis for the determination of the scope of private life.'[73] Although in the context of a natural applicant, the Court in *Niemietz* confirmed that there is 'no reason of principle why' the above understanding of the notion of private life 'should be taken to exclude activities of a professional or business nature since it is, after all, in the course of their working lives that the majority of people have a significant, if not the greatest, opportunity of developing relationships

---

[69] 16.10.2007, no. 74336/01, § 45. Cf *Bernh Larsen Holding AS* v. *Norway*, 14.03.2013, no. 24117/08, § 174.

[70] J. Oster, 'The Criticism of Trading Corporations and their Right to Sue for Defamation', *Journal of European Tort Law*, 2 (2011), 255–279, 262, who writes that a 'company cannot have a "family life"'. See also Emberland, *The Human Rights of Companies*, p. 115 and fn 98 below.

[71] *Axel Springer AG* v. *Germany* [GC], 07.02.2012, no. 39954/08, § 83.

[72] *X* v. *Iceland* (decision), 18.05.1976, no. 6825/74.

[73] L. G. Loukaidēs, *Essays on the Developing Law of Human Rights* (Leiden: Martinus Nijhoff Publishers, 1995), p. 87.

with the outside world.'[74] Corporations have therefore repeatedly sought protection under various aspects of the right.[75]

3/33   In *Wieser*, however, it was the respondent government that assumed that the *search and seizure* at issue interfered with the applicants' private life and home, one of which was a limited liability company. The Court decided to see it as an interference with the applicants' right to respect for their 'correspondence' instead which, as seen earlier, applies equally to communications originating from private and business premises. It thus did not consider it necessary to examine whether there was also an interference with 'private life'.[76]

3/34   Although the Court has ruled that '[t]elephone, facsimile and e-mail communications are covered by the notions of "private life" and "correspondence" within the meaning of Article 8',[77] there is lingering doubt as to whether companies can rely on the former aspect. In *Association for European Integration and Human Rights and Ekimdzhiev* v. *Bulgaria*, the complaint was in respect of a piece of legislation which exposed the applicants, among them a legal person, to possible *surveillance* at any point in time without notification. While upholding the allegation, the Strasbourg Court noted that 'it may be *open to doubt* whether, being such a person, it can have a "private life" within the meaning of that provision'.[78] On the facts it considered that the association's mail and other communications were covered by the notion of 'correspondence'.

3/35   Another aspect of private life that corporations are likely to invoke relates to *reputational infringement*. There is no doubt that individuals can now engage art. 8 ECHR for the purpose of safeguarding attacks on their reputations. This is so despite the fact that the sole mention of the term under the Convention appears in art. 10(2) ECHR. Art. 10(1) ECHR guarantees the right to freedom of expression subject to art. 10(2) ECHR which admits possible limitations, inter alia, in the interest of protecting the reputation of others. The effect was that while freedom of speech

---

[74] 16.12.1992, no. 13710/88, § 29.

[75] Indeed in some legal systems, e.g. Belgium, 'the protection of a company's inner workings' has been considered 'an aspect of the protection of the right to "private life"': C. von Bar and E. Clive (eds.), *Principles, Definitions and Model Rules of European Private Law: Draft Common Frame of Reference*, 6 vols. (Munich: Sellier, 2009), vol. 4, p. 3172. Cf Emberland, *The Human Rights of Companies*, p. 115 and fn 98 below.

[76] 16.10.2007, no. 74336/01, § 45.

[77] *Liberty* v. *the United Kingdom*, 01.07.2008, no. 58243/00, § 56. See Observations of the Swedish government on the admissibility of *Centrum för rättvisa* v. *Sweden*, 14.10.2014, no. 35252/08. See also *Big Brother Watch* v. *the United Kingdom*, 09.01.2014, no. 58170/13.

[78] 28.06.2007, no. 62540/00, § 60. Emphasis added.

was expressly guaranteed by the Convention, the protection of reputation was 'simply a ground of permissible restriction' on the right in art. 10(1) ECHR.[79] In many cases, therefore, freedom of speech was given primary importance. The Court recently felt that such an approach could not be in line with the spirit of the Convention. Consequentially, it has ruled that 'the right to protection of one's *reputation* is of course one of the rights guaranteed by Article 8 of the Convention, as one element of the right to respect for *private life*.'[80]

3/36   As the Court noted in *Pfeifer* v. *Austria*, a person's reputation forms 'part of his or her *personal identity* and *psychological integrity*'[81] and in *Karakó* v. *Hungary*[82] it went on to add that the notion of private life would only be extended to include reputation, where a publication undermined one's *personal integrity*. Although questionable,[83] the basis for the requirement of an interference with personal integrity is that reputation has 'only been deemed to be an independent right sporadically . . . and mostly when the factual allegations were of such a seriously offensive nature that their publication had an inevitable direct effect on the applicant's private life'.[84] Unlike traditional notions of reputation which are protected by the law of defamation domestically as a matter related *primarily to financial interests or social* status, more was required to protect it under art. 8 ECHR, namely an interference with an inalienable interest. A final prerequisite is that the attack on reputation must exceed a certain level of seriousness or gravity 'in a manner causing prejudice to personal enjoyment of the right to respect for private life'.[85] The seriousness threshold is one that arose

---

[79] Concurring opinion of Judge Loucaides in *Lindon, Otchakovsky-Laurens and July* v. *France* [GC], 22.10.2007, no. 21279/02; 36448/02.

[80] *Radio France* v. *France*, 30.03.2004, no. 53984/00, § 31 among other authorities. Emphasis added.

[81] 15.11.2007, no. 12556/03, § 35. Emphasis added.

[82] *Karakó* v. *Hungary*, 28.04.2009, no. 39311/05, §§ 21–28.

[83] The Court reached its conclusion by having regard to the fact that reference to 'personal integrity' was made in § 50 of its *Von Hannover* v. *Germany*, 24.06.2004, no. 59320/00, judgment. However, a reading of *Von Hannover* reveals the terms 'personal identity' and 'physical and psychological integrity' not 'personal integrity'. This mistake was pointed out by Judge Jociene in his partly concurring opinion in *Karakó*. Though cited in some cases, for example, *Putistin* v. *Ukraine*, 21.11.2013, no. 16882/03, § 32, *Karakó* has been omitted from others, including the Grand Chamber decision of *Axel Springer AG* v. *Germany* [GC], 07.02.2012, no. 39954/08, § 83. That said, the Court there referred to *Polanco Torres and Movilla Polanco* v. *Spain*, 21.09.2010, no. 34147/06, § 40 which in turn mentioned a need for the compromise of *intégrité personnelle* in light of *Karakó*.

[84] *Karakó* v. *Hungary*, 28.04.2009, no. 39311/05, § 23. Cf Judge Jociene's partly concurring opinion.

[85] *Axel Springer AG* v. *Germany* [GC], 07.02.2012, no. 39954/08, § 83.

out of *A* v. *Norway*.[86] There, the Court had regard to the fact that, unlike art. 12 Universal Declaration of Human Rights[87] or art. 17 International Covenant on Civil and Political Rights of the United Nations,[88] the progenitors of the Convention made a conscious decision to omit reference to 'honour and reputation' from art. 8 ECHR.

3/37   As regards corporations, there is no doubt that the Court recognises the need to safeguard their reputations, and indeed damages have been awarded where violations of other articles, for example, art. 6 ECHR adversely affected an entity's reputation (no. 4/30). The question here is whether a stand-alone action for the violation of reputation would succeed under art. 8 ECHR. There are arguments both for and against such a conclusion. It is not inconceivable to conclude that a company, which has a name, ought to benefit from protection of that interest as part of its identity and personality, albeit a corporate identity and personality.[89] The difficulty comes when one turns to references to psychological and personal integrity. On the basis of the Court's case law on arts. 2, 3 and 5 ECHR above it would seem that the intrinsic nature of the corporate form would prevent such notions from attaching to it. On the other hand since, as will be illustrated below, the Commission and the Strasbourg bench have found companies capable of harm peculiar to individuals (no. 4/31–4/34), one cannot rule out such a finding. That said, it would not be consistent with the view of those who argue that a corporation is an entity whose rights receive autonomous protection under the Convention,[90] to impute the integrity aspects of those within the company to it for the sake of entitling it to pursue the action under art. 8 ECHR (Chapter 7, in particular no. 7/23). As such, both domestic courts[91] and

---

[86] 09.04.2009, no. 28070/06, §§ 63–64 citing *Sidabras and Džiautas* v. *Lithuania*, 27.07.2004, no. 55480/00; 59330/00, § 49.

[87] Adopted 12 December 1948, UN Doc A/180 (1948).

[88] Adopted 16 December 1966, entered into force 23 March 1976, 999 UNTS 171.

[89] Cf G. Brüggemeier, A. Colombi Ciacchi and P. O'Callaghan, 'A Common Core of Personality Protection' in G. Brüggemeier, A. Colombi Ciacchi and P. O'Callaghan (eds.), *Personality Rights in European Tort Law* (Cambridge University Press, 2010), p. 575 who write that it is 'still questionable whether... the right to identity, can be extended to commercial or non-commercial organisations.'

[90] The concurring opinion of Judge Rozakis joined by Judges Sir Nicolas Bratza, Caflisch and Vajić in *Comingersoll SA* v. *Portugal* [GC], 06.04.2000, no. 35382/97.

[91] In *Euromoney Institutional Investor plc* v. *Aviation News Ltd* [2013] EWHC 1505, para. 20, Tugendhat J., an English judge, opined: 'in the context of a *defamation* claim, a corporate claimant does not have relevant rights under ECHR Art. 8.' Emphasis added. This is in line with his earlier decision in *Thornton* v. *Telegraph Media Group Ltd* [2011] 1 WLR 1985, para. 39: 'if an alleged defamation engages only a person's professional attributes,

scholars[92] doubt that a corporation's claim to reputation would succeed here, preferring instead for them to engage only commercial or property rights which are rights under art. 1 of Protocol No. 1. Indeed, the European Court of Justice (ECJ) case of *Varec SA* v. *Belgium*,[93] which endorses the opposite view, clearly 'goes much further than the European Court of Human Rights'.[94] While the Court is yet to rule on the notion of corporate reputation as property what is certain, however, is that it recognises goodwill as property (no. 5/47).[95]

H   Art. 9 ECHR

3/38   Insofar as art. 9 ECHR (on freedom of thought, conscience and religion) is concerned, the Commission considered 'that a distinction must be made... between the freedom of conscience and the freedom of religion'.[96] As opposed to the former, which by its very nature is limited to humans, claims by organisations for violations of freedom of religion are permissible.[97] It is clear, however, that the provision does not extend to companies. This puzzlingly strict view was expressed in *Company X* v. *Switzerland*.[98] A company may, however, avail itself under art. 10 ECHR.

---

then what is at stake is less likely to engage their rights under article 8, but may engage only their commercial or property rights (which are Convention rights, if at all, under article 1 of the First Protocol)'.

[92] See A. Mullis and A. Scott, 'The Swing of the Pendulum: Reputation, Expression and the Re-Centring of English Libel Law' in D. Capper (ed.), *Modern Defamation Law: Balancing Reputation and Free Expression* (Queens University Belfast Press, 2012), pp. 41–42, 50–51 and Oster, 'The Criticism of Trading Corporations and their Right to Sue for Defamation', 262–265.

[93] Case C-450/06, [2008] ECR I-581, para. 48.

[94] T. Aplin, L. Bently, P. Johnson and S. Malynicz, *Gurry on Breach of Confidence: The Protection of Confidential Information*, 2nd edn (Oxford University Press, 2012), para. 6.189. In that case, the ECJ ruled 'that the notion of "private life" cannot be taken to mean that the professional or commercial activities of either natural *or legal persons* are excluded', quoting *Niemietz* and *Société Colas*, cases on other aspects of art. 8 ECHR, as authority.

[95] *Van Marle* v. *the Netherlands*, 26.06.1986, no. 8543/79; 8674/79; 8675/79; 8685/79, § 41.

[96] *Verein Kontakt-Information-Therapie (KIT) and Hagen* v. *Austria* (decision), 12.10.1988, no. 11921/86, § 1.

[97] See *Church of Scientology of Paris* v. *France* (decision), 09.01.1995, no. 19509/92, § 2 where the Commission ruled that 'under Article 9 of the Convention a church is capable of possessing and exercising the right to freedom of religion in its own capacity as a representative of its members and the entire functioning of churches depends on respect for this right'.

[98] 27.02.1979, no. 7865/77. The Commission concluded that 'a limited company given the fact that it concerns a profit-making corporate body, can neither enjoy nor rely on the rights referred to in Article 9, paragraph 1, of the Convention'. See also *X and Church of*

I Art. 10 ECHR

3/39   Art. 10 ECHR (freedom of expression) is sufficiently broad in its drafting to accommodate companies. The provision thus applies to '"everyone", whether natural or legal persons.'[99] In *Markt Intern Verlag and Klaus
Beermann* v. *Germany*, therefore, the Commission reiterated that a text
could not be excluded from the scope of art. 10(1) ECHR on the basis of
the commercial nature of the information conveyed as art. 10(1) ECHR
does not apply solely to certain types of information or ideas or forms of
expression.[100]

J Art. 11 ECHR

3/40   It would seem, given the decision in *A Association and H* v. *Austria*,
that an action by a legal person for the violation of art. 11 ECHR (on the
freedom of assembly and association) would stand.[101]

K Art. 12 ECHR

3/41   It is evident that a corporation cannot bring an action under
art. 12 ECHR (the right to marry) since the provision refers to 'men
and women of marriageable age'.[102]

L Art. 13 ECHR

3/42   Although some rights have no independent existence and can only be
applied in conjunction with substantive ones, among them the right to
an effective remedy under art. 13 ECHR, companies can also lodge claims
in respect of them.[103]

Scientology v. *Sweden* (decision), 05.05.197, no. 97806/77, § 2. Cf the English approach
in *Exmoor Coast Boat Cruises Ltd* v. *Revenue and Customs Commissioners* [2014] UKFTT
1103 (TC), para. 72 per HHJ Mosedale: 'Therefore, while it is ludicrous to suggest a
company has a religion, or private life or family, nevertheless a company which is the alter
ego of a person can be a victim of a breach of A9 (the right to manifest its religion) if,
were it not so protected, that person's human rights would be breached.'

[99] *Autronic AG* v. *Switzerland*, 22.05.1990, no. 12726/87, § 47.

[100] 20.11.1989, no. 10572/83, § 26.

[101] 15.03.1984, no. 9905/82, § 2. It was held there that 'Article 11 of the Convention, can be
exercised both by the organiser of a meeting, even if it should be a legal person as in the
present case, and by the individual participants'.

[102] Emberland, *The Human Rights of Companies*, p. 33.

[103] *ZIT Company* v. *Serbia*, 27.11.2007, no. 37343/05, § 65 and *Iza Ltd and Makrakhidze* v.
Georgia, 27.09.2005, no. 28537/02, §§ 48–49 among other authorities.

M   Art. 14 ECHR

3/43   Like art. 13 ECHR, art. 14 ECHR (prohibition of discrimination) is not autonomous. It 'constitutes one particular element (non-discrimination) of each of the rights safeguarded by the Convention'.[104] As long as such a claim is in conjunction with other rights that are applicable to them, companies can indeed petition the Court following discrimination.[105]

N   Art. 34 ECHR

3/44   In addition, failure to observe the procedural right of petition under art. 34 ECHR (individual applications) can result in a valid claim by companies.[106] The relevant part reads: 'The High Contracting Parties undertake not to hinder in any way the effective exercise of this right.'

O   Art. 41 ECHR

3/45   Art. 41 ECHR (on just satisfaction) undoubtedly applies to companies. As a central theme in this book, it is given detailed treatment in Section V below.

P   Protocols to the ECHR

3/46   Of all the Protocols to the Convention, Protocol Nos. 10, 15 and 16 are yet to enter into force and like Protocol Nos. 2, 3, 5, 8, 9, 11 and 14 do not confer substantive rights. The paragraphs which follow thus focus on the others.

3/47   Companies can avail themselves of the right to protection of property under art. 1, *Protocol No. 1*.[107] Indeed art. 1, Protocol No. 1 is one of few Convention provisions drafted with reference to corporations, and it expressly refers to the entitlement of the latter (in addition to natural persons) to the peaceful enjoyment of their possessions. While the access to education limb of art. 2 of Protocol No. 1 (the right to education), is clearly not applicable to companies (since it is aimed at children), the

---

[104]   *Airey* v. *Ireland*, 09.10.1979, no. 6289/73, § 30.

[105]   See *Lithgow* v. *the United Kingdom*, 08.07.1986, no. 9006/80; 9262/81; 9263/81; 9265/81; 9266/81; 9313/81; 9405/81, § 177 where the Court, in plenary session, held that art. 14 ECHR 'safeguards persons (including *legal persons*)...against discriminatory differences of treatment'. Emphasis added.

[106]   *Oferta Plus SRL* v. *Moldova*, 19.12.2006, no. 14385/04, § 156.

[107]   CETS No.: 009. See *Iza Ltd and Makrakhidze* v. *Georgia*, 27.09.2005, no. 28537/02, § 54 among other authorities.

Commission repeatedly ruled that the article also guarantees the right to start and run a private school.[108] Thus, it would appear that companies can lodge a claim where their right to provide education is violated. Art. 3 of Protocol No. 1 (the right to free elections) guarantees the right to vote and the right to stand as a candidate at the election of the legislative body. Although the right to stand for elections has been invoked by a political party,[109] it remains to be seen whether companies would be considered victims under this provision.

3/48   In light of the Court's interpretation of 'deprivation of liberty' in art. 5 ECHR, it stands to reason that art. 1, *Protocol No. 4* (on the prohibition of imprisonment for debt) is limited to natural persons.[110] Indeed, the Explanatory Report to the Protocol expressly states that it was designed to reinforce the terms of art. 5 ECHR. The provision prohibits such deprivation merely on the ground of inability to fulfil a contractual obligation. It would appear that companies cannot seek to rely on art. 2 of Protocol No. 4 (liberty of movement and freedom of choice of residence).[111] The position with respect to art. 3 (prohibition of expulsion of nationals)[112] is, as the Commission has ruled, that it only applies to natural persons. It would appear that companies cannot rely upon art. 4 Protocol No. 4 (on the prohibition of collective expulsion of aliens) since in international law the term 'alien' is generally limited to natural persons.[113]

---

[108] *Ingrid Jordebo Foundation of Christian Schools and Ingrid Jordebo* v. *Sweden* (decision), 06.03.1987, no. 11533/85, § 1; *Verein Gemeinsam Lernen* v. *Austria* (decision), 06.09.1995, no. 23419/94. As regards the limitation of the first sentence of art. 2 of Protocol No. 1 to children see *Campbell and Cosans* v. *the United Kingdom*, 25.02.1982, no. 7511/76; 7743/76, § 40. The second sentence of the article is an adjunct of the fundamental right to education and concerns the right of parents. *X* v. *Sweden* (partial decision), 19.07.1971, no. 4733/71 is authority for the proposition that the right is not available to companies.

[109] See *Fryske Nasionale Partij* v. *the Netherlands* (decision), 12.12.1985, no. 11100/84, § 2. The applicant party was successful in *Russian Conservative Party of Entrepreneurs and Others* v. *Russia*, 11.01.2007, no. 55066/00; 55638/00, § 67.

[110] CETS No.: 046.

[111] Dijk, Hoof, Rijn and Zwaak, *Theory and Practice of the European Convention on Human Rights*, 4th edn (Antwerpen/Oxford: Intersentia, 2006), p. 54 cite *X Union* v. *France* (decision), 04.05.1983, no. 9900/82 as authority for the preposition that companies cannot rely on the provision.

[112] See *Association 'Regele Mihai'* v. *Romania* (decision), 04.09.1995, no. 26916/95. See also W. A. Schabas, *The European Convention on Human Rights: A Commentary* (Oxford University Press, 2015), p. 1072.

[113] E. Biglieri and G. Prati, *Encyclopedia of Public International Law* (North Holland: Elsevier, 2014), p. 6 write that: 'In the strict sense of the term, a foreign corporation is not an alien'. In any case the UK had not ratified Protocol No. 4.

3/49   Given the ruling on art. 2 ECHR it stands to follow that a corporate action in respect of *Protocol No. 6* (concerning the abolition of the death penalty) would not succeed.[114]

3/50   Like art. 4 Protocol No. 4, one can conclude that companies cannot seek to rely on art. 1 of *Protocol No. 7* (on procedural safeguards relating to the expulsion of aliens).[115] On the other hand, arts. 2 (the right of appeal in criminal matters)[116] and 3 (compensation for wrongful conviction) are likely of practical relevance to them in light of the Court's conclusions on arts. 6 and 13 ECHR. Indeed, the Court has confirmed this as far as art. 4 of Protocol No. 7 (on the right not to be tried or punished twice respectively) is concerned.[117] The right is non-derogable under art. 4(3) of the Protocol. Art. 5 of the Protocol (equality between spouses) would on the contrary not apply.

3/51   *Protocol No. 12* (general prohibition of discrimination) almost replicates art. 14 ECHR; if anything it is intended to be more expansive in its application since it is not limited to application with other rights under the Convention. For that reason, it would seem that companies can rely upon it.[118]

3/52   *Protocol No. 13* (abolition of the death penalty) distinguishes itself from Protocol No. 6 in that it concerns not just the abolition of the death penalty but its abolition *in all circumstances*. Thus unlike Protocol No. 6, there can be no death penalty in time of war under Protocol No. 13.[119] Again an analogous application of art. 2 ECHR leads one to conclude that the Protocol does not contemplate claims by corporate applicants.

Q   Conclusion

3/53   The above discussion thus puts the hierarchical value of corporate rights into context. Although barred from pursuing rights of foremost fundamental values under the Convention (namely, arts. 2, 3 and 5 ECHR) they are nonetheless permitted to petition the Court in respect of provisions which, given their non-derogable nature, are clearly high up in the

---

[114] CETS No.: 114.   [115] CETS No.: 117. The UK is yet to sign and ratify the Protocol.

[116] See *Fortum Oil and Gas Oy* v. *Finland* (decision), 12.11.2002, no. 32559/96, on art. 2 of Protocol No. 7 where the Court did not question the companies' rights to rely on the provision.

[117] *Grande Stevens* v. *Italy*, 04.03.2014, no. 18640/10, § 228.

[118] CETS No.: 177. Only a handful of applicants have pursued an action under the Protocol. Again, along with most jurisdictions, the UK has not signed or ratified it.

[119] CETS No.: 187.

hierarchy (e.g. art. 7 ECHR). In reaching its conclusions on the applicability of certain Convention articles to legal persons, the Court has repeatedly had regard, first to the 'intrinsic' or 'very nature' of the right: i.e. whether the right seeks to protect an attribute peculiar to human beings; and second to the inherent nature of the corporation (as to which, see Chapter 5). Seen in this way, the Human Rights Court conceives corporations as legal creations endowed with legal form for reasons of practicality. The above two-stage test is consistent with domestic practices and is usually, though not invariably, a useful indicator of how the Court would rule in respect of Convention articles or Protocols yet to be brought before it by company applicants.

V   Just Satisfaction

3/54   Once the merits of an application have been heard and a violation has been found in respect of any one or more of the above Convention articles or Protocols, the next step is an enquiry into the appropriate remedy. This necessitates an examination of the preparatory work leading to the Convention and the Court's jurisprudence on the clause on just satisfaction (art. 41 ECHR).

A   Legislative History

3/55   In the course of elaborating the future treaty, the Convention's drafters considered how to impugn States that disregarded the enumerated rights and freedoms within it. In art. 13(b) of its draft Convention, the European Movement envisaged broad powers: 'The Court may either prescribe measures of *reparation* or may require that the State concerned shall take *penal* or *administrative action* in regard to the persons responsible for the infringement, or it may *demand the repeal, cancellation* or *amendment* of the act.'[120] This view did not accord with all, however. Relying on the goodwill of the Contracting States, Churchill, for example, was of the opinion that the future court should 'have no sanctions and [that

---

[120] Council of Europe, *Collected Edition of the 'Travaux Préparatoires' of the European Convention*, vol. 1, pp. 300–302. Emphasis added. See also Recommendation 1(b) of the conclusions and recommendations adopted at the International Council of the European Movement (Brussels, 25–28 February 1949) (cited in fn 31) which preceded the above text: 'If the Court determines that there has been an infringement, it may either provide for reparations or require that the national authorities shall take either penal or administrative action in regard to the persons responsible therefore, or prescribe that the invalid act shall be repealed, cancelled or amended.'

its judges] would depend for the enforcement of their judgment on the individual decisions of the States now banded together in this Council of Europe.'[121] Norton preferred an approach that compelled 'by moral pressure, the affiliated nations to respect the Convention to which they have subscribed.'[122]

3/56 At the fifth sitting of the Committee on Legal and Administrative Questions of the Consultative Assembly of the Council of Europe, Teitgen, in his report on behalf of the Committee, initially proposed the extensive powers envisaged by the European Movement.[123] This was subsequently watered down in the final version of the report, giving full satisfaction to an entreaty that the Human Rights court should in no way be a court of appellate jurisdiction having the above authority.[124] The competence of the future court to pronounce judgments awarding reparation resurfaced, however, in a meeting of the Committee of Experts on Human Rights – which took over the task of drafting the Convention. There, the Secretary General of the Council of Europe raised the possibility of the court awarding 'damages, restitution in kind … or moral damages' in line with art. 39(1)–(3) of 'the International Criminal Code'.[125] Ultimately, it was the Italians who would dictate the scope of the sanction to be wielded by the court. That the 'decision of the Court shall, if necessary, afford just satisfaction to the injured party' was proposed by Perassi, an expert on international law, on 7 February 1950.[126] Such an approach accorded with international law relating to the violation of obligations by the State. Thus, to Teitgen's distress,[127] the power of the court to declare null or void or amend Acts emanating from the public bodies of Signatory States was

[121] Council of Europe, *Collected Edition of the 'Travaux Préparatoires' of the European Convention*, vol. 1, p. 34.
[122] Council of Europe, *Collected Edition of the 'Travaux Préparatoires' of the European Convention*, vol. 1, p. 132.
[123] Art. 24: 'The verdict of the Court shall order the State concerned: (1) To annul, suspend or amend the incriminating decision; (2) To make reparation for damage caused; (3) To require the appropriate penal, administrative or civil sanctions to be applied to the person or persons responsible'. Council of Europe, *Collected Edition of the 'Travaux Préparatoires' of the European Convention*, vol. 1, p. 212.
[124] See art. 26. *Council of Europe, Collected Edition of the 'Travaux Préparatoires' of the European Convention*, vol. 1, pp. 226–228.
[125] Preparatory Work on Article 50 of the European Convention on Human Rights of 30 April 1970, CDH (70) 17, p. 17.
[126] Preparatory Work on Article 50 of the European Convention on Human Rights of 30 April 1970, CDH (70) 17, pp. 18–20.
[127] Preparatory Work on Article 50 of the European Convention on Human Rights of 30 April 1970, CDH (70) 17, pp. 26–27.

considered undesirable.[128] Though out of respect for States' sovereignty, such a limitation of jurisdiction to mere 'compensation' was thought to be an 'outstanding defect' by Teitgen.[129] The wordy art. 50 ECHR[130] was nonetheless adopted. Following the entry into force of Protocol No. 11 in 1998,[131] art. 50 ECHR was replaced by the more succinct art. 41 ECHR which reads: 'If the Court finds that there has been a violation of the Convention or the protocols thereto, and if the internal law of the High Contracting Party concerned allows only partial reparation to be made, the Court shall, if necessary, afford just satisfaction to the injured party.'

B   The EctHR's Early Jurisprudence on Damages

3/57   Although art. 41 ECHR does not specifically refer to the nature of the damages awardable against recalcitrant States, the Court has since stated that just satisfaction can be awarded in respect of 'pecuniary damage, non-pecuniary damage and costs and expenses'.[132] Yet it was not until the early 1970s that the Court for the first time granted just satisfaction by way of *monetary compensation*. In *Ringeisen* v. *Austria* (Article 50) it awarded DM 20,000 in non-material damages to the applicant for a violation of art. 5(3) ECHR, following the excessive length of the applicant's detention on remand.[133] While the Court was endowed limited powers in the field of redress, in *Neumeister* v. *Austria* (Article 50), where it sat to adjudicate the issue of remedies for the third time, it voiced that its power under (former) art. 50 ECHR was broad. Thus, the Court would from then on act in the 'exercise of the wide competence conferred upon it'.[134]

---

[128] Preparatory Work on Article 50 of the European Convention on Human Rights of 30 April 1970, CDH (70) 17, p. 21.

[129] Preparatory Work on Article 50 of the European Convention on Human Rights of 30 April 1970, CDH (70) 17, p. 27. For a more detailed insight into the drafting history of art. 50 ECHR see E. Steiner, 'Just Satisfaction under Art. 41 ECHR: A Compromise in 1950 – Problematic Now' in A. Fenyves, E. Karner, H. Koziol and E. Steiner (eds.), *Tort Law in the Jurisprudence of the European Court of Human Rights* (Berlin/Boston: De Gruyter, 2011).

[130] 'If the Court finds that a decision or a measure taken by a legal authority or any other authority of a High Contracting Party, is completely or partially in conflict with the obligations arising from the present Convention, and if the internal law of the said Party allows only partial reparation to be made for the consequences of this decision or measure, the decision of the Court shall, if necessary, afford just satisfaction to the injured party.'

[131] ETS No. 155.

[132] *Practice Direction on Just Satisfaction Claims* (2016), para. 6.

[133] 22.06.1972, no. 2614/65, § 26.   [134] 07.05.1974, no. 1936/63, § 30.

3/58   It was accepted in the *Vagrancy* case,[135] the second in which the Court dealt with the issue of damages, that the term 'victim' within the meaning of then art. 25 ECHR (now art. 34 ECHR on the right to petition the Court: see no. 3/10) was synonymous with 'injured party' in the context of art. 50 ECHR, which provided that 'the decision of the Court shall, if necessary, afford just satisfaction to the injured party.' Since the Court had already confirmed that a corporation was capable of victim-status in *Sunday Times* in 1979 (no. 3/15), it was only a matter of time before an appropriate case would be brought by a company claiming to be an *injured party* for the purposes of art. 50 ECHR. Such a case came thirteen years later – in *Open Door and Dublin Well Woman* v. *Ireland* – and even then, redress was for pecuniary loss. In *Sunday Times* v. *the United Kingdom* (Article 50), as in several cases involving companies at the time, no claim was made for damages for pecuniary or non-pecuniary loss.[136] In *Open Door*, however, an action brought by two companies and four individuals for an alleged violation of art. 10 ECHR, the Court awarded the second applicant company IR£25,000 in damages for pecuniary loss.[137] The question on the possibility for a juristic person to be awarded monetary compensation for non-pecuniary loss would be left open for another eight years (nos. 4/10–4/19).

C   *Non-Pecuniary Loss and Damages for Such Loss before the EctHR*

3/59   The starting point is that to qualify for damages, a clear causal link must exist between the violation and damage arising and in addition para. 14 of the Court's Practice Direction on Just Satisfaction Claims conditions the Court's award of damages for non-pecuniary loss on the establishment by the claimant 'of the existence of such damage'. The Court accepts on the other hand that the very nature of non-pecuniary loss is such as not to lend itself to precise calculation.[138] It goes further in its case law by stating that non-pecuniary loss, as a 'subjective-measure', is not 'amenable to

---

[135] *De Wilde, Ooms and Versyp (Vagrancy)* v. *Belgium* (Article 50), 10.03.1972, no. 2832/66; 2835/66; 2899/66, § 23. On the facts, the Court concluded that the applicant's claims for damages were not well-founded.

[136] *Sunday Times* v. *the United Kingdom* (Article 50), 06.11.1980, no. 6538/74. The Court did accept, though only in part, the applicants' claims for reimbursement of the costs they had incurred in the domestic and the Strasbourg proceedings.

[137] *Open Door and Dublin Well Woman* v. *Ireland*, 29.10.1992, no. 14234/88; 14235/88, § 87.

[138] *Practice Direction on Just Satisfaction Claims* (2016), para.14.

proof'[139] so that an 'applicant cannot be required to furnish any proof of the non-pecuniary damage he sustained.'[140] It is this very vulnerability of such damage that exposes damages for non-pecuniary loss to potential abuse. Various considerations have been identified as relevant factors in determining the appropriate quantum of an award of damages for non-pecuniary loss; namely, the seriousness and duration of the injury, *the personal characteristics* (age, health, etc.) of the applicant, the standard of living and economic indicators in the applicant's country and the victim's behaviour. The hierarchical significance of the Convention right in question also influences the size of the award.[141] Considering the Court's stance on companies under arts. 2, 3 and 5 ECHR, it would seem to follow that the measure of damages for non-pecuniary loss awardable to them would be on the low side in comparison to their natural counterparts (cf Chapter 4).

D   A Finding as Sufficient Just Satisfaction

3/60   The Court has developed a *sui generis* remedy which has been said amounts to 'a mere handout of legal idiom'.[142] EctHR judges themselves have contested the Court's practice of finding a violation in itself to constitute just satisfaction. In *Engel* v. *the Netherlands* (Article 50), Judges Ganshof van Der Meersch and Evrigenis found it was 'difficult to accept the proposition that the finding by the Court of a breach of the substantive provisions of the Convention, whilst constituting a condition for the application of Article 50 (art. 50), can at the same time be the consequence in law following from that same provision.'[143] Others, however,

---

[139] *Korchagin* v. *Russia*, 01.06.2006, no. 19798/04, § 25.

[140] *Belousov* v. *Russia*, 02.10.2008, no. 1748/02, § 78. See also *Gridin* v. *Russia*, 01.06.2006, no. 4171/04, § 20. It would seem that what the Court really means here is that an applicant cannot be required to furnish any 'conclusive or concrete proof' as without this addition the logic of the Court's thinking would seem to preclude the applicant from showing that he had suffered more loss than one would expect. Moreover, para. 14 *Practice Direction on Just Satisfaction Claims* goes on to state: '*If the existence of such damage is established,* and if the Court considers that a monetary award is necessary, it will make an assessment on an equitable basis, having regard to the standards which emerge from its case-law.' Emphasis added.

[141] C. Kissling and D. Kelliher, 'Compensation for Pecuniary and Non-Pecuniary Loss' in A. Fenyves, E. Karner, H. Koziol and E. Steiner (eds.), *Tort Law in the Jurisprudence of the European Court of Human Rights* (Berlin/Boston: De Gruyter, 2011), nos. 11/129–11/154.

[142] Partly dissenting opinion of Judge Bonello in *Aquilina* v. *Malta*, 29.04.1999, no. 25642/94. See also O. Ichim, *Just Satisfaction under the European Convention on Human Rights* (Cambridge University Press, 2014).

[143] 23.11.1976, no. 5100/71; 5101/71; 5102/71; 5354/72; 5370/72.

have embraced this practice on the basis that '[d]amages need not ordinarily be awarded to encourage high standards of compliance by member states, since they are already bound in international law to perform their duties under the Convention in good faith'.[144] Such a non-monetary remedy is clearly less intrusive than an award of damages. It is a remedy which must be seen in light of the fact that a judgment in which the Court finds a breach imposes on the respondent State a legal obligation (supervised by the Committee of Ministers of the Council of Europe, acting under art. 46 ECHR) to put an end to the breach.

3/61   Such a finding, as Józon observes, does not derive from the Convention itself but has been developed by the Court[145] and is said to be distinguishable from declarations which are common at domestic level.[146] This has led to a drive to qualify the nature of this practice. According to Bydlinski, a finding as sufficient satisfaction is a form of restitution in kind resorted to most especially in facts concerning infringements of a merely procedural nature. Such a finding, as the Court has repeatedly ruled, usually seeks to redress *non-pecuniary loss* sustained.[147] In Bydlinski's words: 'By means of the authoritative finding of the Convention infringement, the applicant is namely given *emotional satisfaction*, which compensates the offence suffered as well as this is possible. Any damage going beyond this, however, requires financial compensation.'[148] Koziol elucidates Bydlinski's position further:

> If and insofar as the negative *psychological* effects of the violation per se are directly concerned, i.e. the injury to the victim's sense of justice, 'satisfaction' in the strictest sense is obtained for the victim in that he is found authoritatively to be in the right, and his opponent to be in the wrong, which must cause positive reactions in the victim to counter the negative *upset* about the violation, or which come as near as possible to so

---

[144] *R v. Secretary of State for the Home Department, ex parte Greenfield* [2005] 1 WLR 673, para. 19 per Lord Bingham.

[145] M. Józon, 'Satisfaction by Finding a Violation' in A. Fenyves, E. Karner, H. Koziol and E. Steiner (eds.), *Tort Law in the Jurisprudence of the European Court of Human Rights* (Berlin/Boston: De Gruyter, 2011).

[146] See F. Bydlinski, 'Methodological Approaches to the Tort Law of the ECHR' in A. Fenyves, E. Karner, H. Koziol and E. Steiner (eds.), *Tort Law in the Jurisprudence of the European Court of Human Rights* (Berlin/Boston: De Gruyter, 2011), no. 2/255.

[147] In *WB v. Poland*, 10.01.2006, no. 34090/96, § 75, however, the Court concluded that both the *pecuniary* and non-pecuniary loss claimed by the applicant was adequately compensated by the finding of a violation of art. 5(3) ECHR.

[148] Bydlinski, 'Methodological Approaches to the Tort Law of the ECHR', no. 2/284. Emphasis added.

doing. Insofar the mere finding of the breach can be an acceptable *variant of compensation for certain non-pecuniary loss.*[149]

3/62   This of necessity means one of two things: in the first case, since the Court extends this practice to corporate entities (as to which, see nos. 4/4–4/5 and 4/9) we are led to conclude that corporate entities are capable of sustaining non-pecuniary loss of a psychological or emotional nature. The propriety of such an understanding is broached in nos. 4/37–4/38. An alternative reading – and one consistent with Bydlinki's 'if and insofar as' prefix – is that a finding is broader in scope than envisaged above, leaving us to determine its precise nature.

VI Conclusion

3/63   In light of inherent shortcomings of the legislative process, it is inescapable that the eventual scope of protection of the rights conferred or duties imposed by legislative instruments will be determined to a large extent by interpreting bodies. Despite bold attempts by its authors, this is equally the case with the European Convention on Human Rights. Although these considerations necessarily imply a static text, the European Court of Human Rights has ruled otherwise. In the Court's view, the ECHR must be interpreted in light of present-day conditions and in accordance with developments in international law so as to reflect the increasingly high standard being required in the area of the protection of human rights. These and other canons of construction applied by the Court have emboldened it to creatively expand the boundaries of the Convention, both in respect of natural and legal persons and across not just substantive but also procedural and remedial rights.

3/64   Having regard to the wording of the Convention, its Protocols and its overriding purpose, as set out in its Preamble, it seems right that companies should come within the purview of its protection. Considering its contextual setting, however, it is equally legitimate that certain provisions do not and cannot apply to corporate beings.

3/65   Where a State is under an obligation to give effect to the rights and freedoms guaranteed under the Convention and/or its Protocols to corporate

---

[149] H. Koziol, 'Concluding Remarks on Compensatory and Non-Compensatory Remedies' in A. Fenyves, E. Karner, H. Koziol and E. Steiner (eds.), *Tort Law in the Jurisprudence of the European Court of Human Rights* (Berlin/Boston: De Gruyter, 2011), no. 22/23. Emphasis added. See also Bydlinski, 'Methodological Approaches to the Tort Law of the ECHR', no. 2/257 for the full text.

enterprises, and the former falls short, it is appropriate for corporations to seek redress under the Strasbourg mechanism set up for the specific purpose. The extent of such redress once a claim has been successfully adjudicated is what is called into question. It is worth emphasising that the very first award of monetary compensation by the Court was in respect of non-pecuniary loss. Its jurisprudence on the subject is thus ripe for reflection. Following the trajectory of the Strasbourg Court's doctrine, in particular the Court's perception of corporate entities as incapable of the pains to which a natural person is subject, a reasonable assumption would be that similar limitations apply on the issue of just satisfaction. This is particularly so when mapped against the fact that non-pecuniary loss involves interference with one's bodily, mental, emotional and/or personality spheres. As will be seen, however, this is not the view taken by the Court or indeed the former Commission (Chapter 4).

3/66   It seems expedient to now turn to the current jurisprudence of the Court with respect to corporate claims for redress for non-pecuniary loss. In doing so, it is worth recalling that while on the one hand, the Court was curtailed in its ability to declare null or void or amend Acts emanating from the public bodies of Signatory States, on the other within two years of its first award of damages, it took the opportunity in *Neumeister* to authoritatively state that the competence conferred upon it to award just satisfaction was very broad indeed, a statement which – as will be seen – it evidently put into practice.

4

EctHR's Approach to Corporate Non-Pecuniary Loss

I Introduction

4/1   Since the seminal case of *Comingersoll SA* v. *Portugal*,[1] the European Court of Human Rights has periodically awarded damages for non-pecuniary loss to companies alleging a violation of their fundamental rights and freedoms. It is convenient to record the Court's jurisprudence in this area and in particular to begin with significant decisions handed down prior to *Comingersoll* before turning to it proper.

II The State of Affairs Pre-*Comingersoll*

A   Tentative Beginnings

4/2   It should be noted at the onset that the practice of recognising corporations as capable of sustaining non-pecuniary loss was not unprecedented in the early case law of the Commission and Court. At the very least, such a possibility was not ruled out.

4/3   Thus, in *Sunday Times* v. *the United Kingdom* (Article 50) the Commission's Delegates repeatedly expressed the view that, in principle, some monetary satisfaction was called for in respect of the '*moral damage* suffered by the applicants', one of which was a company.[2] As none was claimed, however, none was awarded.[3] This is consistent with the principle of *ne ultra petitum* in respect of which a court may not decide more than it has been asked to notwithstanding the victim may be entitled to it.[4] Equally, in *Open Door and Dublin Well Woman* v. *Ireland*, the first

---

[1]   06.04.2000, no. 35382/97.   [2]   06.11.1980, no. 6538/74, §§ 11, 14.

[3]   See r. 60 (on claims for just satisfaction) of the Rules of Court (2016).

[4]   See V. Wilcox, 'Punitive and Nominal Damages' in A. Fenyves, E. Karner, H. Koziol and E. Steiner (eds.), *Tort Law in the Jurisprudence of the European Court of Human Rights* (Berlin/Boston: De Gruyter, 2011), no. 12/24. In exceptional cases, however, the Court does examine, on its own motion, whether to award the applicant damages for non-pecuniary loss for the violation found: *Chamber* v. *Russia*, 03.07.2008, no. 7188/03, § 77;

case in which (pecuniary) compensation was granted to a company, the forward-looking Judge Matscher in his dissenting opinion also felt that there was no reason to deny companies such damages. Although accepting the position of the majority of the Court as regards the substance of the case, he could not agree with the pecuniary sum awarded to Dublin Well Woman Centre Ltd stating: 'at the most it might have been possible to envisage the award of compensation for *non-pecuniary damage*, if such a claim had been submitted [by it]'.[5]

B   A Finding as Sufficient Just Satisfaction

4/4   In fact, Judge Matscher's position was not based on some arbitrary fantasy but in all likelihood emerged from the Court's own transcripts. Two days prior to the decision in *Open Door*, the Court had decided *Idrocalce Srl* v. *Italy*. Having found that the length of civil proceedings in respect of the applicant company could not be regarded as reasonable within the meaning of art. 6(1) ECHR, the Court *unanimously* went on to share the view of the Italian government that a finding of a violation would constitute just satisfaction *as regards non-pecuniary loss*.[6] One could speculate that the absence of an award of damages owed to the Court's finding that the applicant company also contributed to the slowness of proceedings of which it complained.

4/5   In *Manifattura FL* v. *Italy*, a judgment delivered on the same day and by the same panel as *Idrocalce*, having established a violation of art. 6(1) ECHR in respect of the length of proceedings in question, the Court went on to consider the Commission's view that 'the company was entitled to reparation for non-pecuniary damage'.[7] The Court concluded: 'As to the non-pecuniary damage alleged, *assuming that Manifattura FL, a commercial company, was capable of suffering such damage* . . . the finding of a violation of Article 6 para. 1 (art. 6-1) in itself provides sufficient just satisfaction for the purposes of Article 50 (art. 50).'[8] Other cases prior to *Comingersoll* followed these precedents.[9]

X v. *Croatia*, 17.07.2008, no. 11223/04, § 63. In *Cyprus* v. *Turkey* [GC], 12.05.2014, no. 25781/94, Judge Pinto de Albuquerque, joined by Judge Vučinić, opined that where the Court orders compensation without any claim for just satisfaction being lodged by the applicant or where it does so in an amount higher than the alleged damage, such damages are punitive.

[5] 29.10.1992, no. 14234/88; 14235/88. Emphasis added.

[6] 27.02.1992, no. 12088/86, §§ 21–22.   [7] 27.02.1992, no. 12407/86, § 21.

[8] 27.02.1992, no. 12407/86, § 22. Emphasis added.

[9] Among them *Pressos Compania Naviera SA* v. *Belgium* (Article 50), 03.07.1997, no. 17849/91, § 21; *News Verlags GmbH & Co. KG* v. *Austria*, 11.01.2000, no. 31457/96, § 66.

C   Damages for Non-Pecuniary Loss to Corporations?

4/6   *Matos e Silva, Lda* v. *Portugal*, decided in 1993, marked a significant
turn. The application was brought by two limited companies and a Portuguese national who managed both companies. She, along with the second applicant company, was a shareholder in the first applicant. Having
succeeded in convincing the Court that their rights under art. 1, Protocol No. 1 and art. 6(1) ECHR had been violated, the applicants sought
damages for pecuniary and non-pecuniary loss in the later case since
the dispute in question 'had caused them feelings of frustration, pow-
erlessness, suffering and revolt given the brutal manner in which their
rights had been "trampled on" and the discriminatory treatment they
had received.'[10] Assessing the various items of damage on an equitable
basis, the Court considered that 'the *applicants* should be awarded satisfaction of PTE 10,000,000'.[11] That the award evidently contained an
element of damages for non-pecuniary loss is inferable from the Court's
judgment: 'The breaches found . . . make it incumbent on the Court to
assess the damage as a whole *having regard to the uncertainty created by
the length of the proceedings* and to the interferences with the free use
of the property.'[12] As will be seen, the Court conceives of uncertainty
in decision-planning as one of several categories of non-pecuniary loss
(no. 4/31). It could be contended that, given the joint award, the Court
had in mind to exclude the corporate applicants from enjoying the non-
pecuniary ingredient. However, there is evidence to support the opposite
case: the respondent State in *Matos e Silva* specifically argued that 'only
individuals could suffer anxiety and distress because of the uncertainty
into which the length of proceedings plunged them.'[13] No response was
given by the Court. If this was not mere loose use of terminology, it may
be the first instance in which damages for non-pecuniary loss in money
were awarded to a corporate applicant.

D   Other Instructive Cases

4/7   The prospects now promising, companies – and indeed the Commission's Delegate itself – repeatedly sought to petition the Court, though
unsuccessfully, for damages for non-pecuniary loss suffered. *Dombo
Beheer BV* v. *the Netherlands* decided in 1993, for example, was a case
involving the breach of a company's right to a fair trial as guaranteed

---

[10] 16.09.1996, no. 15777/89, § 98.   [11] 16.09.1996, no. 15777/89, § 101. Emphasis added.
[12] 16.09.1996, no. 15777/89, § 101. Emphasis added.   [13] 16.09.1996, no. 15777/89, § 99.

by art. 6(1) ECHR. The Delegate of the Commission recommended an award of damages for non-pecuniary loss to compensate the *'feelings* of unequal treatment by way of non-pecuniary *damage'.*[14] However, the Court dismissed the applicant's claim for just satisfaction on the facts.

4/8   The Court was again presented with the opportunity to determine the propriety of awards of damages for non-pecuniary loss to companies in 1997 in *Garyfallou AEBE* v. *Greece.* The applicant company had sought compensation for alleged damage in the amount of GRD 3,000,000 for a violation of the reasonable time requirement under art. 6(1) ECHR. Although the applicant did not specify the precise nature of the former sum, the Delegate of the Commission submitted that 'some compensation for *moral damage* might be justified given the extremely lengthy proceedings to which the applicant company had been and continued to be subjected.'[15] While granting the claimant's costs, the Court found the applicant company's claims for damages unsubstantiated.

E   Conclusion

4/9   It can thus be seen that the notion that companies are capable of suffering non-pecuniary loss is one that has a long standing in the Court's jurisprudence. A number of observations should be recorded: first, it is the Commission, often via its Delegates, or in *Idrocalce*, for example, the respondent government itself, that were instrumental in persuading the Court to recognise corporations as possible victims of non-pecuniary loss following violations of Convention rights. As will be demonstrated, the Court, in broadening Convention rights, whether substantive, procedural or remedial, places great emphasis on the objections or lack thereof of Signatory States (no. 4/13) so that it is difficult to argue in retrospect that it has usurped the legislative competence or role that belongs to the Member States of the Council of Europe. Second, the Court does not examine the proposition that companies are capable of suffering non-pecuniary loss at this stage but simply assumes it to be feasible. And since applicants cannot be required to 'furnish any proof' of the 'subjective' non-pecuniary loss sustained (no. 3/59), such a conclusion is easy to reach. As a penultimate remark, the Court underlines its perceived weight of the above assumption by holding a finding of a violation to constitute just satisfaction as regards alleged non-pecuniary loss. This raises a further point: that insofar as Bydlinski views a mere finding as a means to compensate

[14] 27.10.1993, no. 14448/88, § 39. Emphasis added.
[15] 24.09.1997, no. 18996/91, § 48. Emphasis added.

emotional or other *psychological suffering* (no. 3/61), his analysis accords with the Delegate of the Commission's approach in cases such as *Dombo Beheer* where it advocated compensation for injury to the *feelings* of the corporate applicant. This, however, seems inconsistent with the Court's emphasis of various rights not being susceptible by their very nature of being exercised by a company (see nos. 3/21–3/22 and 3/24, for example). Finally, the importance of *Matos e Silva* will not be exaggerated as its place in the chronology of cases in which damages for non-pecuniary loss have been awarded to corporations is not altogether decisive.

III   *Comingersoll SA v. Portugal*

A   *The Facts and Reasoning*

4/10   The facts in *Comingersoll* can be stated summarily: a company successfully brought an action under art. 6(1) ECHR and was awarded PTE 1,500,000 for non-pecuniary loss. In arriving at its decision, the Court was guided by the following factors: (a) the practice of the Committee of Ministers acting on proposals put forward by the European Commission of Human Rights; (b) and in the above connection, the fact that respondent governments at no stage challenged the Committee's power to make awards of damages for non-pecuniary loss to companies in earlier cases; (c) its previous case law on a looser organisation; (d) the practice of the Member States of the Council of Europe of awarding companies damages for non-pecuniary loss; and (e) the need for the Convention to be interpreted and applied in such a way as to guarantee rights that are practical and effective.

1   The Practice of the Committee of Ministers

4/11   The Court founded its authority to award damages for non-pecuniary loss in *Comingersoll* on the strength of the fact that: 'Under the former Convention system, the Committee of Ministers, acting on proposals put forward by the European Commission of Human Rights, ha[d] in a number of cases awarded compensation for the non-pecuniary damage sustained by commercial companies as a result of the excessive length of proceedings.'[16] The Committee of Ministers, being a political body, normally confines itself to confirming the conclusions reached by the Commission. That the European Commission of Human Rights was at the forefront of efforts to promote the equality of treatment between

---

[16] *Comingersoll SA v. Portugal* [GC], 06.04.2000, no. 35382/97, § 33.

natural and juristic persons in this field has already been noted earlier. In practice, however, the Commission is likely to have taken the lead from the Court's acceptance in cases like *Idrocalce* and *Manifattura* that companies could presumably suffer damage of a non-pecuniary nature.

4/12   Under the terms of then art. 32(4) of the Convention,[17] the Committee thus agreed with the Commission's proposals to award damages for non-pecuniary loss against Portugal for art. 6(1) ECHR violations on two occasions: in *Dias E Costa LDA* v. *Portugal*[18] and *Biscoiteria LDA* v. *Portugal*,[19] the applicant companies were awarded PTE 585,000 and PTE 540,000 respectively. On the facts, it is unclear quite how the Commission arrived at its conclusion to award damages for non-pecuniary loss and for what they sought to remedy. The opacity is compounded by the fact that the Commission's report is classified.

2   States' Responses or Lack Thereof

4/13   The Court in its case law has on a number of occasions taken into consideration the lack of challenge by respondent governments to the decisions of Convention bodies. Thus, in *Comingersoll*, it justified itself, inter alia, on the basis that 'the Governments themselves have at no stage challenged the Committee of Ministers' power to make such awards in other Portuguese cases in which it has taken such decisions'.[20] Indeed, nor did the governments in *Idrocalce* and *Manifattura* challenge the possibility of a company to sustain non-pecuniary loss. Actually, in the first of the cases listed, it was the government that pursued the argument. On the other hand, objections appeared to have made no difference in fact as the futile government protests in *Matos e Silva* and *Comingersoll* prove. In the latter case, Portugal contended that:

> the purpose of awarding compensation for non-pecuniary damage for an alleged violation of the right to a hearing within a reasonable time [is] to provide *reparation for anxiety, the mental stress* of having to wait for the outcome of the case and uncertainty.... *[S]uch feelings [are] peculiar to natural persons* and [can] under no circumstances entitle a juristic person to compensation.[21]

---

[17] 'The High Contracting Parties undertake to regard as binding on them any decision which the Committee of Ministers may take in application of the preceding paragraphs'.
[18] Resolution DH(96)604 of 15 November 1996.
[19] Resolution DH(99)708 of 3 December 1999.
[20] 06.04.2000, no. 35382/97, § 33. The Court was referring here to *Dias E Costa LDA* and *Biscoiteria LDA*.
[21] *Comingersoll SA* v. *Portugal* [GC], 06.04.2000, no. 35382/97, § 28.

3   The Previous Case Law of the EctHR

4/14   Among the reasons the Court gave in its *Comingersoll* ruling for awarding the company damages for non-pecuniary loss was *its* own case law
and practice: *Vereinigung Demokratischer Soldaten Österreichs (VDSÖ)
and Gubi* v. *Austria* involved a successful action under art. 10 ECHR (and
art. 13 ECHR in the case of the first applicant) by a private association
under Austrian law, the VDSÖ and Mr Berthold Gubi, one of its members, in respect of distribution prohibitions imposed on the association's
magazine. The latter, published monthly, was aimed at soldiers serving
in the Austrian army and contained information and articles – often of
a critical nature – on military life. The VDSÖ and the second applicant's
claim for damages for non-pecuniary loss, in an amount which they left
to the discretion of the Court, was supported by the Delegate of the Commission and the Court concluded that a finding of a violation afforded
both applicants sufficient just satisfaction for any 'non-pecuniary damage
that *they* may have suffered'.[22] The decision is seminal in that it marks the
first instance in which the Court itself acknowledged the capacity for an
association to suffer 'non-pecuniary damage', albeit redressed by way of
words.

4/15   *Freedom and Democracy Party (ÖZDEP)* v. *Turkey* was the earliest
instance in which the Court awarded pecuniary compensation for non-
pecuniary loss in a case brought by a *political party*. The ÖZDEP was a
Turkish party which, acting through its chairman, lodged an application
claiming a violation of its members' rights to freedom of association
under art. 11 ECHR after the party was forced to dissolve itself. The Court
ordered an award of FRF 30,000 for non-pecuniary loss. In so doing, it
had recourse to the fact that the dissolution, which was carried out under
threat by the Constitutional Court, must have been *highly frustrating*
for the 'founders and members' of the party.[23] It distinctively articulated
that the award, to be paid to the ÖZDEP's chairman, was to compensate
the non-pecuniary loss sustained by the 'founders and members' of the
applicant party.

4/16   While the decision reached in *Comingersoll* appears to logically pro-
gress from the Court's case law on looser organisations, in reality, the legal
foundation for the advancement of damages for non-pecuniary loss to
companies preceded *VDSÖ* and *ÖZDEP*. Although not cited in *Comingersoll*, it is cases like *Idrocalce* and *Manifattura*, delivered prior to *VDSÖ*

---

[22]   19.12.1994, no. 15153/89, § 62. Emphasis added.
[23]   08.12.1999, no. 23885/94, § 57.

and *ÖZDEP* that are instructive illustrations of the resolution of the Convention's earlier stewards to redress Convention violations, albeit through the adoption of assumptive means. In this respect, the Grand Chamber in *Comingersoll* seems to have overlooked its earlier precedents.

4   The Practice of the Member States of the Council of Europe

4/17   At the time *Comingersoll* came before the Court, it was clear that a number of constituent Council of Europe States already endorsed the practice of awarding companies damages for non-pecuniary loss (see no. 3/8 above on reference to domestic law and practice). Although the Court in *Comingersoll* stated that it was 'difficult to identify a precise rule common to all the member States', it reasoned that compensation for non-pecuniary loss could not be ruled out.[24] In the absence of access to the above comparative exercise, Chapter 8 attempts to gain insight into the approach taken to the topic at hand in key Council of Europe States with an eye to assessing the efficacy of the EctHR's jurisprudence in this field.

5   The Need to Guarantee Rights that are Practical and Effective

4/18   To support its above findings, the Court in *Comingersoll* also looked to its interpretive methods. A grounding reason for the Court's finding that a juristic person may be awarded compensation for non-pecuniary loss arose as a result of the application of the effectiveness principle (no. 3/7). The Court stated that '*since the principal form of redress which the Court may order is pecuniary compensation*, it must necessarily be empowered, if the right guaranteed by Article 6 of the Convention is to be *effective*, to award pecuniary compensation for non-pecuniary damage to commercial companies, too.'[25] The effectiveness principle was thus cited as a means to overcome the historical limitations placed on the Court's remedial jurisdictions at the time the Convention was drafted (nos. 3/54–3/57).

B   The Decision and Dissenting Opinion

4/19   There are two aspects to the *Comingersoll* ruling: not only is it authority for the proposition that corporations are capable of (direct) non-pecuniary loss but in addition, the case set the precedent of what we will here refer to as the 'attribution theory or doctrine' (i.e. that they can also sustain indirect non-pecuniary loss). In particular, the Court in

---

[24] 06.04.2000, no. 35382/97, § 34.   [25] 06.04.2000, no. 35382/97, § 35. Emphasis added.

Comingersoll ruled that, in computing the appropriate amount of damages for non-pecuniary loss owed, account should be taken, inter alia, of 'uncertainty in decision-planning' and 'the anxiety and inconvenience caused to the members of the management team'[26] as a result of the breach (see Section V). The dissenting judges questioned the Court's reliance on ÖZDEP since the protected right in question there was the freedom of association *of the members of that party* who established and organised it. Unlike a political party, a company is '*an independent living organism,* protected as such by the legal order of the State concerned, and whose rights also receive autonomous protection under the European Convention on Human Rights.'[27] The four judges were thus unable to share the Court's approach and could not see why the latter should be 'prevented from accepting, without any reservation, implied or otherwise, that a company may suffer non-pecuniary damage, not because of the *anxiety* or *uncertainty* felt by its human components, but because, as a legal person, in the society in which it operates, *it has attributes,* such as its own reputation, that may be impaired by acts or omissions of the State.'[28] The significance of this aspect of the ruling and the opinion of the dissenting judges will be considered in more detail in Chapter 7.

IV   Awards of Damages for Non-Pecuniary Loss to Corporations under the ECHR

4/20   Since *Comingersoll,* the Court has been active in awarding damages for non-pecuniary loss to companies. Such is its impact that several friendly settlements on just satisfaction have been reached,[29] and national courts have brought their case law in conformity with its ruling (see nos. 8/12–8/14). Given the Court's case-by-case approach, the parameters of the Convention remain somewhat uncertain; no doubt, however, the list of articles under which damages for non-pecuniary loss have been awarded to companies will increase as appropriate cases present themselves before the Court.

4/21   Of the various Convention provisions, art. 6(1) ECHR, and in particular its length of judicial proceedings aspect, has most occupied the Strasbourg Court in quantitative terms, and this also holds true with

---

[26] 06.04.2000, no. 35382/97, § 35.   [27] Emphasis added.   [28] Emphasis added.

[29] See among others, *Gefima Immobiliare srl* v. *Italy,* 19.04.2001, no. 33943/96, §§ 16–18 and *Immobiliare Anba* v. *Italy,* 04.10.2001, no. 31916/96, §§ 14–16; *Baroul Partner-A* v. *Moldova,* 19.10.2010, no. 39815/07, §§ 4–5.

respect to applications by companies.[30] Incidentally, the backlog at the Strasbourg Court itself is notorious. The Court has also awarded damages for non-pecuniary loss to corporations in respect of other articles including art. 7 ECHR (no punishment without law),[31] aspects of art. 8 ECHR (right to respect for private and family),[32] arts. 10 (freedom of expression),[33] 13 (right to an effective remedy)[34] and 34 (individual applications) ECHR.[35] In addition, it has on a number of occasions considered an award of compensation for non-pecuniary loss justified in respect of corporate applicants under art. 1, Protocol No. 1 (protection of property).[36]

V Objective and Subjective Non-Pecuniary Loss

4/22   Extrajudicially, it has been admitted that 'the number of elements that serve to make up the notion of non-pecuniary damage is high, and the list is rather vague.'[37] A similar observation has also been made in scholarly writings.[38] The Court has, however, attempted to set forth some guidelines. Having determined that it was entirely appropriate to award companies damages for non-pecuniary loss, the Court in *Comingersoll* went on to state that non-pecuniary loss suffered by companies may

---

[30] As was the case in *Comingersoll SA* v. *Portugal* [GC], 06.04.2000, no. 35382/97, §§ 36–37 itself. The European Court has not infrequently awarded damages for non-pecuniary loss to companies where the applicant has been denied access to court and in respect of other fair trial aspects: *Qufaj Co. Shpk* v. *Albania*, 18.11.2004, no. 54268/00, §§ 45, 63; *Marpa Zeeland BV and Metal Welding BV* v. *the Netherlands*, 09.11.2004, no. 46300/99, §§ 51, 64, 71; *Teltronic-CATV* v. *Poland*, 10.01.2006, no. 48140/99, §§ 64, 70 among others.

[31] *Sud Fondi srl* v. *Italy*, 20.01.2009, no. 75909/01, §§ 118, 154.

[32] *Société Colas Est* v. *France*, 16.04.2002, no. 37971/97, §§ 50, 55.

[33] *Meltex Ltd and Mesrop Movsesyan* v. *Armenia*, 17.06.2008, no. 32283/04, §§ 85, 105 and *Centro Europa 7 Srl and Di Stefano* v. *Italy* [GC], 07.06.2012, no. 38433/09, §§ 157, 222 among other authorities.

[34] *Iza Ltd and Makrakhidze* v. *Georgia*, 27.09.2005, no. 28537/02, §§ 49, 63; *Glas Nadezhda EOOD and Elenkov* v. *Bulgaria*, 11.10.2007, no. 14134/02, §§ 71, 75 and *ZIT Company* v. *Serbia*, 27.11.2007, no. 37343/05, §§ 65, 69 among other authorities.

[35] *Oferta Plus SRL* v. *Moldova*, 12.02.2008, no. 14385/04, § 76.

[36] *Dacia SRL* v. *Moldova*, 24.02.2009, no. 3052/04, §§ 2, 62; *Rock Ruby Hotels Ltd* v. *Turkey*, 26.10.2010, no. 46159/99, §§ 2, 36–37; *Centro Europa 7 Srl and Di Stefano* v. *Italy* [GC], 07.06.2012, no. 38433/09, §§ 188, 221–222.

[37] J.-P. Costa, 'The Provision of Compensation under Article 41 of the European Convention on Human Rights' in D. Fairgrieve, M. Andenas and J. Bell (eds.), *Tort Liability of Public Authorities in Comparative Perspective* (London: BIICL, 2002), p. 8.

[38] See, for example, D. Shelton, *Remedies in International Human Rights Law*, 3rd edn (Oxford University Press, 2015) p. 364.

include heads of claim that are to a greater or lesser extent 'objective' or 'subjective'.[39] Regrettably, the Court has not elaborated further on these two categories. It did, however, state that among such heads of claim, account should be taken of:

(a) the company's reputation;
(b) uncertainty in decision-planning;
(c) disruption in the management of the company; and
(d) lastly, albeit to a lesser degree, the anxiety and inconvenience caused to the members of the management team.

4/23   While said in the context of art. 6 ECHR, the above considerations now have general application. The paragraphs which follow examine the Court's case law in a bid to understand the nature of the terms 'objective' and 'subjective' non-pecuniary loss. Since the guidance arose in the context of art. 6 ECHR, the analysis begins there.

A   The Violation of Art. 6 ECHR

4/24   Where the Court finds it appropriate to afford monetary satisfaction for inordinate length of proceedings, several considerations appear to be relevant in calculating the appropriate amount of damages for non-pecuniary loss. Some such factors are closely linked to the Court's finding that there has been a violation on account of the length in the first place. A detailed analysis of the Court's approach under this head leads one to question whether such damages are non-pecuniary at all. This is supported by the fact that, as with English law, no single European tort system traditionally recognised non-pecuniary loss in such cases,[40] although the legal landscape is now changing in response to Strasbourg jurisprudence.

4/25   With respect to the merits, the starting point is that there is no absolute or objective limit to the length of time that can be taken to decide a case. The question whether there has been a delay contrary to the requirements of art. 6(1) ECHR cannot therefore be decided *in abstracto* with reference only to the total length of the proceedings. Whether there has been an unreasonable delay is a matter that must be assessed in the light of the particular facts of the case and having regard to the criteria laid down in

---

[39] *Comingersoll SA* v. *Portugal* [GC], 06.04.2000, no. 35382/97, § 35.
[40] H. Koziol, 'Concluding Remarks on Compensatory and Non-Compensatory Remedies' in A. Fenyves, E. Karner, H. Koziol and E. Steiner (eds.), *Tort Law in the Jurisprudence of the European Court of Human Rights* (Berlin/Boston: De Gruyter, 2011), nos. 22/13–22/16.

the Court's case law, in particular the complexity of the case, the conduct of the applicant and of the relevant authorities and the importance of what was at stake for the applicant in the litigation. Elements of wrongfulness and causation thus come into play.

4/26   As regards complexity, whether factual or legal, a case that is very complex may justify what would otherwise be seen as unreasonably protracted proceedings. As regards conduct, a breach of art. 6(1) ECHR can only be found where it is established that there have been delays attributable to the State; thus even though the dilatory nature of proceedings may, on the face of it, seem unreasonable, the conduct of the applicant may lead the Court to conclude his complaint was unfounded. Finally, as regards what is at stake for the applicant, if the applicant's material interest in the outcome of the proceedings is considerable, the proceedings in question will call for special expedition.

4/27   Once a violation is found, the Court then turns to the measure of just satisfaction to be awarded, if any. To allow for equivalent results in similar cases, damages for non-pecuniary loss under art. 6(1) ECHR have been calculated through compensation scales or tables since the 1990s.[41] These tables are not publicly available. However, it would seem that in the first place the calculation is based on the particular period that was attributed to the State as an unreasonable delay. The longer the delay, the more damages for non-pecuniary loss are due. The Court also takes the number of tiers of proceedings into consideration. A complex case may require a large number of instances before a decision is reached, and if legitimately pursued, this should not be held against a State. Conversely, what was at stake for the applicant appears to increase the total award. In the case of a high number of applicants, the calculation is further complicated by the fact that the overall amount of just satisfaction to be awarded in respect of non-pecuniary loss will very probably be reduced.[42] In the final step the Court applies adjustment rates, taking into account the local economic circumstances in the respondent State to adjust the tabled amount of damages for non-pecuniary loss in some jurisdictions.[43] Unsurprisingly,

---

[41]   *Scordino* v. *Italy (No. 1)* [GC], 29.03.2006, no. 36813/97, § 176 and *Cocchiarella* v. *Italy* [GC], 29.03.2006, no. 64886/01, § 67.

[42]   '[T]he number of participants . . . may influence the level of distress, inconvenience and uncertainty affecting each of them. Thus, a high number of participants will very probably have an impact on the amount of just satisfaction to be awarded in respect of non-pecuniary damage. . . . Membership of a group of people who have resolved to apply to a court on the same factual or legal basis means that both the advantages and disadvantages of common proceedings will be shared.': *Kakamoukas* v. *Greece* [GC], 15.02.2008, no. 38311/02, § 41.

[43]   *Practice Direction on Just Satisfaction Claims* (2016), para. 2.

the Court has itself admitted, in the context of art. 6(1) ECHR, that: 'It is impossible... to account in detail for the relative importance of each of the factors taken into consideration in calculating the amount to be awarded for non-pecuniary damage, an amount which is determined on an equitable basis.'[44]

4/28   The unique application of 'damages for non-pecuniary loss' in this field leads one to speculate on the true nature of the award here. A line worth pursuing is that such damages are what English lawyers term 'general damages'. As mentioned in no. 1/2 earlier, general damages concern themselves with non-pecuniary loss. However, pecuniary loss may also count as general damage where proof of the exact loss sustained is in issue. Indeed, the Strasbourg Court is mindful that assessing damages for pecuniary loss can at times pose formidable hurdles, hence its practice of making a global assessment in respect of pecuniary and non-pecuniary losses. It does this where 'one or more heads of damage cannot be calculated precisely or if the distinction between pecuniary and non-pecuniary damage proves difficult.'[45] Where the damage is *in respect of length only* (as the formula used in the tables detailed earlier suggests) and the damages do not seek to compensate any interference with the bodily, mental, emotional and/or personality spheres, it is submitted that such damage is not 'non-pecuniary' in the narrow sense of the word but rather unquantifiable pecuniary damage (hence the Court's reference to 'objective' non-pecuniary loss).[46] The conclusion applies in respect of both non-natural and natural persons. To the extent that pecuniary loss that is difficult to translate into hard currency is masquerading as objective 'non-pecuniary loss', the receipt of such damages by corporations in respect of such harm raises no issues, except that it would be conducive to clarity to call them damages for pecuniary loss or some term other than 'damages for non-pecuniary loss'. This is because reference to non-pecuniary loss only emphasises one element of such damage – i.e. that it is difficult to calculate – which is also a feature of some types of pecuniary damage. It fails to include the other distinctive feature of non-pecuniary loss, i.e. that it must involve interference with the bodily, mental, emotional and/or personality spheres, most of which are peculiar to human beings.

[44] *Kakamoukas* v. *Greece* [GC], 15.02.2008, no. 38311/02, § 40.
[45] *Comingersoll SA* v. *Portugal* [GC], 06.04.2000, no. 35382/97, § 29.
[46] Incidentally, the Strasbourg Court's approach is actually consistent with the findings of the Royal Commission on Civil Liability and Compensation for Personal Injury in England which identified three aims of damages for non-pecuniary loss, one of which is to *ensure full justice in meeting hidden expenses caused by an injury*: Royal Commission on Civil Liability and Compensation for Personal Injury (1978: Cmnd 7054-I).

4/29   Apart from unquantifiable pecuniary loss, another way of seeing damages awarded for length under art. 6(1) ECHR is as a preventive or punitive instrument. Indeed, although in a different context, several scholars have also recognised the abuse of damages for non-pecuniary loss as damages for pecuniary loss or for punitive purposes.[47] The use of tables to standardise compensation often has the effect of curtailing judicial discretion to award damages in excess of basic compensatory damages. However, in *Scordino* v. *Italy* (No. 1) and *Cocchiarella* v. *Italy*,[48] the Court revealed that the scales led it to award higher levels of compensation than those awarded by the Convention's institutions prior to 1999. It hastened to add that this increase was not a punitive measure. However, this post-transitional augmentation of damages for non-pecuniary loss under art. 6(1) ECHR was never justified. It cannot be explained in terms of inflation, as inflation would apply to swell damages across all the other Convention articles. The increase is in an area which happens to account for a vast majority of the Court's judgments – an area that would benefit from deterrence: a stated goal of punitive damages. Finally, the purpose of the increase is, inter alia, to '*encourage* States to find their own, universally accessible, solution to the problem.'[49] However optimistically nuanced, this practice bears the hallmarks of punitive damages, a head of damages which aims to punish and deter the defendant and mark the judge's disapproval for his reprehensible conduct. Of course, the Court is mindful that such damages do not form part of the laws of the majority of its Member States and so does not award them openly.[50] That said, 'the existence of punitive or exemplary damages under the Convention is a fact in the Court's practice' has been admitted by the Court's own judges and indeed, it is advocated by the Council of Europe.[51] On this conclusion, there is

---

[47] Among them, O. Moréteau and A.-D. On, 'France' in K. Oliphant and B. C. Steininger (eds.), *European Tort Law 2012* (Berlin/Boston: De Gruyter, 2013), no. 45. O. Moréteau, 'France' in H. Koziol (ed.), *Basic Questions of Tort Law from a Comparative Perspective* (Wien: Sramek Verlag, 2015), no. 1/66. See also A. J. Sebok and V. Wilcox, 'Aggravated Damages' in H. Koziol and V. Wilcox, *Punitive Damages: Common Law and Civil Law Perspectives* (Wien/New York: Springer, 2009), no. 27.

[48] *Scordino* v. *Italy (No. 1)* [GC], 29.03.2006, no. 36813/97, § 176 and *Cocchiarella* v. *Italy* [GC], 29.03.2006, no. 64886/01, § 67.

[49] *Musci* v. *Italy* [GC], 29.03.2006, no. 64699/01, § 68. Emphasis added.

[50] As to their suitability at national level see H. Koziol, 'Punitive Damages: Admission into the Seventh Legal Heaven or Eternal Damnation? Comparative Report and Conclusions' in H. Koziol and V. Wilcox, *Punitive Damages: Common Law and Civil Law Perspectives* (Wien/New York: Springer, 2009).

[51] See the concurring opinion of Judge Pinto de Albuquerque, joined by Judge Vučinić in *Cyprus* v. *Turkey* [GC], 12.05.2014, no. 25781/94. In addition to listing the various instances where such damages have been awarded, the judges gave guidance as to when

parity between companies and individuals; the approach explains why such damages are awarded 'almost automatically, without inquiring into the victim's psychological situation.'[52] Given the predominantly civil law composition of Council of Europe States, damages that exceed *restitutio in integrum* will be difficult to sell, however. Moreover, such covert abuse of damages for non-pecuniary loss ought not to be encouraged.

B   The Company's Reputation

4/30   While it is unclear whether the protection of injury to corporate reputation falls within the ambit of art. 8 ECHR (nos. 3/35–3/37), what is evident is that injury to reputation outside that context is generally compensable. Thus, the Court has ruled, inter alia, that a company may validly claim that the length of proceedings has adversely affected its reputation. In *Sovtransavto Holding* v. *Ukraine*,[53] for example, it held that uncertainty undermined the reputation of the company's brand in the eyes of current and potential customers in violation of art. 6 ECHR. However, the Court has said elsewhere that the fact of exceeding the 'reasonable time' requirement does not of itself damage the applicant's reputation.[54] A causal link must be established between the violation in question and the alleged loss of the applicant company's reputation and the events at issue must negatively affect the company's reputation in a marked way. In addition to damages for pecuniary loss, some of which may be difficult to quantify, injury to corporate reputation also sounds in non-pecuniary loss, since it involves injury to the company's personality, and such damages can rightfully be awarded to corporations (nos. 5/45–5/48).

C   Uncertainty in Decision-Planning

4/31   The Court has repeatedly acknowledged that uncertainty can be disruptive and impacts negatively in that a company cannot fully plan its activities. Again, the events at issue must negatively affect planning and

---

they would be appropriate. On the facts, they opined that a € 90 million award of damages for non-pecuniary loss (in an inter-state application) included an element of punitive damages.

[52] K. Oliphant and K. Ludwichowska, 'Damage' in A. Fenyves, E. Karner, H. Koziol and E. Steiner (eds.), *Tort Law in the Jurisprudence of the European Court of Human Rights* (Berlin/Boston: De Gruyter, 2011), no. 6/33.

[53] 02.10.2003, no. 48553/99, § 80.

[54] *König* v. *Germany* (Article 50), 10.03.1980, no. 6232/73, § 19, albeit said in a non-corporate context.

decision making in a sizeable manner. The case law under this head is divided as follows: where the Court perceives that the applicant company itself was placed in a state of uncertainty;[55] where the uncertainty is said to have been caused to the company's management;[56] or the violation is said to have caused uncertainty to the applicant company, its directors and shareholders.[57] Since the notion of 'uncertainty' is one which generally affects the mental and/or emotional spheres, it would seem the damage referred to here is so-called objective 'non-pecuniary' damage in the sense of pecuniary damage that is difficult to quantify or uncertainty felt by the company's human components. Although a novel approach, the 'attribution theory' seems defensible insofar as it is in respect of uncertainty experienced by the company's directors or management team (Chapter 7).

D   Disruption in the Management

4/32   Significant disruption may arise under different guises. For example, failure or delay in enforcing a judgment may result in a company encountering problems with the tax authorities.[58] Alternatively, it may be the company's general plans that are disrupted as a result of the violation.[59] Again, one is inclined to view such damage as unquantifiable pecuniary damage especially where the disruption is to a company's 'economic activities',[60] unless what the Court is doing here is attributing the disruption experienced by the management team to the company.

E   Anxiety and Inconvenience Caused

4/33   Although the phrase used in *Comingersoll* was 'the anxiety and inconvenience caused to the members of the management team', in practice it is not only members of the company's management who are perceived

---

[55]   *Eko-Energie spol sro* v. *the Czech Republic*, 17.05.2005, no. 65191/01, § 40; *Centro Europa 7 Srl and Di Stefano* v. *Italy* [GC], 07.06.2012, no. 38433/09, § 216.

[56]   *Meltex Ltd and Mesrop Movsesyan* v. *Armenia*, 17.06.2008, no. 32283/04, § 105; *Tudor-Comert* v. *Moldova*, 04.11.2008, no. 27888/04, § 46; *Business si Investiţii Pentru Toţi* v. *Moldova*, 13.10.2009, no. 39391/04, § 38.

[57]   *Comingersoll SA* v. *Portugal* [GC], 06.04.2000, no. 35382/97, § 36; *Wohlmeyer Bau GmbH* v. *Austria*, 08.07.2004, no. 20077/02, § 61; *Petikon Oy and Parviainen* v. *Finland*, 27.01.2009, no. 26189/06, § 46; *Rock Ruby Hotels Ltd* v. *Turkey*, 26.10.2010, no. 46159/99, § 36; *Skyropiia Yialias Ltd* v. *Turkey*, 26.10.2010, no. 47884/99, § 37.

[58]   *Iza Ltd and Makrakhidze* v. *Georgia*, 27.09.2005, no. 28537/02, § 63.

[59]   *Business si Investiţii Pentru Toţi* v. *Moldova*, 13.10.2009, no. 39391/04, § 38.

[60]   *Iza Ltd and Makrakhidze* v. *Georgia*, 27.09.2005, no. 28537/02, § 63.

to have suffered such inconvenience.[61] As above, the Court sometimes refers to the company itself[62] or the applicant company, its directors and shareholders.[63] That this is more appropriately assessed as constituting unquantifiable pecuniary damage is shared by Rogers.[64] It may also constitute attributed non-pecuniary loss.

F   Other Suffering

4/34   In addition to the heads of non-pecuniary loss specifically referred to in *Comingersoll*, damages for non-pecuniary loss have also been awarded for other forms of suffering, namely stress,[65] distress,[66] emotional loss[67] and frustration.[68] At times such non-pecuniary injury is said to have been experienced by the *company itself*. This was the case in *Qufaj Shpk* v. *Albania*, for example, where the Court accepted, as regards the non-pecuniary loss, that '*the applicant company* suffered *distress* that would have been avoided had the authorities complied with the final decision.'[69] Similarly in *Centro Europa 7 Srl and Di Stefano* v. *Italy*, the Grand Chamber ruled that the violations it had found of art. 10 ECHR and art. 1, Protocol No. 1 'must have caused *the applicant company . . . feelings of helplessness and frustration*'.[70] Such feelings may also be said to have been caused to the applicant company's management team[71] or to both the applicant company and its human components.[72] Since these refer to

---

[61] *Belvedere Alberghiera Srl* v. *Italy*, 30.10.2003, no. 31524/96, § 41.

[62] *Eko-Energie spol sro* v. *the Czech Republic*, 17.05.2005, no. 65191/01, § 40; *Unistar Ventures Gmbh* v. *Moldova*, 09.12.2008, no. 19245/03, § 106.

[63] *Comingersoll SA* v. *Portugal* [GC], 06.04.2000, no. 35382/97, § 36; *Wohlmeyer Bau GmbH* v. *Austria*, 08.07.2004, no. 20077/02, § 61; *Rock Ruby Hotels Ltd* v. *Turkey*, 26.10.2010, no. 46159/99, § 36.

[64] W. V. H. Rogers, 'Comparative Report' in W. V. Horton Rogers (ed.), *Damages for Non-Pecuniary Loss in Comparative Perspective* (Wien/New York: Springer, 2001), no. 63.

[65] *Deservire SRL* v. *Moldova*, 06.10.2009, no. 17328/04, § 62.

[66] *Alithia Publishing Company* v. *Cyprus*, 11.07.2002, no. 53594/99, § 45.

[67] *Dacia SRL* v. *Moldova*, 24.02.2009, no. 3052/04, § 61.

[68] *Meltex Ltd and Mesrop Movsesyan* v. *Armenia*, 17.06.2008, no. 32283/04, § 105; *Deservire SRL* v. *Moldova*, 06.10.2009, no. 17328/04, § 62.

[69] 18.11.2004, no. 54268/00, 63. Emphasis added. See also *SC Apron Dynamics SRL Baia Mare* v. *Romania*, 02.11.2010, no. 21199/03, § 60.

[70] 07.06.2012, no. 38433/09, § 221. Emphasis added.

[71] *Meltex Ltd and Mesrop Movsesyan* v. *Armenia*, 17.06.2008, no. 32283/04, § 105; *Dacia SRL* v. *Moldova*, 24.02.2009, no. 3052/04, § 61; *Deservire SRL* v. *Moldova*, 06.10.2009, no. 17328/04, § 62; *Bucuria* v. *Moldova*, 05.01.2010, no. 10758/05, § 38.

[72] *Alithia Publishing Company* v. *Cyprus*, 11.07.2002, no. 53594/99, § 45; *Marpa Zeeland BV and Metal Welding BV* v. *the Netherlands*, 09.11.2004, no. 46300/99, § 71.

inherently human characteristics, the Court must of necessity be referring to pecuniary or imputed non-pecuniary harm.

G Loss of (Real) Opportunities

4/35   There is no coherent theory as to the precise nature of this head. As Lord Bingham in *R* v. *Secretary of State for the Home Department, ex parte Greenfield* observed, English lawyers would call them general damages (in the sense of unquantifiable pecuniary loss). The Strasbourg Court 'tends to call [them], but not always consistently, non-pecuniary damage.'[73] In *Markass Car Hire Ltd* v. *Cyprus*, for example, a case on art. 6(1) ECHR, the Court refused to award the applicant company any compensation for pecuniary damage. However, it accepted that it 'suffered damage of a non-pecuniary nature *as well as* a loss of opportunities as a result of the length of the proceedings' and as such awarded it € 15,000 'as compensation for non-pecuniary damage.'[74] Reference to 'as well as' intimates that the Court does not consider damages for loss of opportunity real non-pecuniary loss and mention of the difficulties in evaluating such damage[75] confirms that they do not fall within the core pecuniary sphere. That they are pecuniary in nature, however, has been acknowledged in some Strasbourg cases.[76] To the extent that awards under this head are nothing more than a pragmatic acceptance that some unquantifiable pecuniary damage worthy of damages has arisen, there is no issue with corporations' receipt of them.

H Lack of Reasoning

4/36   In addition to the above, there are numerous instances where the Court does not specifically elaborate on the purpose of the award of damages for non-pecuniary loss in question at all, at times stating that the company 'must have' sustained it as a result of the violation.[77]

---

[73] [2005] 1 WLR 673, para. 12 per Lord Bingham.
[74] 02.07.2002, no. 51591/99, § 50. Emphasis added.
[75] *Paykar Yev Haghtanak Ltd* v. *Armenia*, 20.12.2007, no. 21638/03, § 56.
[76] See *Dombo Beheer BV* v. *the Netherlands*, 27.10.1993, no. 14448/88, § 39, for example, where the Delegate of the Commission suggested that the Court take into account some loss of opportunities by way of *pecuniary damage*.
[77] See *Bielectric Srl* v. *Italy*, 16.11.2000, no. 36811/97, § 28; *Société Colas Est* v. *France*, 16.04.2002, no. 37971/97, § 55 and *EVT Company* v. *Serbia*, 21.06.2007, no. 3102/05, § 58 among other authorities.

VI A Finding as Just Satisfaction

4/37 The preceding paragraphs have concentrated on cases where pecuniary sums were awarded for non-pecuniary losses. To complete the picture, there have been a number of instances where the Court has ruled that its judgment amounted to just satisfaction for any non-pecuniary loss the applicant company sustained as a result of the violation. Indeed, this is the approach the Court took as a starting point in its quest to afford satisfaction for non-pecuniary loss to companies (nos. 4/4–4/5 and 4/9). Occasionally, it points to equity[78] or concludes that the circumstances of the case simply do not disclose any factors justifying the award of compensation for non-pecuniary loss.[79] The Court has also granted a finding as just satisfaction as 'compensation' where it considers that 'the applicant company *may have* suffered non-pecuniary damage.'[80]

4/38 In a bid to come to terms with what has been termed a reproduction of words stored in the Court's word processor,[81] Bydlinski suggested that the 'finding' seeks to assuage negative psychological effects of the violation and to counter the negative upset or emotional damage caused by it (no. 3/61). Such a conclusion is not unreasonable in the case of natural victims whose emotional suffering is recognisable by 'common human experience'.[82] Even then, however, scholars have observed 'the relative ease with which the Court will infer that a victim has suffered distress or frustration, or some other non-pecuniary damage'. This, they say, 'problematises the distinction between violation and damage',[83] especially in the case of companies which have no feelings to hurt (nos. 5/8 and 8/3–8/6). One could surmise that it is the company's human components the Court has regard to in ensuring satisfaction via its judgment. That conclusion ignores the fact, however, that the attribution doctrine

---

[78] *Pekárny a cukrárny Klatovy, as* v. *the Czech Republic*, 12.01.2012, no. 12266/07; 40059/07; 36038/09; 47155/09, § 86–88. As has been observed, the EctHR usually hides behind the cloak of 'equity' in distinguishing cases where damages for non-pecuniary loss are necessary from those where they are not: Shelton, *Remedies in International Human Rights Law*, p. 287.

[79] *Karhuvaara and Iltalehti* v. *Finland*, 16.11.2004, no. 53678/00, § 60; *Rodinná záložna, spořitelní a úvěrní družstvo* v. *the Czech Republic*, 19.01.2012, no. 74152/01, §§ 18–19.

[80] *'Bulves' AD* v. *Bulgaria*, 22.01.2009, no. 3991/03, § 83; *SA Dangeville* v. *France*, 16.04.2002, no. 36677/97, § 70.

[81] *R* v. *Secretary of State for the Home Department, ex parte Greenfield* [2005] 1 WLR 673, para. 15 per Lord Bingham.

[82] Shelton, *Remedies in International Human Rights Law*, p. 351.

[83] Oliphant and Ludwichowska, 'Damage', no. 6/3. Rogers, 'Comparative Report', no. 68 also speaks of the Court's readiness 'to presume compensable anxiety and distress'.

of *Comingersoll* was conceived long *after* the Court devised this non-intrusive remedy. Then again, it is true that judges 'are often led by their intuition'; in reality they 'first think what the law should be and then say that this is actually the law.'[84] The validity of retrospective reasoning in this case need not necessarily be ruled out therefore. A further argument is that non-pecuniary loss is inherent in a violation of the right itself.[85] However, injury to a non-pecuniary interest, which in the case of a company is an interest in its personality sphere (nos. 5/45–5/48 and 8/7–8/11), must still be shown, and the fact is that not all Convention provisions impinge upon corporate personality. That theory is also not supported by the fact that not all violations result in a finding of a violation as sufficient satisfaction as regards non-pecuniary loss (or in a monetary award for non-pecuniary loss) despite the acknowledgement of a violation.[86] Beyond this, the Court may well be recognising minor unquantifiable pecuniary loss, a practice which as argued earlier should be abandoned in favour of more accurate terminology. In conclusion, the absence of a monocausal explanation may well be an accurate reflection of the Court's reasoning and practice with respect to this complex remedy. What is clear, however, is that in striving to give tangible recognition to the value and importance of complainants' fundamental rights the Court should be careful to ensure that resulting practice is coherent and consistent.

VII   Conclusion

4/39   Having demonstrated in Chapter 3 that companies indeed come within the purview of the Convention's protection, the purpose of this Chapter has been to elaborate on the various Convention articles under which non-pecuniary compensation has been awarded and the nature of such compensation. It has been shown that while the Court was prepared to assume companies could suffer such damage, initially its redress was limited to the finding of a violation as just satisfaction in respect of non-pecuniary loss. It was not until *Comingersoll* that it extended its redress mechanisms to include compensation for damages for non-pecuniary loss and elaborated on its reasoning. Since then, the Court's

---

[84] See I. Griss, a former president of the Austrian Supreme Court, in 'How Judges Think: Judicial Reasoning in Tort Cases from a Comparative Perspective', *Journal of European Tort Law*, 4(3) (2013), 247–258, 248–249.

[85] Oliphant and Ludwichowska, 'Damage', no. 6/3.

[86] Among them, *Immobiliare Sole Srl* v. *Italy*, 19.12.2002, no. 32766/96, § 30; *Geni Srl* v. *Italy*, 19.12.2002, no. 32662/96, § 29; *Soc De ro sa* v. *Italy*, 04.12.2002, no. 64449/01, § 33.

jurisprudence in this area has grown, and with that, a number of issues arise. Before going into these, it is useful to summarise the multiple aspects of the *Comingersoll* ruling, namely a recognition that corporations are capable of suffering non-pecuniary loss both directly and indirectly (in the latter instance, through their human components) and secondly that 'non-pecuniary' damage may be objective or subjective.

A   Direct Non-Pecuniary Loss

4/40   First, it seems that *some* direct so-called 'objective' non-pecuniary loss in reality constitutes pecuniary loss that is difficult to quantify. This is especially the case with respect to damage under art. 6(1) ECHR on length of proceedings and loss of opportunities. However, an element of unquantifiable pecuniary damage may also creep into all the other heads of damage. The alternative conclusion, in respect of art. 6(1) ECHR, in particular, is that the violation in question is remedied by damages that are preventive or punitive in nature. These conclusions apply in respect of all applicants generally. To the extent that the above conclusions are correct, a change in terminology would be desirable. That said, no objection can be raised against corporations receiving damages for pecuniary loss since such damage involves a diminution of one's money, property or wealth – assets which the law recognises corporations as capable of possessing. Similarly, there is nothing unsavoury about companies being awarded extra-compensatory damages; those sceptical of punitive damages, however, will certainly object to their use.

4/41   By reference to 'subjective' heads, the Court appears to mean damage that involves interference with the bodily, mental or emotional spheres on the one hand and/or the personality sphere on the other. In the former case, the harm is associated with the victim's personal appreciation of it. Domestic courts also refer to this as 'subjectively' assessed non-pecuniary loss (see, e.g. nos. 5/61 and 8/3–8/6). In the latter case, at least under English law, allowance is made, in the form of additional damages, for a sentient victim that experiences the effects of an injury to their reputation (no. 5/46). This brings us to the crux of this research; the extent to which 'subjective' non-pecuniary loss can properly be suffered by companies – i.e. persons that the law conceives as separate and distinct entities from the sentient individuals who own or manage them – directly. The Court's stance, for example, with respect to arts. 2, 3 and 5 ECHR, where rights are denied to companies owing to the intrinsic nature of the right in question and the very nature of the corporation, seems to reflect acceptance of the view that companies themselves cannot suffer interference with body, mind or emotions. If that is indeed the case, then the intrinsic nature of the damage in question and the very nature of the corporation should also come into play in assessing the extent of damages for non-pecuniary due. This mirror argument as to the *merits* of the case (corporate rights) on the one hand and *remedies* on the other seems legitimate. The Commission's and Court's practices of presuming that companies are capable of suffering interferences in mental or emotional spheres is thus inconsistent with domestic law (nos. 5/8 and 8/3–8/6). As will be seen in due course (nos. 5/45–5/48), interference with corporate personality is a different matter altogether.

B   Indirect Non-Pecuniary Loss

4/42   The following paragraph is limited to indirect 'subjective' non-pecuniary loss. In addition to recognising a company itself as capable of direct non-pecuniary loss, one effect of *Comingersoll* is that the Court can have recourse to the individuals behind the company for the purpose of assessing the latter's non-pecuniary loss. Recourse to the anxieties, etc. of those within the company as opposed to limiting the award to the company's direct non-pecuniary loss seeks to overcome the anomaly caused by the fact that a company cannot suffer direct 'subjective' non-pecuniary loss. Indeed, deeming corporations as capable of indirect 'subjective' non-pecuniary loss undermines the presumption that corporations are capable of interference in the bodily, mental or emotional spheres. Moreover, there is much force in the argument of the minority in *Comingersoll*: a particular concern of the dissenting judges related to *the* fundamental attribute of the corporation, its corporate personality (no. 2/5). Along with this come rights which are independent from those of the individuals who compose the company; rights which also receive autonomous protection under the Convention. In light of these features, the judges were vehemently against the practice of attributing the above forms of emotional suffering to the company, notwithstanding they may well have been genuinely experienced by those within the company. Following the *Comingersoll* ruling, domestic courts have also gone on to embrace the attribution theory (Chapter 8). The practice is one which ultimately seeks to remedy the party affected via thought-provoking reasoning. Chapter 7 investigates whether such imputation is doctrinally legitimate.

PART III

English Law

5

Tort Law and the Corporation

I Introduction

5/1   As has been observed: 'State liability in most legal systems has been built on the framework of tort law which everywhere addresses the same set of problems: the foundation of liability, causation, justification or excuses, and remoteness of damage.'[1] As such, parallels can be drawn between Strasbourg and domestic practices. To date domestic case law on companies seeking damages for non-pecuniary loss in respect of Convention right violations is currently unavailable in England.[2] It must be remembered that, although one of few States in the vanguard in drafting the Convention and one of the first to sign it,[3] British citizens were not afforded the right to individual petition until 1966[4] and it was not until 1974 that English courts first consulted the Convention.[5] It would take another twenty-six years, however, before the Human Rights Act 1998 – which entered into force on 2 October 2000 – would empower individuals to bring human rights cases 'home'; i.e. before English courts.

5/2   In the paragraphs to follow, we thus turn away from public law under the Convention to private rights of action under English law, with a

---

[1] D. Shelton, *Remedies in International Human Rights Law*, 3rd edn (Oxford University Press, 2015) p. 91.

[2] M. Spencer, 'Damages Under the Human Rights Act' in H. McGregor, *McGregor on Damages*, 19th edn (London: Sweet & Maxwell, 2014), para. 48–054.

[3] The UK signed the Convention on 4 November 1950 and ratified it on 8 March 1951 with effect from 3 September 1953.

[4] As Mole writes, this right to petition was prudently delayed to ensure the statutory reversal (by the War Damage Act 1965) of the House of Lords' decision in *Burmah Oil (Burma Trading) Ltd* v. *Lord Advocate* [1965] AC 75 so as to deprive Burmah Oil of its right to compensation for damage caused during WWII. The date chosen – 14 January 1966 – fell outside the six-month limitation period for challenges to the 1965 Act, thus ensuring that Burmah Oil could not bring its case before the Strasbourg Court: See N. Mole, 'International Law, the Individual and A. W. Brian Simpson's Contribution to the Defence of Human Rights' in K. O'Donovan and G. R. Rubin (eds.), *Human Rights and Legal History* (Oxford University Press, 2004), p. 18.

[5] In *Waddington* v. *Miah* [1974] 1 WLR 683.

view to assessing the efficacy of the EctHR's jurisprudence. This seems legitimate given the Human Rights Court has said that it may decide to take guidance from domestic standards in making an award under art. 41 ECHR and also in light of the fact that the Court's decisions affect national approaches (no. 1/5). Chapter 8 looks into the practices of other Council of Europe Member States.

5/3   Despite nineteenth century reforms, the structure of English tort law today is still 'ruled from the grave'[6] by the historical system of the forms of action. With a pardonable degree of levity it has been said by one account that English law knows of '70 or more torts',[7] each with its own rules of substantive law, though for practical purposes in the modern law the real figure is about 20. Not all torts lie against companies, and not all are actionable by the same. Where the law recognises a right in their favour, however, as with individuals, it also aims to give a remedy for its violation. Even so, there may be restrictions on the damages companies can recover. Whether and the extent to which a company can be said to sustain particular heads of non-pecuniary loss requires us first to reflect upon the nature of the corporation.

II   The Corporate Nature

A   The Legal Person

5/4   English law reports reveal much in terms of the common law's conceptualisation of a corporation. Firstly, the law perceives a corporation as a 'person'. As has been said: 'A corporation is a legal *persona* just as much as an individual'.[8] This is collaborated by statute: according to s. 5 and sch. 1 of the Interpretation Act 1978, in every Act of Parliament (whether civil or criminal) the word 'person' includes a corporation, unless the contrary intention appears.[9] Use of the term 'person' is conducive to simplicity: as far as legal theory is concerned, 'a person is any being whom the law

---

[6] F. Maitland, *The Forms of Action at Common Law* (Cambridge University Press, 1909), p. 77.

[7] K. Oliphant, 'England and Wales' in B. Winiger, H. Koziol, B. A. Koch and R. Zimmermann (eds.), *Digest of European Tort Law*, 2 vols. (Berlin/Boston: De Gruyter, 2011), vol. 2, 1/12 no. 1. See also B. Rudden, 'Torticles', *Tulance Civil Law Forum*, 6/7 (1991–1992) 105–130, 110.

[8] *Re Sheffield and South Yorkshire Permanent Building Society* (1889) 22 QBD 470, 476 per Cave J.

[9] See also sch. 2 para. 4(5) and s. 23 on its application to subordinate legislation.

regards as capable of rights and duties.'[10] As already stated, however, not every entity is treated as having a personality independent of those who are from time to time its members – only an entity with legal personality is (no. 2/5). This prompts us to enquire into the specific nature of the corporation.

B Corporate Personality Theories: The Nature and Origins of Corporations

5/5   Much ink has been spilt by several celebrated jurists in seeking to understand the nature of corporate personality. However, the weight to be attributed to these theories must be seen in light of their historical context and the aims they sought to achieve. On the orthodox side of the scale, there were those who advocated the *Fiction Theory*. This was put forward by Sinibaldo Fieschi who, in 1243, became Pope Innocent IV.[11] Though directed at ecclesiastical bodies – on the basis that a fiction, having no body or soul, could not be excommunicated or guilty of a delict or crime – the canonic doctrine was imported into temporal circles and thrived.[12] Having no home-made theory to oppose such a convenient doctrine as the Fiction Theory, English jurists swallowed it whole.[13] The theory went hand in hand with the *Concession* or *Grant Theory*. As has been observed: if 'the personality of the corporation is a legal fiction, it is the gift of the prince'.[14] This was collaborated by Coke who, in

---

[10] J. W. Salmond, *Jurisprudence*, 4th edn (London: Stevens and Haynes, 1913), § 108.

[11] J. Dewey, 'The Historic Background of Corporate Legal Personality', *Yale Law Journal*, 35(6) (1926), 655–673. As Bouckaert notes, 'the origin of the notion of corporate personality cannot be separated from the metaphysical notion of the "Corpus Christi". The distinction between the "persona ficta", whose existence was distinct from the existence of its members, was derived from the belief that all Christians were part of a supernatural community, designed by God and represented by men, who had committed their earthly life to the implementation of God's will on earth': B. Bouckaert, 'Corporate Personality: Myth, Fiction or Reality?', *Israel Law Review*, 25(2) (1991), 156–186.

[12] O. Gierke, *Political Theories of the Middle Ages* (Cambridge University Press, reprint 1922, translated with an introduction by FW Maitland), p. xiv. Friedrich Karl von Savigny was the most prominent exponent of the theory. See *Jural Relations: or, The Roman Law of Persons as Subjects of Jural Relations: Being a Translation of the Second Book of Savigny's System of Modern Roman Law* (London: Wildy & Sons, 1884).

[13] Gierke, *Political Theories of the Middle Ages*, p. xxx. The Fiction Theory was accepted by the likes of Pollock: 'we may say that the artificial person is a fictitious substance conceived as supporting legal attributes': F. Pollock, *Principles of Contract*, 9th edn (London: Stevens and Sons Ltd, 1921), pp. 119–120.

[14] F. W. Maitland, 'Moral Personality and Legal Personality', *Journal of the Society of Comparative Legislation*, 6(2) (1905), 192–200.

The Case of Sutton's Hospital in 1612, said that 'none but the king alone [could] create or make a corporation'.[15] The Glorious Revolution of 1688 permanently affirmed that Parliament had basic sovereignty over the king. Thus, in the time of the State, corporate personality was a gift from the State, 'which ha[d] stepped into the shoes of the prince'.[16] Indeed, Lord Halsbury LC in *Salomon* v. *Salomon & Co. Ltd* described a corporation as a 'creation of the Legislature'.[17] The *Grant Theory* was 'indifferent as to the question of the reality of a corporate body'.[18] What it did insist upon, however, was that its legal power was derived.[19]

5/6   Almost every conceivable view sandwiched the Fiction Theory on the one extreme and the *Realist (or Organic) Theory* on the other.[20] The Real Entity Theory – a theory 'carried to grotesque lengths'[21] by some – was developed in the late nineteenth century, an era marked by the rise to prominence of the corporation as the preferred form of economic enterprise.[22] Gierke, who was the leading exponent of this view, argued that corporate personality was real and not a fiction.[23] A German legal historian, it was Gierke whose theories (which arose in the context of German codification efforts) were majorly influential to Maitland, and it was Maitland who – as well as Freund, who published in the US[24] – imported the Organic Theory into the common law.[25] A second aspect of

---

[15] (1612) 10 Coke Reports 23a. See also *Tipling* v. *Pexall* (1613) 2 Bulst 233, 233 'the King creates them' and *R* v. *The Earl of Dorset* (1665) T. Raymond 154, 157 where it was said that a company is the 'creature of the King'. Although Parliament could create corporations, crown consent was a necessary ingredient.

[16] Maitland, 'Moral Personality and Legal Personality', 196.

[17] [1897] AC 22, 29; *The Mayor, Aldermen and Citizens of the City of Norwich* v. *The Norfolk Railway Company* (1855) 4 El & Bl 397, 432 per Coleridge J; *In re Jubilee Cotton Mills Ltd* [1924] AC 958, 974 per Lord Sumner.

[18] Dewey, 'The Historic Background of Corporate Legal Personality', 667.

[19] Dewey, 'The Historic Background of Corporate Legal Personality', 667.

[20] E. B. Seymour Jr, 'Historical Development of the Common Conception of a Corporation', *The American Law Register*, 51(9) (1903), 529–551.

[21] A. W. Machen Jr, 'Corporate Personality', *Harvard Law Review*, 24(4) (1911), 253–267.

[22] M. J. Horwitz, '*Santa Clara* Revisited: The Development of Corporate Theory', *West Virginia Law Review*, 88(2) (1985), 180. See also D. Millon, 'Theories of the Corporation', *Duke Law Journal*, 1990 (1990), 201–262.

[23] See O. Gierke, *Das Deutsche Genossenschaftsrecht* (1887).

[24] E. Freund, *The Legal Nature of the Corporation* (1897).

[25] F. W. Maitland, 'The Corporation Sole', *Law Quarterly Review*, 16 (1900), 335–354, 358. For further references see R. Harris, 'The Transplantation of a Legal Discourse: Corporate Personality Theories from German Codification to British Political Pluralism and American Big Business', *Washington and Lee Law Review*, 63(4) (2006), 1421–1478, fn 63. See also Maitland, 'Moral Personality and Legal Personality'.

the theory stated that the entity was not created by law. It existed prior to the law; the law, finding it engaged in some common activity, endowed it with legal capacity.[26] Thus, Maitland conceived the corporation as 'no fiction, no symbol, no piece of the State's machinery, no collective name for individuals, but a living organism and a real person, with body and members and a will of its own.'[27] The theory coincided with the decline in chartering by the State and a rise in general incorporation by registration (seen as more administratively efficient). While the Real Entity Theory 'often provoke[d] the humanisation of the company . . . this [w]as neither necessary nor justified.'[28] Indeed, Maitland went on to say, 'Itself can will; itself can act; *it wills and acts by the men who are its organs* as a man wills and acts by brain, mouth and hand.'[29] Nonetheless, the theory gave some substance to the company; this in turn could be applied to its advantage, entitling it to greater autonomy and privileges (an increasing number of which were similar to those granted to individuals).[30]

5/7 With each theory being used to serve one end or the other,[31] it is unsurprising that the lack of general consensus as to the legal nature of the corporation continues to this day. Indeed, judicial pronouncements on the nature of the corporate entity have been just as incoherent as doctrinal discussions of the past. Lord Hoffmann, for example, has said: 'There is in fact no such thing as the company as such, no ding an sich'.[32] While consistent with notions of the corporation as a *persona ficta*[33] – if one accepts that what is fictional is unreal and what is artificial is real[34] – such

---

[26] 'When a body of twenty, or two thousand, or two hundred thousand men bind themselves together to act in a particular way for some common purpose, *they create a body, which by no fiction of law, but by the very nature of things*, differs from the individuals of whom it is constituted'. Emphasis added. A. V. Dicey, 'The Combination Laws as Illustrating the Relation Between Law and Opinion in England During the Nineteenth Century', *Harvard Law Review*, 17 (1903–1904), 511–532, 513.

[27] Gierke, *Political Theories of the Middle Ages*, p. xxvi.

[28] C. Harding, U. Kohl and N. Salmon, *Human Rights in the Market Place: The Exploitation of Rights Protection by Economic Actors* (Aldershot: Ashgate, 2008), p. 41.

[29] Gierke, *Political Theories of the Middle Ages*, p. xxvi. Emphasis added.

[30] Horwitz, 'Santa Clara Revisited', 183.

[31] Dewey, 'The Historic Background of Corporate Legal Personality', 669.

[32] *Meridian Global Funds Management Asia Ltd* v. *Securities Commission* [1995] 2 AC 500, 507.

[33] See references in the House of Lords in *Rae (Inspector of Taxes)* v. *Lazard Investment Co. Ltd* [1963] 1 WLR 555, 573 per Lord Pearce and more recently in *Arab Monetary Fund* v. *Hashim (No. 3)* [1991] 2 AC 114, 133 per Lord Donaldson. See also G. Morse, *Palmer's Company Law* (London: Sweet & Maxwell, 2015), paras. 1.214, 2.1501, 2.1513.

[34] Machen Jr, 'Corporate Personality', 262.

a view seems contrary to the long history of authorities that branded the corporation 'an artificial person'[35] or 'an artificial entity'.[36] Despite lack of agreement, however, Dewey correctly observed that courts and legislators do their work, sometimes without any concept or theory as regards the nature of the corporation.[37] This supports the submissions by some that discussions on corporate theory are of no practical import or interest. As Holdsworth put it, while an interesting philosophical speculation, 'English law has, at all periods of its history, been very lightly touched' by questions as to the corporate personality.[38] Concerned with the sense of justice in concrete cases as opposed to the logical perfection of theories,[39] the metaphysical label has never blurred the evaluation of the functional capacity of a company. Accordingly, the courts preferred to work out the consequences of incorporation and the limitations of the resulting entity. This process has been gradual: 'No one ever sat down and declared what the result would be of creating a corporation.'[40] What is clear is that there is a point where the law's analogy of a corporation in anthropomorphic terms ends so that the corporation can rightly be said to be a person for certain purposes only. This in turn impacts on what rights and remedies (for our purposes, damages for non-pecuniary loss) a company can claim.

5/8   In light of this, the concept of personification has been said to raise the difficulty of understanding the true nature of a corporation. One author has even remarked that terminological reference to a 'legal person' is 'devoid of content'.[41] This is quite expected if one accepts that the phrase 'resulted from a crisis of legal imagination'.[42] Again, such imprecision of language has not got in the way of recognising limits inherent in the corporate form. Thus, it has been said that a corporation

---

[35] *Pharmaceutical Society of Great Britain* v. *London and Provincial Supply Association Ltd* (1880) 5 App Cas 857, 869 per Lord Blackburn. For an academic source see P. L. Davies and S. Worthington, *Gower and Davies: Principles of Modern Company Law*, 9th edn (London: Sweet & Maxwell, 2012), paras. 15–72 and 16–65 among other references.

[36] *R* v. *ICR Haulage Ltd* [1944] KB 551, 554 per Stable J; more recently *Revenue and Customs Commissioners* v. *Holland* [2010] 1 WLR 2793, para. 20 per Lord Hope and para. 97 per Lord Saville.

[37] Dewey, 'The Historic Background of Corporate Legal Personality', 660.

[38] W. Holdsworth, *A History of English Law*, 17 vols. (London: Methuen & Co. Ltd, 1909–1952), vol. IX, pp. 69–70. Modern corporate textbooks barely dedicate a section to the topic, if at all.

[39] Seymour Jr, 'Historical Development of the Common Conception of a Corporation', 542.

[40] *JH Rayner (Mincing Lane) Ltd* v. *Department of Trade and Industry* [1990] 2 AC 418, 460.

[41] G. A. Mark, 'The Personification of the Business Corporation in American Law', *University of Chicago Law Review*, 54(4) (1987), 1441–1483.

[42] Mark, 'The Personification of the Business Corporation in American Law', 1443.

'has no physical body';[43] 'no corporeal existence'.[44] It 'cannot appear in person';[45] it is invisible.[46] Nor, according to the authorities, can it act,[47] 'give its signature',[48] speak,[49] 'be beaten',[50] be injured in its feelings,[51] suffer pain[52] or a 'death of the natural body'.[53] It is also acknowledged that 'a corporation has no mind'[54] and therefore cannot think,[55] be 'subject to imbecilities'[56] or 'have indecent or vulgar manners'.[57] It has neither conscience[58] nor *mens rea*.[59] It is incapable of 'desires and intentions',[60]

---

[43] *Saccharin Corporation Ltd* v. *Chemische Fabrik Von Heyden Aktiengesellschaft* [1911] 2 KB 516, 521 per Vaughan Williams LJ: 'My Lords, a corporation is an abstraction. It has no mind of its own any more than it has a body of its own': *Lennard's Carrying Co. Ltd* v. *Asiatic Petroleum Co. Ltd* [1915] AC 705, 713 per Viscount Haldane LC.

[44] *Adams* v. *Cape Industries plc* [1990] Ch 433, 519 per Slade LJ; *R* v. *JG Hammond & Co. Ltd* [1914] 2 KB 866, 867 per Darling J.

[45] *Fealtie* (1580) 73 ER 885, 885; *The Case of Sutton's Hospital* (1612) 10 Co Rep 23a, para. 32 b; *Tipling* v. *Pexall* (1613) 2 Bulst 233, 233.

[46] *Tipling* v. *Pexall* (1613) 2 Bulst 233, 233; *Gibson* v. *The East India Company* (1839) 5 Bing NC 262, 269 per Tindal CJ.

[47] *Yarborough* v. *Bank of England* (1812) 16 East 6, 7 per Lord Ellenborough CJ; *Director of Public Prosecutions* v. *Kent and Sussex Contractors Co. Ltd* [1944] KB 146, 155 per Viscount Caldecote CJ.

[48] *R* v. *The Worksop Local Board of Health* (1865) 5 B & S 951, 964 per Blackburn J. See also *In re Pilkington Brothers Ld Workmen's Pension Fund* [1953] 1 WLR 1084, 1088 per Danckwerts J.

[49] *Tipling* v. *Pexall* (1613) 2 Bulst 233, 233; *Croydon Hospital* v. *Farley* (1816) 6 Taunt 467, 481 per Gibbs CJ; *Director of Public Prosecutions* v. *Kent and Sussex Contractors Co. Ltd* [1944] KB 146, 155 per Viscount Caldecote CJ.

[50] *Eastern Counties Railway Company and Richardson* v. *Broom* (1851) 6 Ex 314, 325 per Patteson J.

[51] See Chapter 6.

[52] *Triplex Safety Glass Co. Ltd* v. *Lancegaye Safety Glass (1934) Ltd* [1939] 2 KB 395, 409 per Du Parcq LJ.

[53] *The Case of Sutton's Hospital* (1612) 10 Co Rep 23a, para. 32 b; *Green* v. *The London General Omnibus Company Ltd* (1859) 7 CB NS 290, 294.

[54] *Stevens* v. *The Midland Counties Railway Company and Lander* (1854) 10 Ex 352, 356 per Alderson B; *Edwards* v. *Midland Railway Company* (1880) 6 QBD 287, 288 per Fry J; *Lennard's Carrying Co. Ltd* v. *Asiatic Petroleum Co. Ltd* [1915] AC 705, 713 per Viscount Haldane LC.

[55] *Director of Public Prosecutions* v. *Kent and Sussex Contractors Co. Ltd* [1944] KB 146, 156 per Viscount Caldecote CJ.

[56] *The Case of Sutton's Hospital* (1612) 10 Co Rep 23a, para. 32 b; *Green* v. *The London General Omnibus Company Ltd* (1859) 7 CB NS 290, 294.

[57] *South Hetton Coal Company Ltd* v. *North Eastern News Association Ltd* [1894] 1 QB 133, 138 per Lord Esher MR.

[58] *Tipling* v. *Pexall* (1613) 2 Bulst 233, 233.

[59] *Edwards* v. *Midland Railway Company* (1880) 6 QBD 287, 288 per Fry J; *Pharmaceutical Society of Great Britain* v. *London and Provincial Supply Association Ltd* (1880) 5 QBD 310, 313 per Bramwell LJ.

[60] *Commissioners of Inland Revenue* v. *Fisher's Executors* [1926] AC 395, 411 per Lord Sumner.

'malice or motive'.[61] A corporation, not being a physical person, 'cannot have a religion'[62] and in any case it has no 'soul to be damned'.[63] It has no heirs.[64] In short, the corporation is a thing which the world knows of but only the eyes of the law can perceive.[65] Despite numerous limitations, there are attributes favourable to a company that are singular to them. Thus, among other things, unlike natural persons, corporations enjoy potential perpetuity – a consequence of the personality conferred on them. Moreover, once a company has ceased to exist it may be restored to life,[66] a feat few humans can boast.

5/9   If logically worked out, the incorporeal nature of the corporation would abolish its liability, not only in the case of tort but also in criminal law, contract law, and so on. To avoid such an untenable prospect, the law has found ways to overcome any technical difficulties by accepting that the company exercises its rights and executes its duties through natural persons. As Lord Hoffmann put it: 'Any statement about what a company has or has not done, or can or cannot do, is necessarily a reference to the rules of attribution [e.g. agency] as they apply to that company.'[67]

C   Conclusion

5/10   In Lord Halsbury LC's famous words in *Salomon's* case, once a company is 'legally incorporated it *must be treated like* any other independent person with its rights and liabilities *appropriate to itself*' (no. 2/5). This echoes Coke's judgment over 280 years prior, in *The Case of Sutton's Hospital*. While opining that a corporation 'is a fiction, a shade, a nonentity', he concluded that it is 'a reality for legal purposes'.[68] What is decisive, therefore, is that the law is prepared to *deem* that a company has certain capacities of its own, and the law's starting point is to uphold this principle.

---

[61] *Abrath* v. *North Eastern Railway Co.* (1886) 11 App Cas 247, 251 per Lord Bramwell.

[62] *McGrath* v. *Dawkins* [2012] Info TLR 72, para. 81 per HHJ Moloney.

[63] The words of the extra-judicial quotation are often attributed to Lord Thurlow. Quoted in M. A. King, *Public Policy and the Corporation I* (London: Chapman and Hall, 1977), p. 1. See also *The Case of Sutton's Hospital* (1612) 10 Co Rep 23a, para. 32 b; *Tipling* v. *Pexall* (1613) 2 Bulst 233, 233 'a corporation, is a body aggregate, none can create soules but God, but the King creates them, and therefore they have no soules'.

[64] *Kemp* v. *Magistrates of Largs*, 1938 SC 652, 679 per Lord Mackay.

[65] Salmond, *Jurisprudence*, § 114.

[66] Companies Act 2006, s. 1024(1) provides that: 'An application may be made to the registrar to restore to the register a company that has been struck off the register'.

[67] *Meridian Global Funds Management Asia Ltd* v. *Securities Commission* [1995] 2 AC 500, 506.

[68] *The Case of Sutton's Hospital* (1612) 10 Rep. 32 b.

As to the source of a company's legal powers, modern authorities seem consistent in attributing it to Parliament[69] so the 'State has largely won the battle, in the UK certainly, and elsewhere.'[70] As indicated in no. 2/2, by far the vast majority of companies are incorporated by statute. Thus, the company is 'clothed' by the law. It cannot exist outside the law but must act within the company law framework, mainly the Companies Act 2006, and within its constitution, as permitted by the law. Increasingly, however, Parliament is in turn steered by corporate legislation from Brussels and by the growing jurisprudence of courts, including the Human Rights Court in Strasbourg.

III   Torts Committed against Corporations

5/11   When it comes to *imposing liability*, the law looks to the conduct of the individuals within the company, resulting either in primary (direct) liability or secondary (vicarious) liability being imposed on the company (see Chapter 7). When it comes to the *capacity to be the subject of a legal right*, however, the approach is not to look to the natural persons behind the company – at least not under English law. Thus, although it is true that a company has whatever rights the law says it can have and technically these *could be* all the rights available to natural persons, the current practice is to expand the law only insofar as is consistent with the tort in question (and the interests it seeks to protect) and the nature of companies (i.e. whether they can conceivably suffer the sort of damage in question). Before turning to the question of awarding damages for non-pecuniary loss to corporations, it is thus necessary to determine which specific torts can be committed against them.[71] The *starting* point is that a company can bring an action in respect of a tort in the same way as an individual, save for torts of a purely personal nature.[72] Companies, being

---

[69] See, for example, *Rae (Inspector of Taxes)* v. *Lazard Investment Co. Ltd* [1963] 1 WLR 555, 573 per Lord Pearce: the corporation 'owes its existence to the law under which it is created and cannot act except in accordance with it' and *JH Rayner (Mincing Lane) Ltd* v. *Department of Trade and Industry* [1989] Ch 72, 167 per Kerr LJ: 'Under the law of this country a legal entity in the form of a persona ficta can only be created by legislation or Royal Charter, and no such entities are known to English law other than bodies corporate'.

[70] B. Pettet, *Company Law*, 2nd edn, (Essex: Pearson Education, 2005), p. 50.

[71] The classificatory scheme below is inspired by C. A. Witting (ed.), *Halsbury's Laws Commentary on Torts* (London: LexisNexis Butterworths, 2015), vol. 97, paras. 491–810. There is some overlap in the categories.

[72] *South Hetton Coal Company Ltd* v. *North Eastern News Association Ltd* [1894] 1 QB 133, 141 per Lopes LJ: 'a corporation cannot maintain an action for libel in respect of anything reflecting upon them personally'.

capable of acquiring, possessing and transmitting property, can maintain an action for torts affecting property or rights of a proprietary nature. Difficulties arise when dealing with a wrong 'not strictly in the nature of an invasion of proprietary rights.'[73] The issue of whether *a corporation* would qualify for an award of aggravated damages in respect of the torts discussed below is broached in Chapter 6.

A   General Tortious Liabilities

1   Negligence

5/12   Negligence serves as the basis for most personal injury claims, and non-pecuniary losses play a major role there. A corporation, which has no corporeal existence, cannot sue in respect of such injuries but can of course bring an action for property damage as well as pure economic loss, interests which the tort also protects. Outside personal injury, damages for non-pecuniary loss in negligence actions are available under the following heads: physical inconvenience and discomfort, mental distress (in limited cases) and bereavement damages, categories closed to companies. Injury to reputation may also be actionable in negligence.[74] It is common, albeit contested, ground that aggravated damages are not generally available in negligence actions.[75] For some, the assumptions upon which this conclusion is based (i.e. that 'negligence is only committed through inadvertent or otherwise non-intentional conduct'[76]) are unfounded.[77]

---

[73] H. A. Smith, *The Law of Associations: Corporate and Unincorporated* (Oxford: Clarendon Press, 1914), p. 775.

[74] In *Verderame* v. *Commercial Union Assurance Co. plc* [1955–95] PNLR 612 it was decided, in light of the position in contract law, that there would be no recovery for mental distress where the negligence resulted in economic loss alone. For the position on injury to reputation see *Spring* v. *Guardian Assurance plc* [1995] 2 AC 296. See nos. 5/60–5/67 for the various recognised heads of non-pecuniary loss under English law.

[75] See *Kralj* v. *McGrath* [1986] 1 All ER 54, 60 where Lord Woolf said: 'It is my view that it would be wholly inappropriate to introduce into claims of this sort, for breach of contract and negligence, the concept of aggravated damages'. Stuart-Smith LJ agreed with this in *AB* v. *South West Water Services* [1993] QB 507, 528. Cf The Law Commission, *Aggravated, Exemplary and Restitutionary Damages*, Law Com 247 (1997), para. 1.36, p. 25: 'we cannot detect any good reason why aggravated damages should not be available for the tort of negligence or for breach of contract'.

[76] J. Murphy, 'The Nature and Domain of Aggravated Damages', *Cambridge Law Journal*, 69(2) (2010), 353–377.

[77] See Cf *Prison Service* v. *Johnson* [1997] ICR 275, 286–287 in fn 83 below. In *Ashley* v. *Chief Constable of Sussex Police* [2008] 1 AC 962, the Chief Constable agreed that the issue of aggravated damages would be dealt with as if they were available in the tort of negligence and agreed to pay them. Lord Neuberger (at para. 102) stated: 'I cannot see

2 Public Nuisance

5/13 It has been said that '[p]ublic and private nuisances are not in reality two species of the same genus at all'[78] and indeed, a firm distinction was drawn in *In re Corby Group Litigation*. Dyson LJ there ruled that while private nuisance involves interference with someone's private right to enjoy his own land, public nuisance involves the endangering of 'life, safety, health, property or comfort of the public.'[79] Since public nuisance is primarily a criminal matter, public officials normally bring enforcement proceedings. Where, however, an individual or indeed a company is appreciably more affected by a defendant's behaviour than the general public, they are accorded a cause of action. Damages for non-pecuniary loss are available for personal injury,[80] physical inconvenience and discomfort[81] and mental distress[82] and loss of society in the case of death. In light of the corporate form an action in public nuisance would be limited to interests over property. As a claimant in an action for public nuisance need not have an interest in land, however, it would seem that individuals within the company can sue for nuisance affecting their life, safety, health or comfort. There is conflicting authority as to whether aggravated damages are available.[83]

3 Special Liability Regimes and Breach of Statutory Duty

5/14 It is evident that some special liability regimes, such as that in respect of defective products, are not open to companies to pursue. In the latter case, the enactment aims at the protection of *consumers*. In any case, actionable damage is limited to death, personal injury or loss of or

why such [aggravated] damages should not logically be recoverable in some categories of negligence claims'. Similarly, Murphy, 'The Nature and Domain of Aggravated Damages', 369–372.

[78] R. E. V. Heuston and R. A. Buckley, *Salmond & Heuston on the Law of Torts*, 21st edn (London: Sweet & Maxwell, 1996), p. 54.

[79] [2009] QB 335, para. 27. See *Hunter* v. *Canary Wharf Ltd* [1997] AC 655, 692 per Lord Goff.

[80] *In re Corby Group Litigation* [2009] QB 335, para. 22 per Dyson LJ.

[81] E. Finch and S. Fafinski, *Tort Law* (Pearson Education, 2009), p. 111.

[82] *AB* v. *South West Water Services* [1993] QB 507, 528 per Stuart-Smith LJ.

[83] *AB* v. *South West Water Services* [1993] QB 507, 528 per Stuart-Smith LJ and 532 per Sir Thomas Bingham MR. Cf *Prison Service* v. *Johnson* [1997] ICR 275, 286–287 where the court ruled that Sir Thomas Bingham MR's remarks in *AB* v. *South West Water Services* which were made in the context of a claim for damages for personal injury based upon the torts of negligence, non-intentional nuisance and non-intentional breach of statutory duty were not of general application: 'The decision in *A.B. v. South West Water Services Ltd.* turns upon the non-intentional nature of the torts sued upon and the limited basis upon which the plaintiffs were able to advance their claim for aggravated damages'.

damage to property ordinarily intended for private use, occupation or consumption.[84] Companies fall within the purview of other regimes, such as the Human Rights Act 1998, and can claim damages for non-pecuniary loss where appropriate.[85] As to the common law action of breach of statutory duty, i.e. where statutory provisions are silent on 'the question whether breach of obligations contained in them should be actionable in damages, whether so as to confirm the existence of a civil remedy or to rule it out',[86] companies can sue provided that the provision was intended to confer private rights of action upon a class of persons of which the company was one and the latter suffered injury of a kind the statute was designed to guard against. The action is likely to be confined to damages for pecuniary loss, except where reputation is at stake. The authorities as to whether the breach may be aggravated by the defendant's conduct are inconsistent.[87]

4   Misrepresentation

5/15   Deceit, negligence and malicious falsehood may give rise to liability for misrepresentation. Statutory liability for misrepresentation may also arise under the Misrepresentation Act 1967. A corporation is entitled to sue in respect of actions under the false representations umbrella.

(a)   Deceit

5/16   Actionable damage for the tort of fraudulent misrepresentation or deceit extends to pecuniary and non-pecuniary loss.[88] In the latter instance, damages are available for pain and suffering and loss of amenities (in the rare case),[89] physical inconvenience[90] and mental suffering,[91] all of

---

[84] Consumer Protection Act 1987, s. 5.   [85] See s. 8(4).

[86] M. Lunney and K. Oliphant, *Tort Law: Text and Materials* (Oxford University Press, 2013), p. 596.

[87] See fn 83.

[88] The tort is committed where 'a false representation has been made (1) knowingly, or (2) without belief in its truth, or (3) recklessly, careless whether it be true or false' and intending that the representee should act in reliance on it, and the representee does so rely and suffers loss as a result: *Derry* v. *Peek* (1889) 14 App Cas 337, 374 per Lord Herschell.

[89] H. McGregor, *McGregor on Damages*, 19th edn (London: Sweet & Maxwell, 2014), para. 47–041.

[90] *Mafo* v. *Adams* [1970] 1 QB 548.

[91] In *Doyle* v. *Olby (Ironmongers) Ltd* [1969] 2 QB 158, 170 Winn LJ thought that damages 'for worry, strain, anxiety and unhappiness' may well be appropriate in deceit. This was the case, for example, in *Shelley* v. *Paddock* [1979] QB 120 (at 131 per Bristow J) and *A* v. *B* [2007] EWHC 1246 (a test confirmed that A was not the biological father of a child he had supported financially; held: A felt a deep sense of loss and suffered great unhappiness).

which are not compatible with the corporate form. Aggravated damages are also awardable.[92]

(b) Negligent Misrepresentation

5/17   Tortious liability through negligent misrepresentation is founded on the case of *Hedley Byrne & Co. Ltd* v. *Heller & Partners Ltd.*[93] The House of Lords held there that where a duty of care arises from a special relationship there could be liability for damages in tort for economic loss caused by a negligent misrepresentation. Damage to property caused as a result of the misrepresentation is recoverable. In the rare case where a negligent misstatement results in personal injury, damages will also be recoverable. In addition, damages for non-pecuniary loss for physical inconvenience and mental distress (in appropriate cases) can be pursued.[94] A company's claim would consequentially be limited to damages for pecuniary loss. As indicated earlier, it is thought that aggravated damages are not appropriate in negligence actions.

(c) Misrepresentation Act 1967

5/18   The 1967 Act applies only where there is a contract. In particular, s. 2(1) provides for liability for *negligent* and *innocent* misrepresentations which induce a party to enter into such a contract.[95] While damages for both pecuniary and non-pecuniary loss can be claimed for negligent misrepresentation,[96] a company can only recover the former. Rescission is

---

[92] *Archer* v. *Brown* [1985] QB 401. For a more detailed account on the damages for non-pecuniary loss available see McGregor, *McGregor on Damages*, para. 47–041.

[93] [1964] AC 465.

[94] In *McNally* v. *Welltrade International* [1978] IRLR 497, the claimant who travelled to Libya based on the details of the job offered by the defendants and was repatriated within two weeks for want of experience was awarded € 400 in 'general damages' for worry and inconvenience. See McGregor, *McGregor on Damages*, paras. 47–061 and 47–065. Cf *Verderame* v. *Commercial Union Assurance Co. plc* [1955–95] PNLR 612 on mental distress in negligence actions in fn 74.

[95] The very wordy provision reads: 'Where a person has entered into a contract after a misrepresentation has been made to him by another party thereto and as a result thereof he has suffered loss, then, if the person making the misrepresentation would be liable to damages in respect thereof had the misrepresentation been made fraudulently, that person shall be so liable notwithstanding that the misrepresentation was not made fraudulently, unless he proves that he had reasonable ground to believe and did believe up to the time the contract was made the facts represented were true'.

[96] As to the latter see *McNally* v. *Welltrade International* [1978] IRLR 497 which was based on both the common law and the 1967 Act. See also *Chesneau* v. *Interhome* [1983] 134 NLJ 341. Cf *Verderame* v. *Commercial Union Assurance Co. plc* [1955-95] PNLR 612 on mental distress in negligence actions in fn 74.

the primary remedy for innocent misrepresentation. Aggravated damages are likely to be limited to intentional misstatements.

(d)   Malicious Falsehood

5/19   This Section will be given detailed consideration since it was argued during the reforms leading to the introduction of the Defamation Act 2013 that corporations were best served by the tort of malicious (sometimes labelled 'injurious') falsehood, which is a closely related tort to defamation. Unlike defamation, however, malicious falsehood does *not* admit damages for non-pecuniary loss.[97] The tort encompasses slander of title, slander of goods and other malicious falsehoods. To support an action, the claimant must show that the defendant *maliciously published* a *false* oral or written statement to third parties which *referred to him, his property or business* and *special (or pecuniary) damage* arose as a result.[98]

5/20   The essential differences between the torts of defamation and malicious falsehood were conveniently summarised in an early edition of Duncan and Neill on Defamation as: (a) the shift in the burden of proof: in defamation the defendant has to prove that the defamatory words were true (see s. 2 Defamation Act 2013); in malicious falsehood the claimant must prove that the words were false; (b) unlike in defamation, in an action for malicious falsehood the claimant has to prove malice; and (c) damage is not presumed in the case of malicious falsehood as it was, until recently, in libel and slander actionable *per se*. A recent interpretation of s. 1 Defamation Act 2013 removes the presumption there (no. 5/39). In any case, the severity of the rule in malicious falsehood cases is mitigated by s. 3 of the Defamation Act 1952, which dispenses with the need to prove special damage if the words are calculated to cause pecuniary damage to the plaintiff and are published in writing or other permanent form or if the said words are calculated to cause pecuniary damage to the claimant in respect of any office, profession, calling, trade or

---

[97]   As Lord Denning MR said in *Fielding* v. *Variety Inc* [1967] 2 QB 841, 850: 'The plaintiffs on this head of claim [i.e. injurious falsehood] can only recover damages for their probable money loss, and not for their injured feelings'. ; Cf *Joyce* v. *Sengupta* [1993] 1 WLR 337, 347–349 per Sir Donald Nicholls VC who advocated the recoverability of damages for anxiety and distress for malicious falsehood if pecuniary loss is established but not for injury to reputation: 'It would be going too far to hold that all non-pecuniary loss suffered by a plaintiff is recoverable in a malicious falsehood action, because that would include injury to reputation at large....; the remedy for such loss is an action for defamation in which, incidentally, damages for injury to feelings may be included in a general award of damages'. This was said *obiter* however. See also McGregor, *McGregor on Damages*, paras. 46–012–46–015.

[98]   *Ratcliffe* v. *Evans* [1892] 2 QB 524.

business held or carried on by him at the time of the publication.[99] To the above may be added that a malicious falsehood need not be defamatory in itself as the tort does not seek to protect reputations.[100] Moreover, there is no right to a trial by jury in an action for malicious falsehood; though the right has also recently been removed for defamation, the court may order otherwise.[101] Once liability is established, a separate sum may be awarded to reflect the aggravating features of the defendant's conduct.[102]

B   Torts to Specific Interests

1   Torts Affecting Land

(a)   Trespass to Land

5/21   Trespasses, generally, are ancient wrongs which have their roots in criminal law and criminal procedure. Traces of the semi-criminal nature of trespass are evidenced by the fact that the tort is actionable without proof of loss. However, in that case, the award will only be nominal. The tort of trespass to land protects against physical (and usually intentional) interference with another's rights over land and thus the latter's right of possession. Where special damage is shown, damages for pecuniary loss are available, and naturally this extends to companies too. Damages for non-pecuniary loss may also be awarded. However, this remedy is available to natural persons only. In a case on wrongful occupancy of land, the court in *Inverugie Investments* v. *Hackett* held that the ordinary letting value of the property would determine the amount of the damages.[103] While this was accepted in the subsequent case of *Davies* v. *Ilieff*,[104] the judge in *Davies* held that the assessment in *Inverugie* was simply the starting point

---

[99]   See Balcome LJ in *Derbyshire County Council* v. *Times Newspapers Ltd* [1992] QB 770, 817 referring to an earlier edition of B. Neill and R. Rampton (eds.), *Duncan and Neill on Defamation*, 2nd edn (London: Butterworths, 1983), para. 2.03.

[100]   *Ratcliffe* v. *Evans* [1892] 2 QB 524, 529 per Bowen LJ. See also fn 97 above and A. Mullis and K. Oliphant, *Torts*, 4th edn (Basingstoke: Palgrave Macmillan, 2011) para. 20.1.1 on the tort's limited protection of reputation.

[101]   A further advantage under defamation was the right to trial by jury under s. 69(1)(b) of the Senior Courts Act 1981 and s. 66(3)(b) of the County Courts Act 1984 unlike in malicious falsehood cases. This is now removed by s. 11 Defamation Act 2013.

[102]   Indeed the practice of denying damages for non-pecuniary loss as a head of loss in a tort then awarding aggravated damages, a species of damages for non-pecuniary loss, once the cause of action is established, was thought odd by Sir Donald Nicholls VC in *Joyce* v. *Sengupta* [1993] 1 WLR 337, 348–349. See *Khodaparast* v. *Shad* [2000] 1 WLR 618, 631 where aggravated damages for injury to feelings were said to be appropriate in an action for malicious falsehood (in line with Sir Michael Kerr's approach in *Joyce*, at 351). Cf McGregor, *McGregor on Damages*, paras. 46–012–46–015. See also Chapter 6.

[103]   [1995] 1 WLR 713.   [104]   2000 WL 33201551 (Official Transcript).

since *Inverugie* was a case on trespass to *commercial* residential premises. In the case of an individual's home, containing all their personal and private possessions, it was thought appropriate to entitle the latter to a sum of 'general damages' proportionate to the insult and distress the individual suffered. On the right set of facts, account of any aggravating features could properly be taken into consideration.[105]

(b) Private Nuisance

5/22   In the case of nuisance one might wonder whether a company, with its lack of human attributes, can have a lawful action where the disturbance is caused by noise, odours, etc. or other nuisance resulting in 'sensible' personal discomfort. Although the point is yet to be decided, it appears they can. Private nuisance is a tort to land or more accurately, 'a tort directed against the claimant's enjoyment of rights over land'.[106] Generally, proof of damage is essential, although there will be instances where the law presumes injury from the mere fact of encroachment. There was some inclination to view Lord Westbury's judgment in the case of *St Helen's Smelting* v. *Tipping*[107] as having divided nuisance into two torts, one of causing material injury to the property (such as flooding) and the other in respect of personal discomfort (such as excessive noise or smells) or even personal injury. In *Hunter* v. *Canary Wharf Ltd* such a premise was considered 'quite mistaken', however.[108] Lord Hoffmann ruled that, in the case of nuisances productive of 'sensible' personal discomfort, the action is not for causing discomfort to the person but for causing injury to the land: 'True it is that the land has not suffered "sensible" injury, but its utility has been diminished by the existence of the nuisance. It is for an unlawful threat to the utility of his land that the possessor or occupier is entitled to an injunction and it is for the diminution in such utility that he is entitled to compensation.'[109]

---

[105] See A. Tettenborn, *Halsbury's Laws Commentary on Damages* (London: LexisNexis Butterworths, 2014), vol. 29, para. 323, fn 13 for a list of cases that support this proposition.

[106] See F. H. Newark, 'The Boundaries of Nuisance', *Law Quartely Review*, 65 (1949), 480–490 as approved by Lord Goff in *Hunter* v. *Canary Wharf* Ltd [1997] AC 655, 688 (and Phill LJ at 671).

[107] (1865) 11 HL Cas 642.   [108] [1997] AC 655, 706 per Lord Hoffmann.

[109] [1997] AC 655, 706 per Lord Hoffmann. Cf K. Oliphant, 'Unblurring the Boundaries of Nuisance' [A Commentary on Hunter v. Canary Wharf], *Tort Law Review*, 6 (1998), 21–28 who avers that '[w]here actual inconvenience is in fact suffered, it is entirely legitimate to treat it as consequential upon the nuisance'. J. O'Sullivan, 'Nuisance in the House of Lords – Normal Service Resumed', *Cambridge Law Journal*, 56(3) (1997) 483–485, 485 states that the above view is artificial: 'What precisely is it about, for example, a horrible

5/23   Thus, notwithstanding companies cannot by their very nature experience such nuisance, a corporate action would not give rise to any mischief as the injury is to the land, not the individuals on the land.[110] In the case of a business, compensation would include damages for the diminution in the amenity or utility value of the property during the period for which the noise or other nuisance persisted, notwithstanding this involves placing a value upon intangibles. The damages here are for unquantifiable pecuniary loss.

5/24   As only a person with an interest in the land can sue, individuals within the company are not entitled to an action. The same principles apply to claims under the rule in *Rylands* v. *Fletcher*[111] which is a subspecies of private nuisance. There is conflicting authority as to whether aggravating aspects can be reflected in an award for private nuisance and in *Rylands*.[112]

2   Wrongful Interference with Goods

5/25   Without going into too much detail here, corporations can pursue damages for wrongful interference which includes the specific torts of trespass to goods, conversion and wrongful distress, all of which are in respect of *pecuniary damage only*.[113] Despite this, in the case of trespass to goods, aggravated damages are known to have been awarded.[114] In principle, actions for conversion and wrongful distress may merit an award of such damages.[115]

---

smell that is deserving of legal sanction? Surely the fact that *human beings* are adversely affected by it'. Emphasis added.

[110] M. Lunney, 'Capacity to Commit a Tort and to Sue' in K. Oliphant (ed.), *The Law of Tort*, 2nd edn (London: LexisNexis Butterworths, 2007), para. 2.55, fn 1.

[111] (1868) LR 3 HL 330. S. Deakin, A. Johnston and B. Markesinis, *Markesinis and Deakin's Tort Law* (Oxford University Press, 2012), p. 438.

[112] See fn 83 above.

[113] 'The action in conversion is a purely personal action and results in a judgment for pecuniary damages only'. : *General and Finance Facilities Ltd* v. *Cooks Cars (Romford) Ltd* [1963] 1 WLR 644, 649 per Lord Diplock. As with nuisance, the award for loss of use is in respect of unquantifiable pecuniary loss. *The Medina* [1900] AC 113, 117 f per Earl LC. See S. Douglas, *Liability for Wrongful Interference with Chattels* (Oxford: Hart Publishing Ltd, 2011).

[114] *IRC* v. *Rossminster* [1980] AC 952, 1000–1001 per Lord Wilberforce.

[115] As to the former see City Law School, *Remedies* (Oxford University Press, 2014), para. 10.4.6.8.

3   Intellectual Property Torts

(a)   Infringement of Copyrights, Patents and Trademarks

5/26   Corporations can hold intellectual property rights and as such can seek to defend infringements of the same. As McGregor notes, damages for non-pecuniary loss do not generally feature in awards for the infringement of copyrights, patents and trademarks as the invasion of a proprietary right is unlikely to lead to such a loss.[116] Under the Patents Act 1977[117] and the Copyright, Designs and Patents Act 1988[118] a court may, in an action for infringement having regard to all the circumstances and in particular to the flagrancy of the infringement and any benefit accruing to the defendant by reason of the infringement, award such *additional damages* as the justice of the case may require.[119] Following decades of debate as to the nature of such damages, the law seems settled by the ruling in *Nottinghamshire Healthcare NHS Trust* v. *News Group Newspapers Ltd.*[120] There Pumfrey J equated them to 'aggravated damages and such amount by way of restitution'.[121] Chapter 6 details the availability of aggravated damages for corporate victims.

5/27   Outside such economic rights are moral rights. Although protected in part by various torts under the common law, moral rights are now regulated under the 1988 Act (in implementation of international laws). These are: (a) the right of paternity (the right to be identified as an author of a copyright literary, dramatic, musical or artistic work, director of a copyright film or as a performer);[122] (b) the integrity right (the right of the above to object to derogatory treatment of their work, film or performance);[123] (c) the right not to have a work or a film falsely attributed to one as its author or director;[124] and (d) the right to privacy of a person who *for private and domestic purposes* commissions the taking of a

---

[116] McGregor, *McGregor on Damages*, para. 46–034.

[117] Sch. A1, para. 12(4).   [118] Section 97(2). See also ss. 191J and 229.

[119] In *Ravenscroft* v. *Herbert and New English Library Ltd* [1980] RPC 193, 208 Brightman J ruled that 'flagrancy' implied the existence of scandalous conduct, deceit and such like; it included deliberate and calculated infringements, and 'benefit' implied that the defendant had reaped a pecuniary advantage in excess of the damages he would otherwise have to pay.

[120] [2002] EMLR 33, para. 51.   [121] See cl. 9(3)(b) Draft Civil Law Reform Bill of 2009.

[122] Copyright, Designs and Patents Act 1988, s. 77. See also the right to be identified as a performer under s. 205C.

[123] Copyright, Designs and Patents Act 1988, s. 80. Under s. 80(2), 'treatment', defined in s. 80(1), is derogatory if it amounts to distortion or mutilation of the work or is otherwise prejudicial to the honour or reputation of the author or director. See also s. 205F in relation to performers' rights.

[124] Copyright, Designs and Patents Act 1988, s. 84.

photograph or the making of a film.[125] (d) is clearly not addressed to companies. As regards (a) to (c) some scholars are of the view that moral rights or some such rights can only be invoked by natural persons. Performers, who have paternity and integrity rights, must clearly be natural persons. What is also clear, is that while not assignable *inter vivos* (by virtue of ss. 94 and 205L), the effect of ss. 95 and 205M is to entitle a company, for our purposes, 'by succession to exercise the paternity right [and indeed other moral rights, with the exception of that in (c) above] after the death' of the original holder.[126] Section 78(2) establishes the manner of asserting moral rights. Under ss. 176 and 210A this requirement is satisfied in the case of a body corporate by signature on behalf of the body or by the affixing of its seal. A company entitled to assert moral rights can claim damages for breach of statutory duty among other remedies.[127] Damage need not be proved. Infringements of moral rights may attract damages for damage to reputation, injured feelings and annoyance.[128] Since an action does not lie for defamation of the dead,[129] however, an individual's reputational infringement would not be actionable by the company post-mortem. Moreover, any claims for damages for mental distress that survive the deceased are not actionable as damages for non-pecuniary loss to the company itself but rather to the former.

(b) Passing off

5/28   The action, clearly available to corporations, is rooted in the nineteenth century. It sought to prevent a trader from using the trade name or trademark of a rival trader to induce potential purchasers to believe that his goods were those of the rival trader, thus cashing in on a rival's goodwill (as to which, see no. 5/47). The tort was expanded to include cases of a manufacturer selling goods which are correctly described as being made by that manufacturer but falsely suggesting that their business is connected

---

[125] Copyright, Designs and Patents Act 1988, s. 85.

[126] K. Garnett, G. Davies, and G. Harbottle, *Copinger & Skone James on Copyright*, 16th edn (London: Sweet & Maxwell, 2010), para. 11–19, fn 105. See also para. 11–72. As regards moral rights and natural persons see T. Aplin and J. Davis, *Intellectual Property Law: Text, Cases, and Materials* (Oxford University Press, 2013), p. 119 and the reference therein. As regards performers, see reference to 'qualifying performance' in ss. 205C and 205F Copyright, Designs and Patents Act 1988 and the definition of that term in s. 181. See also s. 206(1).

[127] Copyright, Designs and Patents Act 1988, ss. 103(1) and 205N.

[128] M. Vitoria et al, *Laddie, Prescott & Vitoria: The Modern Law of Copyright and Designs*, 4th edn (London: LexisNexis Butterworths, 2011), para. 63.57.

[129] Law Reform (Miscellaneous Provisions) Act 1934, s. 1(1).

with another's.[130] Damages are for pecuniary loss and loss of profits may be inferred.[131] Aggravated damages ought to be available here in light of their availability in (a) above.

4   Economic Torts

(a) Conspiracy

5/29   Corporations have standing to sue under the tort and, as with other claimants, must prove actual pecuniary loss.[132] The action arises where two or more persons agree to do acts, whether lawful (lawful means conspiracy) or unlawful (unlawful means conspiracy) in themselves, for the sole or predominant purpose of causing injury to the claimant and which in fact cause pecuniary loss to the claimant. Damages for injury to reputation and emotional harm (e.g. injury to feelings) are not sufficient to ground an action for conspiracy and no award can be made in respect of such injury. A claimant who seeks such damages must do so in an action for defamation, where applicable.[133] Where actual pecuniary loss is proved, damages are at large, in the sense that they are not limited to a precise calculation of the amount of the pecuniary loss actually proved. Consequently, a claimant may be entitled to aggravated damages.[134]

(b) Inducement of Breach of Contract

5/30   An action lies in favour of a company against a person who induces or procures another to commit a breach of contract concluded between that person and the company.[135] While actual damage is the gist of the claim,[136] it has been held that, if the breach will 'in the ordinary course of business'

---

[130] The 'classic trinity' in an action for passing off are: (a) the claimant's goods or services have acquired a goodwill in the market and are known by some distinguishing name, mark or other *indicium*; (b) there is a misrepresentation by the defendant (whether or not intentional) leading or likely to lead the public to believe that goods or services offered by the defendant are goods or services of the claimant; and (c) the claimant has suffered or is likely to suffer damage as a result of the erroneous belief engendered by the defendant's misrepresentation: R. Arnold, *Halsbury's Laws Commentary on Trade Marks and Trade Names* (London: LexisNexis Butterworths, 2014), vol. 97A, para. 287.

[131] *Draper* v. *Trist* (1939) 56 RPC 429, 442 per Lord Goddard.

[132] *Quinn* v. *Leathem* [1901] AC 495, 498 as approved in 508 by Lord Halsbury LC and by other members of the House of Lords.

[133] *Lonrho plc* v. *Fayed (No. 5)* [1993] 1 WLR 1489, 1496 per Dillon LJ.

[134] *Huntley* v. *Thornton* [1957] 1 WLR 321; *Pratt* v. *British Medical Association* [1919] 1 KB 244. See Tettenborn, *Halsbury's Laws Commentary on Damages*, para 323, fn 16.

[135] *Lumley* v. *Gye* (1853) 2 E & B 216.

[136] *Exchange Telegraph Co. Ltd* v. *Gregory & Co. Ltd* [1896] 1 QB 147, 156–157 per Kay LJ.

cause damage, special damage need not be proved.[137] Oliphant opines that emotional injuries falling short of recognised medical conditions ought not ordinarily to constitute actionable damages under this head.[138] As damages are at large, aggravated damages may be awarded in the appropriate case.[139]

(c) Unlawful Interference with Economic Interests

5/31   In order to maintain an action under this head (once termed unlawful interference with trade), proof of the intentional infliction of harm by the use of unlawful means is essential.[140] Damages for mere emotional distress are not available.[141] Aggravated damages may, however, be awarded.[142]

(d) Intimidation

5/32   That the tort of intimidation was an established tort was confirmed in *Rookes* v. *Barnard*.[143] It is actionable by companies. Proof of damage is required. While there is authority that damage need not be limited to economic loss,[144] it has been argued that where the intimidation directly results in injury to the claimant's health, the case should be brought under the separate principle of liability for intentional interference with the person.[145] Aggravated damages may be awarded.[146]

---

[137] See *Goldsoll* v. *Goldman* [1914] 2 Ch 603, 615 per Neville J; *Exchange Telegraph Co. Ltd* v. *Gregory & Co. Ltd* [1896] 1 QB 147, 156–157 per Kay LJ.

[138] K. Oliphant, 'The Economic Torts' in K. Oliphant (ed.), *The Law of Tort*, 2nd edn (London: LexisNexis Butterworths, 2007), para. 29.46. See also *SOS Kinderdorf International* v. *Bittaye* [1996] 1 WLR 987.

[139] *Pratt* v. *British Medical Association* [1919] I KB 244, 282 per McCardie J where damages were awarded for the deliberate and relentless vigour with which the defendants sought to achieve the infliction of the claimants' complete ruin and the long period for which they respectively suffered humiliation and menace.

[140] *OBG Ltd* v. *Allan* [2008] 1 AC 1.

[141] According to Oliphant, cases in which damages for non-pecuniary loss have apparently been awarded in such actions can be explained on the basis that the underlying loss was in reality pecuniary or that the cause of action was really for interference with the person: Oliphant (ed.), *The Law of Tort*, para. 29.87. *Mbasogo* v. *Logo Ltd* [2007] QB 846.

[142] *Messenger Newspapers Group Ltd* v. *National Graphical Association* [1984] IRLR 397.

[143] *Rookes* v. *Barnard* [1964] AC 1129. It is in essence the use of unlawful threat to compel another to act or refrain from acting in a manner which causes loss to himself (two-party intimidation) or another (three-party intimidation).

[144] *Godwin* v. *Uzoigwe* [1993] Fam Law 65.

[145] Oliphant (ed.), *The Law of Tort*, para. 29.57.

[146] *Rookes* v. *Barnard* [1964] AC 1129; *Messenger Newspaper Group Ltd* v. *National Graphical Association* [1984] IRLR 397; *Godwin* v. *Uzoigwe* [1993] Fam Law 65.

5   Torts to Reputation and Privacy

(a)   Defamation

5/33   While there is much discomfort in the notion of corporations suffering interference in the bodily, mental or emotional spheres, legal systems (see nos. 8/7–8/11), including England, readily accept that they are capable of suffering injury to the personality sphere. This practice and the imbalance it was perceived to encourage was, however, the subject of reform campaigns which resulted in the passing of the Defamation Act 2013. A detailed review of this area is thus made inevitable by the enactment of the statute which entered into force on 1 January 2014.

(i)   Prerequisites

5/34   Defamation law in England consists of libel (which concerns itself with publications of a permanent form such as written allegations) and slander (which concerns itself with less permanent or transient kinds of communication such as oral conversations).[147] For an action in defamation to succeed, a claimant must establish that: (a) the statement was defamatory; (b) it referred to him; and (c) it was published (in the sense of disclosed to a third party). Various tests were formulated over the years as determinative of a defamatory statement – all of which were objectively assessed. Among these, words were said to be defamatory if they had a *tendency* to: (a) expose the claimant to hatred, contempt, or ridicule;[148] (b) cause others to shun and avoid the claimant;[149] or (c) lower the claimant's reputation in the estimation of right-thinking members of society generally.[150] As will be seen in *(iv)* below, whether a statement was defamatory is assessed differently under the 2013 Act.

(ii)   The Expansion of the Law from Sole Traders to Corporations

5/35   It was established early on that, where defamation was in respect of a sole trader's business, an action would lie whether special damage was

---

[147] Note that broadcasting is libel by statute: see s. 166(1) Broadcasting Act 1990 and s. 4 Theatres Act 1968.

[148] *Parmiter* v. *Coupland* (1840) 6 M & W 105, 108 per Parke B.

[149] The Court of Appeal in *Tournier* v. *National Provincial and Union Bank of England* [1924] 1 KB 461 thought that the 'ancient formula' in (a) above was too narrow. Scrutton LJ opined (at 477) that it was not 'sufficient in all cases, for words may damage the reputation of a man as a business man, which no one would connect with hatred, ridicule, or contempt.' In *Youssoupoff* v. *Metro-Goldwyn-Mayer Pictures Ltd* (1934) 50 TLR 581, 587, Slesser LJ took the opportunity to expand the test.

[150] *Sim* v. *Stretch* [1936] 2 All ER 1237, 1240 per Lord Atkin. See *Thornton* v. *Telegraph Media Group* [2011] 1 WLR 1985 per Tugendhat J at paras. 27–49, for discussion of the formulations.

shown or not.[151] Although having no separate personality, this rule was extended to partnerships (where the defamation was on the whole body in the way of their trade and not on members of the firm in their individual capacities) so that an action could and indeed still can be brought in the partnership's name.[152] It was not until *Metropolitan Saloon Omnibus Company Ltd* v. *Hawkins*, however, that standing was extended to corporations. The court for the first time ruled there that: 'That a corporation at common law can sue in respect of a libel there is no doubt.'[153] On the facts, it was not necessary to decide whether or not proof of special damage was necessary because special damage was alleged. *Metropolitan Saloon* was confirmed in *South Hetton Coal Company Ltd* v. *North Eastern News Association Ltd* where the court reasoned that the law of libel is one and the same as to all plaintiffs whether 'a person, a firm, or a company'.[154] Significantly, the court added that a suit would lie for a trading company in respect of a libel *without proof of special damage*[155] provided that the words imputed scandal to collective rights and interests as distinct from those of the individuals who composed it. It was irrelevant to the finding of *liability*, as counsel for the defendant had contended, that a company has no feelings which may be hurt or irritated or that it has no *moral* character which could be besmirched. For a corporation has a '*trading* character, the defamation of which may ruin it'.[156] Where, however, as the case was in *South Hetton*, no damage was proved, it was held that the damages given would probably be small.[157] It is only a defamation which is *related to its business* that a company can complain of and not

---

[151] *Ingram* v. *Lawson* (1840) 6 Bing NC 212, 215 per Bosanquet J and 216 per Coltman J.

[152] 'I believe it to be clear law, that wherever slanderous words are spoken of partners in the way of their trade, they may maintain a joint action for them, though they do not state special damage': *Forster* v. *Lawson* (1826) 3 Bing 452, 457 per Park J. See also *Williams* v. *Beaumont* (1833) 10 Bing 260, 270 per Tindal CJ. This continues to be the case today. Para. 5A.3 of Practice Direction 7A, Civil Procedure Rules reads: 'Where that partnership has a name, unless it is inappropriate to do so, claims must be brought in or against the name under which that partnership carried on business at the time the cause of action accrued.'

[153] (1859) 4 Hurl & N 87, 90 per Pollock CB.

[154] [1894] 1 QB 133, 138 per Lord Esher MR.

[155] 'It is not necessary to prove any particular damage': *South Hetton Coal Company Ltd* v. *North Eastern News Association Ltd* [1894] 1 QB 133, 139 per Lord Esher MR. Lopes LJ also ruled (at 141) that a cooperation 'can maintain an action for a libel reflecting on the management of their trade or business, and this without alleging or proving special damage'.

[156] *South Hetton Coal Company Ltd* v. *North-Eastern News Association Ltd* [1894] 1 QB 133, 145 per Kay LJ. Emphasis added.

[157] *South Hetton Coal Company Ltd* v. *North-Eastern News Association Ltd* [1894] 1 QB 133, 148 per Kay LJ.

in respect of acts that cannot be attributed to it. Thus, in *D & L Cater-*
ers v. *D'Ajou* Lord Goddard explained: 'If one said of a company "It is
a murderer"' there is 'no doubt that the company could not bring an
action, because . . . a company cannot murder'.[158] That case is important
for extending the principle in *South Hetton* to slanders.

(iii)   The Criticism of South Hetton

5/36   Although English law has accepted the rule in *South Hetton* for well
over a hundred years – with the exception that governmental authorities (since 1993)[159] and political parties (since 1997)[160] cannot sue for
defamation – it is one that has since then, as today, been criticised. There
was lingering doubt as to the propriety of presuming a corporation had
suffered damage, in particular non-pecuniary loss, once a libel or slander
per se had been established, without it being pleaded or proved that the
publication complained of caused it any damage at all. The argument
in favour of such a presumption was that: 'It is impossible to track the
scandal, to know what quarters the poison may reach';[161] i.e. it was unreasonable to require the claimant, whether corporate or natural, to prove
such damage. In fact, once an action was brought it was not open to
a defendant to prove that no loss followed or that the defamation was
'followed by a pecuniary *benefit*.'[162] The criticism went that while there

---

[158]   [1945] KB 364, 366. Nor, as Pollock CB pointed out in *Metropolitan Saloon Omnibus Com-*
pany Ltd v. *Hawkins* (1859) 4 Hurl & N 87, 90, can a company sue in respect of 'an imputation of . . . incest, or adultery, because it could not commit those crimes . . . although
the individuals composing it may'. A company can, however, commit manslaughter (see
R v. *P&O European Ferries* (1990) 93 Cr App R 72 and the offence under the Corporate
Manslaughter and Corporate Homicide Act 2007).

[159]   I.e. central and local government authorities. In *Derbyshire County Council* v. *Times*
Newspapers Ltd [1993] AC 534, 547 the House of Lords overruled the earlier authority
of *Bognor Regis Urban Distinct Council* v. *Campion* [1972] 2 QB 169, reasoning that it
is 'of the highest public importance that a democratically elected governmental body,
or indeed any governmental body, should be open to uninhibited public criticism. The
threat of a civil action for defamation must inevitably have an inhibiting effect on freedom
of speech'. (per Lord Keith). Having said that, the decision does not seem to preclude
an employee of a government body who considers that they have been defamed, from
pursuing an action in his own name. See *McLaughlin* v. *London Borough of Lambeth*
[2011] EMLR 8.

[160]   *Goldsmith* v. *Bhoyrul* [1998] QB 459.

[161]   *Ley* v. *Hamilton* (1935) 153 LT 384, 386 per Lord Atkin.

[162]   V. V. Veeder, 'The History and Theory of the Law of Defamation II', *Columbia Law*
Review, 4(1) (1904), 33–56. Emphasis added. Anderson observes that: 'The presumption
of causation was so strong at common law that it not only relieved the plaintiff of the
need to establish causation and to negate the existence of other possible causes of injury,
but it even prevented the defendant from introducing evidence of alternative theories of

was still justification for absolving a human claimant from the need to prove harm, the Court of Appeal in *South Hetton* was wrong to extend this privilege to a trading company. Weir, for example, noted that in the former case the individual '*will feel bad* and *others will think badly of him*: the first need not be proved and the second cannot be.' All that a trading company can experience is harm to its commercial relations. This *can* and therefore should be proved.[163] There was also the problem of inequality of arms. Companies with deep pockets might threaten defamation, thus abusing the action to chill opponents' freedom of expression. That nuisance was aggravated by the fact that litigation costs were 'likely to be set off against the company's profits for tax purposes and the Value Added Tax could be reclaimed, neither of which advantage tended to be available to non-corporate defendants.'[164] Some therefore argued against the presumptive rule on damages for corporations,[165] others called for companies to lose their right to seek damages for non-pecuniary loss,[166] indeed damages generally in defamatory actions.[167] They added that complete or partial ban, said to be consistent with the Australian approach on defamation claims by corporations,[168] would still leave companies with other remedies (e.g. a declaration of falsity or an action in malicious falsehood, notwithstanding the difficulties in proving malice[169]). Moreover it was contended that leading figures in such corporations could sue.[170]

---

causation'. D. A. Anderson, 'Reputation, Compensation and Proof', *William and Mary Law Review*, 25(5) (1984), 747–778. Cf the effect of s. 1 Defamation Act 2013.

[163] J. A. Weir, 'Local Authority v. Critical Ratepayer – a Suit in Defamation', *Cambridge Law Journal* [1972A] 238, 239–240. See also proposal by The Faulks Committee's Report on Defamation (1975: Cmnd 5909), para. 336.

[164] D. Hooper, K. Waite and O. Murphy, 'Defamation Act 2013 – What Difference Will it Really Make', *Entertainment Law Review*, 24(6) (2013), 199–206, 200.

[165] See the opinion of the dissenting judges in *Jameel* v. *Wall Street Journal* [2007] 1 AC 359, for example.

[166] See no. 5/47 below for those who argued that corporate reputation is property and as such, corporate actions should be limited to damages for pecuniary loss.

[167] House of Lords and House of Commons, *Joint Committee on the Draft Defamation Bill*, HL Paper 203, HC 930–I, October 2011, para. 113.

[168] House of Lords and House of Commons, *Joint Committee on the Draft Defamation Bill*, HL Paper 203, HC 930–I, October 2011, paras. 111 and 113. See also fn 45 of no. 8/11 below.

[169] *Jameel* v. *Wall Street Journal* [2007] 1 AC 359, para. 91 per Lord Hoffmann. See also D. Howarth, 'Libel: Its Purpose and Reform', *Modern Law Review*, 74(6) (2011), 845–877. Cf G. Phillipson, 'The "Global Pariah", the Defamation Bill and the Human Rights Act' in D. Capper (ed.), *Modern Defamation Law: Balancing Reputation and Free Expression* (Queens University Belfast Press, 2012), p. 189, fn 262.

[170] Although such figures may indeed by implicated in a statement about the company (as was the case in *Aspro Travel* v. *Owners Abroad* [1996] 1 WLR 132 where it was accepted

5/37   Despite such calls, courts were slow to interfere with the law as pro-
        pounded in *South Hetton*.[171] And indeed, the House of Lords affirmed
        the entitlement of a company to recover general damages in *Jameel* v.
        Wall Street Journal,[172] albeit by a narrow margin, leaving it to Parliament
        to abrogate or modify the law. Such intervention came in the form of
        a Private Member's Bill[173] moved by Lord Lester – a huge champion of
        freedom and rights – and subsequently, the Defamation Act 2013.

        (iv)   The Defamation Act 2013 and its Application
5/38   The 2013 Act was the product of extensive parliamentary scrutiny
        and compromise.[174] By s. 1(1): 'A statement is not defamatory unless *its
        publication has caused or is likely to cause serious harm* to the reputation
        of the claimant.'[175] *All* claimants, namely both natural and legal persons,
        must satisfy this test which builds on the common law.[176] In addition,
        Parliament legislated to require a *trading corporation* to adduce evidence
        under s. 1(2) that the statement *has caused or is likely to cause* it serious
        financial loss before it qualified as defamatory. Section 1(2) does not extend
        to not-for-profit corporations, such as charities and nongovernmental
        organisations since, as was argued, any 'damage from a defamatory attack
        on the credibility of their work' would 'not necessarily have a financial
        impact on their resources and future capability.'[177] This was not the view
        taken by Lord Hope who observed in *Jameel* that injury to the reputation
        of charities or other non-trading companies may also result in financial

---

        as one of several preliminary points that a statement about a small family company could
        be understood to refer to the individual directors), this is not necessarily so: see *Jameel*
        v. *Wall Street Journal* [2007] 1 AC 359, para. 25 per Lord Bingham. In any case, such an
        individual would not be entitled to claim for the corporation's loss: House of Lords and
        House of Commons, *Joint Committee on the Draft Defamation Bill*, HL Paper 203, HC
        930–I, October 2011, para. 112.
[171]   See *Derbyshire County Council* v. *Times Newspaper Ltd* [1993] AC 534, 547 per Lord Keith.
        In *Shevill* v. *Presse Alliance SA* [1996] AC 959 a presumption of damage was also treated
        as correct in a case where one of the claimants was a trading corporation.
[172]   [2007] 1 AC 359.   [173] [HL] 2010–12.
[174]   See J. Price and F. McMahon, *The Blackstone's Guide to the Defamaton Act 2013* (Oxford
        University Press, 2013), pp. 13–25 which includes a section on the Act's history.
[175]   Emphasis added. As Lunney and Oliphant, *Tort Law: Text and Materials*, p. 699 observed,
        the new test 'seems to blur the distinction between the questions of whether a statement
        is defamatory and the damage flowing from it'.
[176]   See s. 1 Explanatory Notes to the Act.
[177]   Draft Defamation Bill – Joint Committee on the Draft Defamation Bill (2011), para. 118.
        On the merits of s. 1(2) see E. Descheemaeker, 'Three Errors in the Defamation Act 2013',
        Journal of European Tort Law, 6(1) (2015), 1–25.

or pecuniary damage. As such, he saw 'no good reason why trading companies should be treated differently from the rest.'[178]

5/39   Happily, cases have now started to emerge which shed light on both limbs of the test. In *Cooke* v. *MGN Ltd*, the first case to interpret the Act, Bean J gave guidance on s. 1(1); the ruling *Lachaux* v. *Independent Print Ltd* is more significant, however, since Warby J concluded there that libel is no longer actionable without proof of damage. It is insufficient for a claimant to show that the words complained of had a *tendency* to cause serious harm to his reputation. Actual or likely serious harm must be proved (on the balance of probabilities) or at least be inferable (cf no. 5/20).[179] Also germane here is the decision in *ReachLocal UK Ltd* v. *Bennett*.[180] After the introduction of the 2013 Act it was unclear whether damages for non-pecuniary loss would continue to be available to trading corporations to pursue even once the test in s. 1(2) was satisfied. This was because s. 1(2) drew inspiration from cl. 11 of Lord Lester's Defamation Bill of 2010, which in turn was heavily influenced by the position in New Zealand. Significantly, the Court of Appeal there ruled: 'Although not entirely clear on [the wording of the applicable Act], we have *no doubt* that the legislative intent was to *limit compensatory relief for a corporate plaintiff to pecuniary loss*.'[181]

5/40   Per contra, in *ReachLocal UK Ltd* v. *Bennett*, an English High Court decision, the claimant company was awarded £75,000 in general damages, the company having shown, inter alia, that several customers no longer wished to use its services as a direct result of the defamatory publications in question. The second claimant, the first claimant's parent company, did not trade in the UK and was awarded a nominal sum of £100 by way of general damages, the court concluding in any case that the defamatory words were understood to refer primarily to the first claimant. Significantly, the court entered into detail on the issue of why corporate claimants should continue to be entitled to damages for non-pecuniary loss once s. 1 of the 2013 Act is satisfied: in the first place,

---

[178]   [2007] 1 AC 359, para. 101.
[179]   *Cooke* v. *MGN Ltd* [2015] 1 WLR 895 and *Lachaux* v. *Independent Print Ltd* [2016] QB 402.
[180]   [2015] EMLR 7. As to the serious financial loss requirement see *Brett Wilson* v. *Persons Unknown* [2016] 4 WLR 69.
[181]   *Midland Metals Overseas Pte Ltd* v. *The Christchurch Press Co. Ltd* [2002] 2 NZLR 289, para. 12. Emphasis added. The Act in question is the Defamation Act 1992, s. 6 of which reads that an action by a body corporate shall fail unless it proves that the publication of the matter has caused or is likely to cause pecuniary loss.

HHJ Parkes QC echoed several of their Lordship's statements in *Jameel* that a company's good name was a thing of value. As Lord Bingham had ruled there:

> A damaging libel may lower [a company's] standing in the eyes of the public and even its own staff, make people less ready to deal with it, less willing or less proud to work for it. If this were not so, corporations would not go to the lengths they do to protect and burnish their corporate images. I find nothing repugnant in the notion that this is a value which the law should protect.[182]

5/41   Second, HHJ Parkes QC referred to the vindicatory role of damages for defamation, saying that although a company could 'only be hit in its pocket', that was 'not to say that its good name might not merit vindication'.[183] That vindication is *the primary purpose* of an award of damages in a libel action has been repeatedly acknowledged.[184] As Tugendhat J in *McLaughlin* v. *Lambeth BC* explained:

> Vindication includes preventing, or reducing the risk of, future publications of the words complained of. The fact that the damage suffered so far may be small (if it is), is no indication of the extent of the damage which is prevented from occurring in the future, when a claimant in a libel action obtains a public retraction or a judgment in his favour from the court.[185]

---

[182] [2007] 1 AC 359, para. 26. Lord Scott also observed (at para. 120) that: 'If reputation suffers, sponsorship invitations may be reduced, advertising opportunities may become difficult, customers may take their custom elsewhere. If trade suffers, profits suffer'.

[183] [2015] EMLR 7, para. 54.

[184] In *Broome* v. *Cassell & Ltd (No. 1)* [1972] AC 1027, 1071 reference was made to *Uren* v. *John Fairfax & Sons Pty Ltd* (1966) 117 CLR 115, 150 an Australian case in which Windeyer J spoke of non-pecuniary compensation in defamation cases operating, inter alia, as 'a *vindication* of the plaintiff to the public' and emphasised that they are awarded not so much to compensate the plaintiff '*for* his damaged reputation' but '*because* he was injured in his reputation'; 'that is simply because he was publicly defamed'. Emphasis added. See also *Jameel* v. *Wall Street Journal* [2007] 1 AC 359, para. 123 per Lord Scott: 'the primary purpose of an award of damages in a libel action . . . is not compensation but vindication of reputation'.; *Clarke (t/a Elumina Iberica UK)* v. *Bain* [2008] EWHC 2636, para. 54 per Tugendhat J: 'Defamation actions are not primarily about recovering money damages, but about vindication of a claimant's reputation'.; *McLaughlin* BC [2011] EMLR 8, para. 112 per Tugendhat J: 'the main point of defamation proceedings is vindication'. It is also worth noting that the power under s. 12 of the Defamation Act 2013 (which builds on s. 9 Defamation Act 1996) to order publication of the court's judgment arguably goes some way to providing non-monetary vindication. See also s. 13 of the Act. Cf *Cruddas* v. *Adams* [2013] EWHC 145.

[185] [2011] EMLR 8, para. 112.

5/42   HHJ Parkes QC concluded – quoting *Purnell* v. *Business Magazine Ltd*[186] – that, while a reasoned judgment might in principle provide some degree of vindication, in the case before him, given that the court's judgment was not a contested decision on the merits, any vindicatory effect of the judgment was bound to be marginal.[187] He continued that although the very size of the special damages awarded to the first claimant was likely to provide some measure of vindication, any award of general damages had to be sufficient to enable the first claimant to counter the defendants' campaign and to show beyond argument to those who operated in its area of business that the allegations made against it had been baseless.

5/43   Several factors were said to be relevant to the level of general damages awarded in *ReachLocal UK Ltd* v. *Bennett*: (a) the gravity of the allegation; (b) the extent of publication, including the fact of dissemination via the internet. In particular, HHJ Parkes QC highlighted the fact that such campaigns can easily go viral and are difficult to remove completely out of the public arena; (c) the fact that the first claimant was not a long-established business and that it operated in a very new field. It had thus not 'had the opportunity to build up for generations an established standing associated with integrity from which those with whom it is dealing would immediately recognise that any wrongdoing was entirely uncharacteristic of it';[188] (d) and finally, the overriding principle that, in order to comply with art. 10 of the European Convention on Human Rights, an award of damages must be proportionate to the legitimate aim of providing vindication.

5/44   In the case of a successful claim for defamation, the court may find it appropriate to award aggravated damages.[189] Corporate entitlement to such damages is considered in Chapter 6.

---

[186] [2008] 1 WLR 1. This was a libel action before the Court of Appeal. The only live ground was whether the judge was wrong in allowing the jury to include any element of vindication in its award since, as was argued, a prior reasoned judgment rejecting a justification defence and so holding that the claimant had been libelled had 'provided all the vindication that was available' to the claimant. Laws LJ held that, although the effect of a prior reasoned judgment in relation to vindication will 'most likely be marginal', the court in assessing damages must see whether it does in fact provide such vindication, for otherwise it would fail to make a complete or comprehensive judgment and would be at risk of failing in its duty to uphold and apply the European Convention on Human Rights. On the facts, the prior judgment was *insufficient* to constitute all the vindication to which the claimant was entitled to.

[187] As Lord Bingham noted in *Jameel*, 'The ordinary means of vindication is by the verdict of a judge or jury and an award of damages'.: [2007] 1 AC 359, para. 24.

[188] Borrowed from the words of Andrew Smith J in *Jon Richard Ltd* v. *Gornall* [2013] EWHC 1357.

[189] Tettenborn, *Halsbury's Laws Commentary on Damages*, para 323, fn 9.

(v)   Corporate Reputation Examined

5/45   Contrary to those, like Howarth, who found it questionable that pure economic loss in defamation, that is, loss entirely unrelated to sociality or the pain of fearing the loss of social relationships, should be actionable at all by trading companies,[190] the decision by Parliament was not to deprive trading companies of the opportunity to sue and be fully remedied for aspersions on their reputation, and rightly so. The law has acknowledged corporations, created for the promotion of collective interests, as having legal personality; *the* very attribute that distinguishes them from other business forms. The personality that a company enjoys following incorporation is distinct from but overlaps with the concept of 'personality rights' which covers things such as one's name, likeness, publicity rights, voice, signature or other facets of one's identity. As with natural persons, companies have names and consequently, desires for control over that aspect of their personality. This is not inconsistent with the law of defamation and the interest it seeks to protect; nor is it inconsistent with the corporate form. Reputation, after all is *an external construct*; what people *communicate* to third persons about one. Its external nature is underlined first by the need for publication.[191] Second, by the fact that the publication must be to a third party. If made solely to the person claiming to have been defamed, the offending statement – in effect a 'mere personal insult'– is not actionable under English law at least.[192] Admittedly, its objective nature was more nuanced by the old tests for what was defamatory – among them, the *tendency* for a publication to lower the claimant's reputation in the estimation of right-thinking members of society. '[W]hether the publication actually did harm the plaintiff's reputation was irrelevant to the issue of liability; at most it was relevant to the quantum of damages.'[193] Reputation is still objective, however – despite the ruling in

---

[190]   Howarth, 'Libel: Its Purpose and Reform', 874.

[191]   W. B. Odgers, *Libel and Slander* (London: Stevens and Sons Ltd, 1905), p. 150: 'the law permits us to think as badly as we please of our neighbours so long as we keep our uncharitable thoughts to ourselves'.

[192]   For 'undivulged matter is merely the bomb which has not exploded, the caged animal which has not broken loose'.: G. S. Bower, *A Code of the Law of Actionable Defamation: With a Continuous Commentary and Appendices* (London: Butterworth & Co., 1923), p. 259. It is true that before its abolition in 2009, no third-party publication was necessary for criminal libels either: abolished by s. 73 Coroners and Justice Act 2009. In the case of common law libel offences, however, the law was aimed not at the vindication of reputation but at the preservation of breaches of public peace.

[193]   E. Barendt, 'What is the Point of Libel Law?', *Current Legal Problems*, 52(1) (1999), 110–115, 122. *Morgan* v. *Odhams Press* [1971] 1 WLR 1239, 1246 per Lord Reid: 'One of the witnesses thought that the article referred to the appellant but completely *disbelieved it*:

Lachaux where Warby J concluded that it must in fact be seriously harmed in the eyes of those who read the words complained of – and is different from character.[194] despite the ruling in *Lachaux* where Warby J concluded that it must in fact be seriously harmed in the eyes of those who read the words complained of.[195] Character is what a person really is. Not only are reputation and character not synonymous, 'but they may be directly contrary to each other. A man may have a good character and a bad reputation, being unjustly judged by the public; or he may have a bad character and a good reputation, standing in a false light before the public.'[196] Since character is too subjective, too personal as a yardstick to measure, the law has chosen to protect reputation, whether or not this in fact mirrors character.

5/46   That said, 'most men set the utmost value precisely on what other people think' and in so doing regard 'the opinions of others as real existence and their own consciousness as something shadowy'.[197] As well as causing others to dissociate themselves from the defamed, aspersions may have a direct and immediate impact on one insofar as they can hurt their sensibility, lower their dignity and move one to modify who one is, one's character. Hence, the award of damages for non-pecuniary loss to soak up the presumed 'subjective' mess that bad words cause. These 'act as a consolation to the claimant for the distress and embarrassment which he has suffered from the publication of defamatory words'.[198] Since common law defamation is '*not* concerned with the plaintiff's own humiliation, wrath or sorrow, except as an element of "parasitic" damages attached

---

he thought it was rubbish. It was argued that he must be left out of account because no tort is committed by making a defamatory statement about X to a person who utterly disbelieves it. *That is plainly wrong'.* Emphasis added.

[194] In *Plato Films Ltd* v. *Speidel* [1961] AC 1090, 1129 Lord Radcliffe observed the lack of any clear distinction between disposition or character on the one hand and reputation on the other in many of the earlier cases and also the absence of the different ideas which they convey. Similarly, Lord Denning (at 1138) stated: 'A man's "character", it is sometimes said, is *what he in fact is,* whereas his "reputation" is what *other people think he is'.* Emphasis added. Therefore, 'a libel action is concerned only with a man's reputation, that is, with what people think of him: and it is for damage to his reputation, that is, to his esteem in the eyes of others, that he can sue, and not for damage to his own personality or disposition'. See also Doley et al. (eds.), C. Doley, A. Mullis and Carter-Ruck (eds.), *Carter-Ruck on Libel and Privacy,* 6th edn (LexisNexis Butterworths, 2010), para. 2.3 and Barendt, 'What is the Point of Libel Law?', 115.

[195] [2016] QB 402, para. 59.

[196] Veeder, 'The History and Theory of the Law of Defamation II', 33.

[197] A. Schopenhauer, *The Wisdom of Life and Counsels and Maxims* (New York: Prometheus Books, 1995), p. 55.

[198] *ReachLocal UK Ltd* v. *Bennett* [2015] EMLR 7, para. 53 per HHJ Parkes QC.

to an independent cause of action',[199] it follows that corporate bodies, with no feelings to injure, can nonetheless sue for the two other functions which non-pecuniary damages for defamation serve: 'to compensate for the injury to the claimant's reputation; and . . . to act as vindication for his reputation',[200] matters of objective assessment.

5/47   Earlier English authorities which conceived reputation as a 'species' of property did so for perverse reasons.[201] Thankfully, these opinions have not prevailed so that today most accept that such a view – though supported by eminent minds[202] – is incomplete insofar as it 'mistakes the consequences of the harm libel causes for the harm itself.'[203] Despite this, scholars continue to insist that 'the fact that a corporation can, under English law, sue for defamation can only be explained if reputation is conceived as property.'[204] Such writers appear to confuse corporate

---

[199] Emphasis added. W. Page Keeton et al., *Prosser and Keeton on The Law of Torts*, 5th edn (St Paul: West Publishing Co., 1984), § 111, p. 771. D. Price, K. Duodu, N. Cain, *Defamation: Law Procedure and Practice*, 4th edn (London: Sweet & Maxwell, 2010), para. 20-03. See also E. Descheemaeker, 'Three Keys to Defamation: Media 24 in a Comparative Perspective', *South African Law Journal*, 130(2)(2013), 435–448.

[200] *ReachLocal UK Ltd* v. *Bennett* [2015] EMLR 7, para. 53 per HHJ Parkes QC.

[201] The context in which the cases took place is crucial to understanding the reasoning therein: it is one that dates back to the separate jurisdictions of the court of equity, or the Court of Chancery, and the common law courts. Unlike the common law courts, the court of equity could grant injunctions and order specific performance. In *Du Bost* v. *Beresford* (1810) 2 Campbell 511 and *Gee* v. *Pritchard* (1818) 2 Swanston 402, the courts were taken as laying down the proposition that the office of equity was *limited to protecting rights over property*. On the facts in *Gee*, the court went on to secure an interest in personality leading to the conclusion that reputation was property. However, this was in fact a way for equity to expand its jurisdiction and in so doing achieve justice for claimants. The passing of the Judicature Acts did away with the jurisdictional battle and with it, the need to force the concept of reputation into the category of 'property'. The dominant view of the English authorities is thus in line with *Prudential Assurance Co.* v. *Knott* (1874-75) LR 10 Ch App 142; that reputation in itself is not property. It will be remembered, moreover, that *Prudential* concerned corporate reputation.

[202] Among them R. C. Post, 'The Social Foundations of Defamation Law: Reputation and the Constitution', *California Law Review*, 74(3) (1986), 691–742. Bower, *A Code of the Law of Actionable Defamation*, pp. 240–244, with some reservations. R. Pound, 'Interests of Personality', *Harvard Law Review*, 28(5) (1914–1915), 445–456, also with reservations.

[203] Howarth, 'Libel: Its Purpose and Reform', 853. L. McNamara, *Reputation and Defamation* (Oxford University Press, 2007), p. 42; D. Milo, *Defamation and Freedom of Speech* (Oxford University Press, 2008), p. 30; D. Rolph, *Reputation, Celebrity and Defamation Law* (Hampshire/Burlington: Ashgate, 2008), p. 23; Mullis and Carter-Ruck (eds.), *Carter-Ruck on Libel and Privacy*, para. 2.15.

[204] Mullis and Carter-Ruck (eds.), *Carter-Ruck on Libel and Privacy*, para. 2.13. In line with Pound, 'Interests of Personality', 447: 'a juristic person can have interests of substance only' and elsewhere 'defamation of a juristic person is only cognizable so far as the reputation of the association is an asset and is injuriously affected as such'. See also R. C. Post, 'The Social Foundations of Defamation Law', 717 who concluded that

reputation with goodwill, in the latter case a concept that is well-established *is* property both in legal and accounting terms. This view is best set out by Jacob LJ who in *IN Newman Ltd* v. *Richard T Adlem* ruled that: 'It is trite English law that there is no property in a name as such. But there is property in the goodwill attached to a name. That goodwill is a species of property and that it is the right in that property which is protected by the law of passing off. So much was settled long ago.'[205] Since a company '*must be treated* like any other independent person with its rights and liabilities *appropriate to itself*', as Halsbury LC put it in *Salomon* v. *Salomon & Co. Ltd* (no. 2/5), a company which the law has endowed with legal personality should therefore be entitled to damages for non-pecuniary loss for interference with the non-proprietary aspects of its personality to the extent that this is appropriate to the corporate form (i.e. with the exception of the injury to feelings component).

5/48 The question then arises as to whether damages for the injured feelings of a company's organs should be available to the company following a successful finding of interference with its reputation on the basis of the attribution theory. While there is some merit to the theory, dealt with more fully in Chapter 7, this seems contrary to sound legal principle; firstly, because the company has a personality sphere of its own which the law has seen fit to limit and secondly since damages for injury to feelings in defamation, especially in light of *Lachaux*, seek in essence to remedy an injury to dignity, an inherently human facet (nos. 5/46 and 6/13).

(b) Misuse of Private Information and Related Actions

5/49 Unlike Continental European systems, English law was traditionally slow in protecting privacy outside a group of established torts (e.g. trespass to land, nuisance, harassment and defamation). Indeed, in

the concept of reputation as property explains why corporations and other inanimate entities can sue for defamation. Milo, *Defamation and Freedom of Speech*, pp. 28–29: 'The classic aspect of defamation law that regards reputation as a form of property is the rule that corporations can sue for defamation'. Rolph, *Reputation, Celebrity and Defamation Law*, p. 23: 'Post is clearly correct to observe that certain aspects of defamation are only explicable on the basis that the common law provides protection for reputation as property. The extension of defamation law to protect corporate reputation is the most obvious example of this'. J. Oster, 'The Criticism of Trading Corporations and their Right to Sue for Defamation', *Journal of European Tort Law*, 2 (2011), 255–279, 258–260.

[205] [2006] FSR 16, para. 22. He referred to Lord Diplock's historical account on this question in *Erven Warnink* v. *Townend* [1979] AC 731, 740. See also *Boehringer Ingelheim Ltd* v. *Vetplus Ltd* [2007] Bus LR 1456, para. 37 per Jacob LJ: 'The common law has long recognised that that goodwill is a species of property and one that is protected by the law of passing off.' See also the EctHR's case in no. 3/37 confirming this.

Wainwright v. *Home Office*[206] the House of Lords rejected the previously unknown tort of invasion of privacy. However, in *Campbell* v. *MGN Ltd*[207] their Lordships implicitly recognised a tort of *misuse of private information*, albeit grounded in the doctrine of breach of confidence.[208] Art. 8 of the European Convention on Human Rights was the impetus for this move. As Lord Nicholls noted in *Campbell*, the new 'tort' has 'shaken off the limiting constraint of the need for an initial confidential relationship'.[209] That breach of commercial confidence, aimed at the protection of pecuniary interests, is actionable by companies is trite law.

5/50   The question for our purposes is whether the protection afforded under the tort of misuse of private information extends to corporations. *Douglas* v. *Hello! Ltd* is a good place to begin. In that case, 'OK!' entered into a contract with Michael Douglas and Catherine Zeta-Jones for the exclusive right to publish photographs of their wedding. However, a photographer infiltrated the wedding and took photographs which he sold to 'Hello!', a competing magazine. The Douglases and Northern & Shell plc, which publishes 'OK!' Magazine, sued 'Hello!' for the unauthorised publication. One of the issues on appeal was whether Northern & Shell plc had any right in relation to the photographic images portraying the Douglases. Although the action was framed as one for breach of commercially confidential information Lord Hoffmann nevertheless emphasised that Northern & Shell plc could not sue under misuse of private information on the facts since the photographs in respect of a 'private' aspect of OK!'s business. He stated there that:

> this appeal is *not concerned with the protection of privacy*. Whatever may have been the position of the Douglases, who, as I mentioned, recovered damages for an invasion of their privacy, "OK!'s" *claim is to protect commercially confidential information and nothing more.* So your Lordships need not be concerned with Convention rights. "OK!" has *no claim to privacy under article 8 nor can it make a claim which is parasitic upon*

---

[206] [2004] 2 AC 406.   [207] [2004] 2 AC 457.

[208] See *Douglas* v. *Hello! Ltd,* sub. nom. *OBG Ltd* v. *Allan* [2008] 1 AC 1, para. 118 per Lord Hoffmann citing *Campbell*: 'English law has adapted the action for breach of confidence to provide a remedy for the unauthorized disclosure of personal information'. See also per Lord Nicholls, para. 255 who stated: 'As the law has developed breach of confidence, or misuse of confidential information, now covers two distinct causes of action, protecting two different interests: privacy, and secret ("confidential") information. It is important to keep these two distinct.' In *Vidal Hall* v. *Google Inc* [2015] 3 WLR 409, para. 21 Lord Dyson MR and Sharp LJ ruled, in line with Tugendhat J's conclusion in the lower court, that breach of confidence and misuse of private information were two separate and distinct torts. The latter has no equitable characteristics.

[209] [2004] 2 AC 457, para. 14.

the Douglases' right to privacy. The fact that the information happens to have been about the personal life of the Douglases is irrelevant. It could have been information about anything that a newspaper was willing to pay for. What matters is that the Douglases, by the way they arranged their wedding, were in a position to impose an obligation of confidence. They were in control of the information.[210]

5/51   Northern & Shell plc's claim for the protection of commercially confidential information succeeded, however, since their interest lay in 'maximising the financial advantage flowing from having an exclusive right to publish the authorised pictures'.[211] As such, the tort of misuse of private information has so far been limited to cases involving 'private'[212] or 'personal'[213] information. The question remains, therefore, as to whether corporations have a right to protect their *private, rather than commercial, information.*

5/52   While some doubt that corporations can or indeed need to claim under misuse of private information,[214] it has correctly been observed that there are many things a company may (legitimately or illegitimately) wish to keep private, including their property, meetings and correspondence.[215] That the courts will protect certain aspects of corporations' privacy is confirmed by *R* v. *Broadcasting Standards Commission, ex parte BBC.*[216] The case was one before the Court of Appeal in which the British Broadcasting Corporation (BBC) sought judicial review of the decision of the

[210]   [2008] 1 AC 1, para. 118. Emphasis added.

[211]   Per Lord Nicholls, [2008] 1 AC 1, para. 256, felt that '"OK!'s" interest was wholly commercial, in maximising the financial advantage flowing from having an exclusive right to publish the authorised pictures. Accordingly, as my noble and learned friend, Lord Walker of Gestingthorpe, says, "OK!'s" claim has to be based on a right to short-term confidentiality for a commercial secret'.

[212]   *Douglas* v. *Hello! Ltd (No. 6)* [2006] QB 125, para. 53 per Lord Phillips: 'in so far as *private information* is concerned, we are required to adopt, as the vehicle for performing such duty as falls on the courts in relation to Convention rights, the cause of action formerly described as breach of confidence'. Emphasis added.

[213]   *Campbell* v. *MGN Ltd* [2004] 2 AC 457, para. 51 per Lord Hoffmann: 'The result of these developments has been a shift in the centre of gravity of the action for breach of confidence when it is used as a remedy for the unjustified publication of *personal information*'. Emphasis added.

[214]   See T. Alpin, 'A Right of Privacy for Corporations?' in P. L. C. Torremans (ed.), *Intellectual Property and Human Rights* (Hague/London/New York: Kluwer Law International, 2008), pp. 493–505. See also the discussions on the private life aspect of art. 8 ECHR in nos. 3/32–3/37, albeit in the context of injury to reputation.

[215]   *R* v. *Broadcasting Standards Commission, ex parte BBC* [2001] QB 885, para. 42 per Hale LJ.

[216]   [2001] QB 885.

Broadcasting Standards Commission upholding a complaint by the electronic retailer, Dixons, that secret filming in its stores amounted to an unwarranted infringement of its privacy under s. 110(1)(b) Broadcasting Act 1996. Lord Woolf MR ruled that while intrusions into the privacy of an individual are no doubt more extensive than the infringement of the privacy of a company, a company does have activities of a private nature which need protection from unwarranted intrusion.[217] To provide no protection under the Act, he said, would leave a company at a disadvantage.[218] Hale LJ agreed that such a reading was consistent with the wording of the 1996 Act.[219] She acknowledged, however, that there 'may well be contexts in which the concept should be limited to human beings, whose very humanity is defined by their own particular consciousness of identity and individuality, their own wishes and their feelings.'[220] The extent to which the recognition of corporate privacy is protected outside this limited context is unclear. Hale LJ and Lord Mustill, in particular, emphasised the degree to which the court's conclusion was dependent on *the language and purpose* of the particular statute in the case; that is, *the enforcement of broadcasting standards as opposed to sharp-edged legal rights.*[221] Lord Mustill, for his part, found the concept of a company's privacy hard to grasp:

> To my mind the privacy of a human being denotes at the same time the personal "space" in which the individual is free to be itself, and also the carapace, or shell, or umbrella, or whatever other metaphor is preferred, which protects that space from intrusion. An infringement of *privacy is an affront to the personality*, which is damaged both by the violation and by the demonstration that the personal space is not inviolate. The concept is hard indeed to define, but if this gives something of its flavour *I do not see how it can apply to an impersonal corporate body, which has no sensitivities to wound, and no selfhood to protect.*[222]

---

[217] See also R. B. Stevenson, *Corporations and Information: Secrecy, Access and Disclosure* (Baltimore: Johns Hopkins Press, 1989), p. 51, who writes, in respect of corporations, that it would be 'fallacious to assume that those interests are identical to or deserving of the same protection as the interests of living and breathing persons'.

[218] [2001] QB 885, para. 34.

[219] Section 111(1) provides: 'A fairness complaint may be made by *an individual or by a body of persons, whether incorporated or not*'. Emphasis added. Moreover the words 'Where the person affected is an individual', under s. 111(2) and (3), clearly contemplate that a person affected may not be an individual.

[220] [2001] QB 885, para. 44.

[221] [2001] QB 885, para. 44 per Hale LJ and paras. 46–50 per Lord Mustill.

[222] [2001] QB 885, para. 48. Emphasis added.

5/53   The question of corporate standing here thus turns on the specific interest the privacy law in question seeks to protect. As McGregor states, 'when it comes to damages for an invasion of privacy, non-pecuniary loss by way of injury to feelings and mental distress predominates. Indeed there is hardly ever any claim for pecuniary losses'.[223] This, of course, impacts negatively on the real extent of protection affordable to companies under this head. 'Infringement of privacy is clearly a field ripe for aggravated damages.'[224]

6   Torts to the Person

5/54   As mentioned earlier, the general rule is that torts of a *purely* personal nature are not open for a corporation to pursue; i.e. torts in respect of a personal aspect of one's reputation or ones involving or consisting in an injury to one's person or feelings, as distinguished from an injury or damage to property.[225] Torts to the person, which are included under the umbrella of torts of a *purely* personal nature, encompass trespasses to the person and wrongs to the person not amounting to trespasses.

(a)   Trespasses to the Person

5/55   Trespasses to the person, namely assault, battery and false imprisonment, seek to protect the *body of a person and his liberty*. All three forms of trespass to the person are actionable *per se* so that nominal damages will be awarded in recognition of the violation of the right even in the absence of actual damage. Where real damage is shown, an award of both pecuniary and non-pecuniary loss is available. Assault requires *apprehension* of the infliction of force to one's *body*.[226] Battery requires physical contact with the claimant's *person* – a *corporal* injury.[227] Finally, false imprisonment requires *physical* confinement.[228] By their very nature, therefore, the latter

---

[223]   McGregor, *McGregor on Damages*, paras. 45–002.

[224]   McGregor, *McGregor on Damages*, paras. 45–011.

[225]   *South Hetton Coal Company Ltd* v. *North Eastern News Association Ltd* [1894] 1 QB 133, 141 per Lopes LJ: 'a corporation cannot maintain an action for libel in respect of anything reflecting upon them personally'.

[226]   Damages for non-pecuniary loss are available for mental distress following an assault.

[227]   Damages for non-pecuniary loss for pain and suffering and loss of amenity and mental distress are available under this head.

[228]   Damages for pain and suffering and loss of amenity are available if one can prove injury to health. In addition to damages for physical inconvenience and discomfort, damages for mental distress and injury to reputation are available as the 'wrongful act of the defendant casts an imputation on the reputation of the plaintiff which, ex hypothesi, is not justified'. : *Lonrho plc* v. *Fayed (No. 5)* [1993] 1 WLR 1489, 1504 per Stuart-Smith LJ.

torts can be committed solely against individuals, for a company has no mind;[229] nor can it be beaten or be imprisoned (no. 5/8). The manner in which the above torts are committed may aggravate the level of damages awarded.

(b)   Wrongs to the Person not Amounting to Trespasses

(i)   Intentional Infliction of Physical or Emotional Harm

5/56   The tort of intentional infliction of physical harm other than trespass to the person arises where a defendant has committed a wilful act or made a wilful statement calculated to cause physical or recognised psychiatric harm (i.e. to infringe an individual's 'personal safety') and in fact causes such harm to the claimant.[230] The action is thus not open to corporations to pursue. Damages may be aggravated.

(ii)   Harassment

5/57   Harassment, which is prohibited under s. 1 the Protection from Harassment Act 1997,[231] has been held to be an action against individuals only. Section 7(2) of the Protection from Harassment Act 1997, which does not purport to provide a comprehensive definition of harassment, states that references to harassing a person 'include alarming the person or causing the person distress.' In *Thomas* v. *News Group Newspapers Ltd*, Lord Phillips ruled that harassment 'describes conduct *targeted at an individual* which is calculated to produce the consequences described in section 7 and which is oppressive and unreasonable'.[232] This and other authorities led the court in *Daiichi Pharmaceuticals UK Ltd* v. *Stop Huntingdon*

---

[229]   *South Hetton Coal Company Ltd* v. *North Eastern News Association Ltd* [1894] 1 QB 133, 141 per Lopes LJ: 'A corporation or company could not sue in respect of a charge of . . . an assault'.

[230]   The Rule in *Wilkinson* v. *Downton* [1897] 2 QB 57, 58–59 per Wright J. See, however, the criticism of the gap between this view of the law and the facts expressed in *Wainwright* v. *Home Office* [2004] 2 AC 406, para. 41 per Lord Hoffmann.

[231]   Section 1(1) reads: 'A person must not pursue a course of conduct — (a) which amounts to harassment of another, and (b) which he knows or ought to know amounts to harassment of the other'. Section 1(2) states that the test is objective.

[232]   [2002] EMLR 4, para. 30. Emphasis added. See also *Pratt* v. *Director of Public Prosecutions* (2001) 165 JP 800, 804, para. 12 per Latham LJ: 'The mischief, which the Act is intended to meet, is that persons should not be put in a state of alarm or distress by repetitious behaviour'. In addition, in *Director of Public Prosecutions* v. *Dziurzynski* [2002] EWHC 1380, paras. 32–33, Rose LJ pointed to the use of the words 'him' in s. 4(1) and 'victim' in s. 5(2) of the Act and regard was had to the use of the word 'individual' in references to Scotland in ss. 8 to 11 of the Act. In his view, 'the Act was *not intended by Parliament to embrace*, within the ambit of a criminal offence, *conduct amounting to harassment directed to a limited company* rather than to an individual human being'. Emphasis added.

Animal Cruelty to conclude that the Act does not seek to protect corporate entities from harassment.[233] A number of companies were thus refused injunctive relief under s. 3 of the Act. It was, however, proper for individual or natural claimants to bring proceedings both on their own behalf and on behalf of the employees of the claimant companies because they shared the same interest in not wishing to be harassed by animal rights activists. In *Majrowski* v. *Guy's and St Thomas's NHS Trust*, a case before the House of Lords, Lord Nicholls seems to have given the final word in stating: 'it is now tolerably clear that, although the *victim must be an individual*, the perpetrator may be a corporate body.'[234] By s. 3(2), 'damages may be awarded for (among other things) any anxiety caused by the harassment and any financial loss resulting from the harassment.' The manner in which the harassment was committed may warrant an award of aggravated damages.[235]

7   Malicious use of Process

(a)   Malicious Prosecution and Analogous Actions

5/58   Malicious prosecution, malicious procurement of an arrest warrant and malicious procurement of a search warrant all involve the criminal process: the first, criminal prosecution and the last two, the initiation of a criminal process short of prosecution. With the exception of malicious procurement of an arrest warrant, which is necessarily pursuable by individuals only, an action can be brought by a company. To maintain an action in such cases there must be evidence that the claimant suffered some special damage. Damages for non-pecuniary loss are available, although a company can only claim in respect of injury to reputation.[236] Aggravated damages have been awarded in malicious prosecution settings.[237]

---

[233] [2004] 1 WLR 1503, para. 20 per Owen J. See also *EDO MBM Technology Ltd* v. *Campaign to Smash EDO* [2005] EWHC 837, para. 32 per Gross J.

[234] [2007] 1 AC 224, para. 19. Emphasis added.

[235] *Choudhary* v. *Martins* [2008] 1 WLR 617.

[236] As explained in the dictum of Holt CJ in *Saville* v. *Roberts* (1698) 3 Salk 16, in the context of malicious prosecution, the tort may result in: (a) damage to a man's person, as where a man is put in danger to lose his life or limb or liberty; (b) damage to a man's property, as where he is put to expense to acquit himself of the accusation; and (c) damage to his fair fame. In addition to damages for mental distress and physical inconvenience and discomfort, the courts have held that something akin to damages for pain and suffering is available if a claimant can prove injury to health as a result of a malicious prosecution.

[237] See Tettenborn, *Halsbury's Laws Commentary on Damages*, fn 12.

(b)   Malicious Issue of Civil Proceedings

5/59   In English law, the tort of malicious proceedings is not at present generally actionable in respect of civil proceedings.[238] It has only been admitted in a civil context in a few special cases of abuse of legal process, in particular: (a) malicious institution of bankruptcy or winding-up proceedings; (b) malicious arrest or detention; (c) malicious execution against property; and (d) malicious arrest of a ship. (a), (c) and (d) are not torts to the person and are of course actionable by companies. Normally, in order to maintain the action in malicious proceedings cases there must be evidence that the claimant suffered some special damage. However, in *Quartz Hill Consolidated Gold Mining* v. *Eyre*[239] the court ruled that an action could lie even if no special damage to a company can be proved, for the presentation of the petition is, by its very nature, calculated to injure the credit of the company. Where no damage is proved, the claimant, if he succeeds, is entitled to at least nominal damages. As to damage to fame, in *Gregory* v. *Portsmouth City Council*, Lord Steyn specifically acknowledged that with the exception of the malicious arrest of a ship, where the loss is merely financial, actions for abuse of process in the civil context share a common feature; namely 'immediate and perhaps irreversible damage to the reputation of the victim.'[240] Damage to reputation is thus presumed to flow.[241] The analogy in respect of the presumption of damage to reputation was founded on the law of libel and slander *per se* (cf s. 1 Defamation Act 2013).[242] Any non-pecuniary injury other than that consequential upon injury to reputation will be limited to natural persons.[243] Abuse of process may attract an award of aggravated damages.[244]

---

[238]   See *Crawford Adjusters* v. *Sagicor General Insurance* [2014] AC 366 where a fundamentally divided Privy Council suggested that the tort of malicious prosecution should apply to civil as well as criminal proceedings.

[239]   (1883) 11 QBD 674.   [240]   [2000] 1 AC 419, 427.

[241]   See McGregor, *McGregor on Damages*, para. 42–002 (on the malicious institution of legal proceedings) who notes that: 'The types of proceedings and the types of damage form two sides of the same coin, since it is because these kinds of damage flow from these kinds of legal proceedings that they are made actionable in the first place, and these kinds of damage are then in all cases presumed to flow from these kinds of legal proceedings'.

[242]   *Quartz Hill Consolidated Gold Mining* v. *Eyre* (1883) 11 QBD 674, 692 per Bowen LJ.

[243]   See McGregor, *McGregor on Damages*, para. 42–009: 'Where proceedings related to insolvency are maliciously brought, the principal, and in many cases probably the only, head of damage is injury to the reputation; injury to feelings, with individual as distinct from corporate claimants, perhaps also comes in'.

[244]   See *Columbia Picture Industries Inc* v. *Robinson* [1987] Ch 38 where an Anton Piller order was abused.

IV   Non-Pecuniary Loss and Damages for Such Loss

5/60   Once a tort has been established, the courts turn to the question of damage and damages. McGregor, who authors the leading work on damages in England, enumerates the following heads of non-pecuniary loss: pain and suffering and loss of amenities; physical inconvenience and discomfort; social discredit; and mental distress. In addition, one may claim statutory damages for bereavement. The compensation is normally in respect of the losses arising from injury and not the injury itself. Just as not every tort is actionable by companies, the nature of non-pecuniary loss coupled with that of the corporate form mean that damages for non-pecuniary loss play a very limited role for them.[245] Simply put, the sort of losses that companies are most likely to encounter – namely, interference with property or business interests and contract related losses – are not (readily) protected by such damages. In turning to the above heads, it is convenient to classify damages for non-pecuniary loss into those that entail personal injury to the victim, including recognised psychiatric injury, and those that do not.

A   Personal Injury

1   Physical Impact

(a)   Pain and Suffering

5/61   'Pain' has been defined as 'physical hurt or discomfort attributable to the injury itself or consequent upon it' including 'pain caused by any medical treatment which the plaintiff might have to undergo'[246] as a result of the injury and 'suffering' as mental anguish or emotional distress which the claimant may feel as a consequence of the injury, e.g. anxiety, worry, fear, torment, embarrassment, etc. Loss of life expectancy is also subsumed under this category.[247] The assessment is

---

[245] W. V. H. Rogers, 'England' in W. V. Horton Rogers (ed.), *Damages for Non-Pecuniary Loss in Comparative Perspective* (Wien/New York: Springer, 2001), no. 3.

[246] The Law Commission, *Damages for Personal Injury: Non-Pecuniary Loss*, Law Com Consultation Paper 140 (1995), para. 2.10. See the tariff system for such awards: The Judicial Studies Board's *Guidelines for the Assessment of General Damages in Personal Injury Cases*, 13th edn (Oxford University Press, 2013).

[247] Loss of life expectancy was once considered a separate category under English law: *Flint v. Lovell* [1935] 1 KB 354. Changes ushered in by s. 1(1)(a) Administration of Justice Act 1982 abolished it as a separate head – as knowledge of the loss of life expectancy results in the abovementioned feelings – so that they are now subsumed under the heading of pain and suffering.

subjective.[248] The duration and intensity of the pain and suffering has consistently been cited as a relevant consideration. Consequently, in England there is no scope for any pecuniary recompense for an unconscious person who is spared such feelings or any other person who has no appreciation of their state.[249] Incidentally, damages are also available for pain and suffering and indeed loss of amenities (below) where the personal injury arose out of a breach of contract, whether or not there is a concurrent claim in tort.[250] Given the fact that corporations have no body, on the one hand, and the requirement for subjective injury, on the other, to allow them to benefit under this head would be inequitable for other victims, e.g. comatose patients, who are not entitled to such compensation.[251]

(b)   Loss of Amenities of Life

5/62   Loss of amenities that deprive a person of the ordinary experience of life as a human being, i.e. pleasure or some ability or faculty, is assessed *objectively.*[252] In contrast to pain and suffering, therefore, the effect of unconsciousness does not eliminate the actuality of the deprivation of the ordinary experiences and amenities of life, the loss of a limb say. It would be unprincipled for a company to sue for loss of *amenities of life*, which by its very title suggests that the action is limited to natural persons.

2   Non-Physical Impact

5/63   Where the tort involves interference with one's *physical* state but is unaccompanied by any actual impact, damages can still be awarded under the above categories. Accordingly, damages for non-pecuniary loss for pain and suffering are appropriate where the injury constitutes medically recognised psychiatric illness. To qualify, the claimant must 'establish that he is suffering, not merely grief, distress or any other normal emotion, but a *positive psychiatric illness.*'[253] Damage to health resultant from specific

---

[248] Although the assessment is said to be subjective, in reality the courts resort to objective indicators, including awards in similar cases.

[249] *West* v. *Shephard* [1964] AC 326, 349 per Lord Morris.

[250] McGregor, *McGregor on Damages*, paras. 5–020–5–021.

[251] See also Rogers, 'England', no. 18.

[252] Among other authorities *Wise* v. *Kaye* [1962] 1 QB 638; *West* v. *Shephard* [1964] AC 326; *Lim Poh Choo* v. *Camden and Islington AHA* [1980] AC 174. That said, in assessing the appropriate quantum of damages, the court will take consideration of the effect that the lost amenity will have on the particular individual: *West* v. *Shephard* [1964] AC 326, 365 per Lord Pearce.

[253] *McLoughlin* v. *O'Brian* [1983] 1 AC 410, 431 per Lord Bridge. Emphasis added.

torts, e.g. false imprisonment, public nuisance and breach of contract, will also sound in damages for pain and suffering and where applicable, loss of amenities and expectation of life.[254] Though less likely to happen, damage to health consequential upon injury to property cannot be excluded.[255] Again, in light of their nature and the nature of such damage(s), corporations cannot recover damages for non-pecuniary loss here.

B   Non-Personal Injury

1   Physical Inconvenience and Discomfort

5/64   Damages here have traditionally been awarded in contract cases.[256] In tort, awards have been made, inter alia, in the case of deceit, false imprisonment (i.e. for loss of liberty absent injury to health), public nuisance (in respect of personal discomfort such as excessive noise or smells)[257] and negligence.[258] Though stated in a contractual context, successful tort cases seem to confirm that the cause of the inconvenience or discomfort must be a sensory (sight, touch, hearing, smell, etc.) experience.[259] It is manifest therefore that a corporation cannot be inconvenienced in the sense referred to here. Physical inconvenience and discomfort may well engender mental distress (no. 5/66).

2   Social Discredit

5/65   While vindication of reputation is mainly achieved through an action in defamation, other torts such as malicious prosecution and false imprisonment also protect this aspect of one's personality. Despite its overlap with defamation, one cannot recover damages for injury to reputation in an action for malicious falsehood, since the protection of proprietary

---

[254] McGregor, *McGregor on Damages*, paras. 5–004–5–009, 5–020–5–022.

[255] McGregor, *McGregor on Damages*, para. 5–009.

[256] For example, *Bailey* v. *Bullock* [1950] 2 All ER 1167 (delay by a solicitor in instituting proceedings resulting in his client and the latter's family being forced to move into a single room in his in-law's home).

[257] Oliphant correctly notes that, contrary to McGregor's statement in para. 3–009 (now para. 5–010), personal inconvenience and annoyance is not actionable damage in the tort of private nuisance as private nuisance is a tort to land, not a tort to the person as was decided in *Hunter* v. *Canary Wharf Ltd* [1997] AC 655: K. Oliphant, 'England and Wales' in B. Winiger, H. Koziol, B. A. Koch and R. Zimmermann (eds.), *Digest of European Tort Law*, 2 vols. (Berlin/Boston: De Gruyter, 2011), vol. 2, 11/12 no. 3, fn 213.

[258] McGregor, *McGregor on Damages*, para. 5–010.

[259] *Farley* v. *Skinner (No. 2)* [2002] 2 AC 732, 768 per Lord Scott.

interests lies at the heart of the tort. Similar conclusions apply, inter alia, in respect of torts affecting goods and conspiracy.[260] While damages for non-pecuniary loss for loss of reputation arising from breach of contract have traditionally been denied, the courts have been prepared to retreat from that rule of late.[261] That corporations have a reputation is trite, and indeed this is the one area under which they are currently awarded damages for non-pecuniary loss in England (see nos. 5/33–5/48).

3   Mental Distress

5/66   Mental distress is a broad term for injury short of psychiatric damage, e.g. distress, injury to feelings, frustration, anxiety, displeasure, vexation, tension or aggravation.[262] 'The general principle embedded in the common law [is] that mental suffering caused by grief, fear, anguish and the like is not assessable';[263] or more precisely, that 'the law cannot value, and does not pretend to redress' such complaints 'when the unlawful act complained of causes that loss alone'.[264] Once liability has been established in torts such as libel and slander, malicious prosecution, assault, deceit, misuse of private information, trespass to property, public nuisance, statutory torts involving sex, race and disability discrimination and harassment, damages for non-pecuniary loss for mental distress may, however, be recovered. In the case of breach of contract they may only be recovered if the contract is *personal* as opposed to primarily commercial[265] and its predominant purpose is the provision of some mental satisfaction so that a company has no remedy here and indeed under this head generally.[266] As such damages are only occasionally recoverable in contract, the same rule applies where damages for distress are claimed to have resulted from negligently caused economic loss. They are certainly not available, inter alia, for private nuisance and conspiracy.[267] Damages may

---

[260] *Lonrho plc* v. *Fayed (No. 5)* [1993] 1 WLR 1489, 1496 per Dillon LJ. See also McGregor, *McGregor on Damages*, paras. 5–011 and 8–126–8–127.

[261] McGregor, *McGregor on Damages*, para. 5–035.

[262] *Watts* v. *Morrow* [1991] 1 WLR 1421, 1445 per Bingham LJ.

[263] *Behrens* v. *Bertram Mills Circus Ltd* [1957] 2 QB 1, 28 per Devlin J.

[264] *Lynch* v. *Knight* (1861) 9 HLC 577, 598 per Lord Wensleydale.

[265] *Hayes* v. *James & Charles Dodd* [1990] 2 All ER 815; *Johnson* v. *Gore Wood & Co.* [2002] 2 AC 1.

[266] *Watts* v. *Morrow* [1991] 1 WLR 1421.

[267] McGregor, *McGregor on Damages*, para. 5–012. See also K. Oliphant, 'England and the Commonwealth' in H. Koziol (ed.), *Basic Questions of Tort Law from a Comparative Perspective* (Wien: Sramek Verlag, 2015), no. 5/78.

be aggravated to compensate the claimant for increased mental distress suffered as a result of the defendant's conduct.

4 Bereavement Damages

5/67   As has been written, 'personal injury damages law places a value of £0 on each life involved'.[268] Compensation for loss of life itself is not available under English law since it is 'considered impossible to form an estimate of the value of human life'.[269] Moreover, while accepting the anguish of the loss of a loved one, 'the common law has never awarded damages for the pain of bereavement.'[270] Per contra, bereavement damages (payable for the grief suffered because of a person's death) are statutorily available under the Fatal Accidents Act 1976 (as amended). Under s. 1A, a claim for damages for bereavement can only be for the benefit of the wife, husband or civil partner of the deceased and where the deceased was a minor who was never married or a civil partner, of his parents (if he were legitimate) and of his mother (if he were illegitimate).[271] The Act does not make allowance for corporate claims; this study will thus not pursue this head further.

V Conclusion

5/68   While there is lack of consensus as to the conceptual nature of the company, all accept that it is a reality for legal purposes. Unlike their Strasbourg counterparts, judges in England consistently treat companies like independent persons with rights and duties that are appropriate to them, so that there is a correlation between the nature of the tort and remedy on the one hand and legal subject on the other as determinative of the extent of protection afforded to the latter. Since, as the above analysis reveals, non-pecuniary loss must of necessity involve interference with one's bodily, mental, emotional and/or personality spheres, this necessarily places limitations on the availability of damages for non-pecuniary loss for companies which only posses those attributes necessary to give effect to the purpose for which they are created. As a result, there are

---

[268] S. Hedley, 'Death and Tort' in B. Brooks-Gordon, F. Ebtehaj, J. Herring, M. H. Johnson and M. Richards (eds.), *Death Rites and Rights* (Oxford: Hart Publishing, 2007), p. 251.

[269] *Armsworth* v. *South Eastern Ry Co.* (1847) 11 Jur (OS) 758, 759 per Parke B.

[270] *Hicks* v. *Chief Constable of the South Yorkshire Police* [1992] PIQR 433, 434 per Lord Bridge.

[271] See the Negligence and Damages Bill of 2015–16 for proposed changes to this area of law.

torts that are not open to corporations to pursue: as Table 2 illustrates, this is the case with respect to torts of a purely personal nature: i.e. trespasses to the person (assault, battery and false imprisonment), wrongs to the person not amounting to trespasses (the intentional infliction of physical or emotional harm and harassment) and some torts under the wrongful use of process umbrella (malicious procurement of an arrest warrant and malicious arrest or detention). Incidentally, damages for non-pecuniary loss tend to play a major role here. There are also torts that are available to corporations but imposing limited rights of action or compensation upon them in light of their form: specifically, torts such as negligence, public nuisance, those under the false representations category, trespass to land, copyright related torts, defamation, misuse of private information and the remaining wrongful use of process torts.

5/69   Sometimes it is the nature of the tort, as opposed to the subject, which prevents a claim for damages for non-pecuniary loss (i.e. by both natural and legal persons alike). This is the case with torts of malicious falsehood, private nuisance and the rule in *Rylands* v. *Fletcher*, wrongful interference with goods torts, passing off, economic torts and malicious arrest of a ship.

Table 2. *'Torts Committed Against Corporations and the Availability of Damages for Non-Pecuniary Loss in Respect Thereof'*

Torts		Actionability by corporations	General availability of damages for non-pecuniary loss under the tort	Nature of damages for non-pecuniary loss	Availability of damages for non-pecuniary loss for corporations	General availability of aggravated damages
General tortious liabilities						
Negligence		Yes	Yes	■ Pain and suffering and loss of amenity ■ Physical inconvenience and discomfort ■ Social Discredit ■ Mental distress (in limited cases) ■ Bereavement damages	Yes (social discredit)	Conflicting authorities
Public nuisance		Yes	Yes	■ Pain and suffering and loss of amenity ■ Physical inconvenience and discomfort ■ Mental distress ■ Bereavement damages	No	Conflicting authorities
Special liability regimes and breach of statutory duty		Yes, if contemplated by the statute in question	Yes, if contemplated by the statute in question	■ Depends on the statute in question	Depends on the statute in question	Conflicting authorities
Misrepresentation	Deceit	Yes	Yes	■ Pain and suffering and loss of amenity (rare) ■ Physical inconvenience and discomfort ■ Mental distress	No	Yes
	Negligent misrepresentation	Yes	Yes	■ Pain and suffering and loss of amenity (rare) ■ Physical inconvenience and discomfort ■ Mental distress (in limited cases)	No	Conflicting authorities

(cont.)

Table 2 (cont.)

Torts		Actionability by corporations	General availability of damages for non-pecuniary loss under the tort	Nature of damages for non-pecuniary loss	Availability of damages for non-pecuniary loss for corporations	General availability of aggravated damages
	Misrepresentation Act 1967: Negligent misrepresentation	Yes	Yes	■ Pain and suffering and loss of amenity (rare) ■ Physical inconvenience and discomfort ■ Mental distress (in limited cases)	No	Conflicting authorities
	Malicious falsehood	Yes	No	–	–	Yes
Torts to specific interests						
Torts affecting land						
	Trespass to land	Yes	Yes	■ Mental distress	No	Yes
	Private nuisance	Yes	No	–	–	Conflicting authorities
	Rylands v. Fletcher	Yes	No	–	–	Conflicting authorities
Wrongful interference with goods						
	Trespass to goods	Yes	No	–	–	Yes
	Conversion	Yes	No	–	–	Yes
	Wrongful distress	Yes	No	–	–	Yes
Intellectual property torts						
	Infringement of copyrights, patents and trademarks	Yes	Yes	■ Social discredit ■ Mental distress	Doubted	Yes
	Passing off	Yes	No	–	–	Yes
Economic torts						
	Conspiracy	Yes	No	–	–	Yes
	Inducement of breach of contract	Yes	No	–	–	Yes
	Unlawful interference with economic interests	Yes	No	–	–	Yes
	Intimidation	Yes	Doubted	–	–	Yes

Torts		Actionability by corporations	General availability of damages for non-pecuniary loss under the tort	Nature of damages for non-pecuniary loss	Availability of damages for non-pecuniary loss for corporations	General availability of aggravated damages
Torts to reputation and privacy						
Defamation		Yes	Yes	▪ Social discredit ▪ Mental distress ▪ Loss of standing in the community, dignity (rare)	Yes (social discredit)	Yes
Misuse of private information and related actions		Yes (some aspects)	Yes (some aspects)	▪ Mental distress	No	Yes
Torts to the person						
Trespasses to the person	Assault	No	Yes	▪ Pain and suffering and loss of amenity ▪ Mental distress	–	Yes
	Battery	No	Yes	▪ Pain and suffering and loss of amenity ▪ Mental distress	–	Yes
	False imprisonment	No	Yes	▪ Pain and suffering and loss of amenity ▪ Physical inconvenience and discomfort ▪ Social discredit ▪ Mental distress	–	Yes
Wrongs to the Person not amounting to trespasses	Intentional infliction of physical or emotional harm	No	Yes	▪ Pain and suffering and loss of amenity ▪ Mental distress	–	Yes
	Harassment	No	Yes	▪ Pain and suffering and loss of amenity ▪ Physical inconvenience and discomfort ▪ Mental distress	–	Yes

(cont.)

Table 2 (*cont.*)

Torts			Actionability by corporations	General availability of damages for non-pecuniary loss under the tort	Nature of damages for non-pecuniary loss	Availability of damages for non-pecuniary loss for corporations	General availability of aggravated damages
Wrongful use of process	Malicious prosecution and analogous actions	Malicious prosecution	Yes	Yes	■ Pain and suffering and loss of amenity ■ Physical inconvenience and discomfort ■ Social discredit ■ Mental distress	Yes (social discredit)	Yes
		Malicious procurement of an arrest warrant	No	Yes	■ Pain and suffering and loss of amenity ■ Physical inconvenience and discomfort ■ Social discredit ■ Mental distress	–	Yes
		Malicious procurement of a search warrant	Yes	Yes	■ Pain and suffering and loss of amenity ■ Physical inconvenience and discomfort ■ Social discredit ■ Mental distress	Yes (social discredit)	Yes
	Malicious civil proceedings	Malicious institution of bankruptcy proceedings	Yes	Yes	■ Social discredit ■ Mental distress	Yes (social discredit)	Yes
		Malicious arrest or detention	No	Yes	■ Pain and suffering and loss of amenity ■ Physical inconvenience and discomfort ■ Social discredit ■ Mental distress	–	Yes
		Malicious execution against property	Yes	Yes	■ Social discredit	Yes (social discredit)	Yes
		Malicious arrest of a ship	Yes	No	–	–	yes

6

Aggravated Damages for Corporate Victims?

I Introduction

6/1   It has been shown above that breaches of several torts entitle a victim to add a claim for aggravated damages. 'Aggravated damages', *eo nomine* at least, are peculiar to the common law.[1] They fall within the *compensatory* rationale and refer to the aggravation – etymologically, the making more serious – of injury caused to the claimant by the defendant's conduct where a basic award would not be sufficient. In particular, they are paid for the 'shock, distress, outrage and similar emotions experienced by the claimant'[2] as a result of the aggravating features of the case. Given the function of such damages on the one hand and the nature of the corporation on the other, it would seem unprincipled for such an element to be available to them. Whether aggravated damages can properly be awarded in favour of corporate claimants has been the subject of discussion in reported cases, and at one point Parliament pressed for companies to benefit from such awards. Happily, the reform proposals have come to naught, leaving this area in conformity with the law's general approach to corporate entities.

II Availability

6/2   Aggravated damages are recoverable for those torts for which damages are at large in the sense that a claimant is not limited to a precise calculation of the amount of the pecuniary loss actually proved.[3] Thus, even where the action is limited to pecuniary loss, the amount awarded can still be increased to reflect the claimant's distress. While this may seem a

---

[1] See A. J. Sebok and V. Wilcox, 'Aggravated Damages' in H. Koziol and V. Wilcox, *Punitive Damages: Common Law and Civil Law Perspectives* (Wien/New York: Springer, 2009).

[2] *Ashley* v. *Chief Constable of Sussex Police* [2007] 1 WLR 398, para. 10 per Sir Anthony Clarke MR.

[3] *Rookes* v. *Barnard* [1964] AC 1129, 1221 per Lord Devlin.

contradiction in terms,[4] it is the current law. Although several of the causes of action open to companies – for example, trespass to goods, unlawful interference with economic interests and malicious falsehood – are in respect of pecuniary damage only in theory this alone does not prevent them from seeking aggravated damages (see Table 2).

6/3 Despite a lack of consensus, the current position is that aggravated damages are not generally available under contract law or for negligence, since they seek to tackle particularly egregious conduct. Both are actions upon which corporations frequently base their claim.

III   An Examination of the Cases

6/4 With few exceptions, the view of most authorities has been that a company cannot be injured in its feelings. Although not a case on aggravated damages *per se, In re Lindsay Bowman Ltd* is one of a few decisions that took the other line. The preferred view, however, is that it should be confined to its facts. The action was brought by a contributory (one of the two shareholders in the company) and a company to restore the company, which had been struck off, to the register. The relevant part of s. 353(6) Companies Act 1948 reads: '*If a company* or any member or creditor thereof *feels aggrieved* by the company having been struck off the register, the court on an application made by the company or member or creditor', may, among other things, order the name of the company to be restored to the register.[5] Megarry J ruled: 'In obedience to Parliament, I must assume that the artificial and impersonal entity that we know as a limited company has been endowed with the capacity *not merely of having feelings* but also of *feeling aggrieved* even though it has ceased to exist.'[6] It is clear Parliament did not intend to say that a company had feelings. The confusion was an oversight in legislative drafting and indeed, the wording of the provision was revised in subsequent Companies Acts. In particular, s. 125(1) Companies Act 2006 now provides that 'the person aggrieved,

---

[4] *Joyce* v. *Sengupta* [1993] 1 WLR 337, 348–349 per Sir Donald Nicholls VC: 'I do not see how, if only pecuniary loss is recoverable, the amount awarded can be increased to reflect the plaintiff's distress. That would be a contradiction in terms. It would be to award damages for distress in a disguised fashion. If distress can inflame the damages recoverable for pecuniary loss, the difference between awarding aggravated damages for that reason and awarding damages for distress as a separate head of loss is a difference of words only.' See also H. McGregor, *McGregor on Damages*, 19th edn (London: Sweet & Maxwell, 2014), para. 46–015: 'Since, however, aggravated damages are relevant only to non-pecuniary loss they could only be claimed as a head of damage separate from the damages for the pecuniary loss which they cannot "aggravate".'
[5] Emphasis added.   [6] [1969] 1 WLR 1443, 1448. Emphasis added.

or any member of the company, or the company, may apply to the court for rectification of the register.'

6/5 In *Messenger Newspapers Group* v. *National Graphical Association*, the court was directly faced with the question of whether an award of aggravated damages was appropriate to a corporate claimant. The case was one on unlawful interference with business, nuisance (both private and public) and intimidation. Caulfield J stated: 'Certainly exemplary and aggravated damages can be awarded against inanimate legal entities like limited companies, and I cannot see any reason why the same legal entities cannot be awarded aggravated and exemplary damages.'[7] He thus ruled in favour of an award, having regard to the fact that it was companies generally – though not invariably – that were the sort of claimants that suffered damage from intimidation by trade unions and – invariably – unlawful interference with business. In addition, Caulfield J pointed to the fact that the defendant was reckless in pursuit of its intentions to close down the claimant's business and/or enforce a closed shop, and this it did in defiance of court orders and with open arrogance. In calculating the aggravated amount due, Caulfield J approached the question of quantum from the perspective of 'the *manner* of the doing of the injury' and proceeded to award £10,000 in aggravated damages but not without first having '*eliminated human feelings*' from his award thus supporting the argument that corporations do not have feelings.[8]

6/6 The obvious tension caused by the *Messenger* decision – one which the High Court picked up in the most authoritative case on the matter, *Collins Stewart Ltd* v. *The Financial Times Ltd*[9] – is the lower place given to injured feelings in the two pronged test for aggravated damages. In *Messenger*, Caulfield J opined that '[i]njured feelings of the plaintiff is only one aspect in considering aggravated damages. The more important element is where the injury to the plaintiff has been aggravated by malice or by the manner of doing the injury; that is, the insolence or arrogance by which it is accompanied.'[10] This approach cannot, however, be supported by the authorities, which stipulate that knowledge of the defendant's wrong or motive is so pivotal that without it, a claimant cannot maintain his feelings have been injured by the tort and cannot thus qualify for aggravated damages. Indeed, as the court in *Collins Stewart* held, the concept of injury to feelings runs through the cases. This being so, the 'essence of an award of aggravated damages'[11] must be compensation for

---

[7] [1984] IRLR 397, para. 77.   [8] [1984] IRLR 397, para. 78. Emphasis added.
[9] [2005] EWHC 262.   [10] [1984] IRLR 397, para. 78.
[11] [2005] EWHC 262, para. 30.

extra injury to the claimant's *subjective* feelings. There is no presumption of entitlement to aggravated damages.

6/7   The requirement of injury to feelings is also consistent with the compensatory character of aggravated damages. In the words of Davies LJ in *Broadway Approvals Ltd* v. *Odhams Press Ltd* if the tort outrages the claimant, it is a proper element in compensatory damages, but if it outrages the judge or jury, it is a proper element in punitive damages.[12] This is so because in contrast to punitive damages, where the focus is on the defendant's actions and his motive, aggravated damages are only indirectly grounded in the defendant's behaviour. According to Beever: 'In aggravated damages cases . . . the sole epistemological access to the claimant's injury is through examination of the defendant's actions. This does not show an interest in the defendant's actions *per se*. Rather, the interest in these actions extends *only insofar as they impinge on the claimant*.'[13] This impression is further fortified by Woolf J's words in *Kralj* v. *McGrath*:

> the general approach to damages in this area . . . is to compensate the plaintiff for the loss that she has *actually* suffered, so far as it is possible to do so, by the award of monetary compensation and not to treat [aggravated] damages as being a matter which *reflects the degree of . . . breach of duty of the defendant*. . . . What I am saying is no more than that what the court has to do is to *judge the effect on the particular plaintiff of what happened to her*.[14]

6/8   To diminish the significance of injury to feelings necessarily dictates a return to the state of affairs pre-1964, where the law as regards aggravated and punitive damages was confused. The fact that Caulfield J eliminated from the award of aggravated damages the element of injury to feelings suggests that the additional damages which the judge awarded to the corporate claimant in that case had more in common with exemplary damages. Whether they were in fact exemplary damages, as the court in *Collins Stewart* concluded, is another question. Either way, the decision in *Messenger* is 'considered to be wrong'.[15]

6/9   In its broader reading, *Collins Stewart* is authority for the proposition that aggravated damages are not in principle available to a corporate

---

[12] [1965] 1 WLR 805, 822.

[13] A. Beever, 'The Structure of Aggravated and Exemplary Damages', *Oxford Journal of Legal Studies*, 23(1) (2003), 87–110, 93. Emphasis added.

[14] [1986] 1 All ER 54, 61. Emphasis added.

[15] McGregor, *McGregor on Damages*, para. 5–014, fn 56.

claimant. A company has 'no feelings to injure and cannot suffer distress'.[16] This is consistent with *Lewis* v. *Daily Telegraph* where Lord Reid opined that: 'A company cannot be injured in its feelings, it can only be injured in its pocket'.[17] The view is one that has been echoed elsewhere on a number of occasions.[18] *Collins Stewart* is also consistent with *Columbia Picture Industries Inc* v. *Robinson*, where the court awarded £2,500 to the claimant company and £7,500 to Mr Robinson, expressly stating that the 'split recognises that contumely and affront affect individuals, not inanimate corporations'.[19] In the more recent case of *McKennitt* v. *Ash*, Eady J seemed to endorse these views when he awarded the claimant

---

[16] *Collins Stewart Ltd* v. *The Financial Times Ltd (No. 2)* [2005] EWHC 262, para. 31 per Gray J.

[17] *Lewis* v. *Daily Telegraph* [1964] AC 234, 262 per Lord Reid.

[18] *Lonrho plc* v. *Fayed (No. 5)* [1993] 1 WLR 1489, 1505 per Stuart-Smith LJ: 'In the case of Lonrho [plc], it has no feelings'; *Jameel* v. *Wall Street Journal Europe Sprl* [2007] 1 AC 359, para. 95 per Lord Hope: 'It is obvious, of course, that a trading company has no feelings which are capable of being injured.' See also *Hays plc* v. *Jonathan Hartley* [2010] EWHC 1068, para. 24 per Tugendhat J; *Wallis* v. *Meredith* [2011] EWHC 75, para. 59 per Clarke J; *McGrath* v. *Dawkins* [2012] Info TLR 72, para. 81 per HHJ Moloney QC: 'Since a limited company has no feelings, it cannot recover aggravated damages; see *Collins Stewart* v. *Financial Times* [2006] EMLR 5, Gray J. This is a long-established principle, and C has produced no good reason to doubt its authority or its correctness.'; *Eaton Mansions (Westminster) Ltd* v. *Stinger Compania de Inversion SA* [2013] EWCA Civ 3354: 'It was wrong in principle to award aggravated damages to a corporation, such as E, which could not suffer injury to feelings or damaged pride'. See also *Euromoney Institutional Investor plc* v. *Aviation News Ltd* [2013] EWHC 1505, para. 20 per Tugendhat J: 'A corporate claimant does not have feelings, and cannot therefore suffer the injury to feelings which account for a significant element of awards of damages made in favour of personal claimants.' In *ZAM* v. *CFW* [2013] EMLR 27, para. 70, Tugendhat J said: 'Corporations are different from individuals in that they cannot claim injury to feelings.' *ReachLocal UK Ltd* v. *Bennett* [2015] EMLR 7, para. 54 per HHJ Parkes QC: 'A company stands in a slightly different position from an individual claimant, for it has no feelings to hurt, and it follows that considerations of aggravation which might be relevant if the claimant is an individual do not apply.' The approach has been endorsed by leading scholars: B. Neill, R. Rampton, H. Rogers, T. Atkinson, A. Eardley (eds.), *Duncan and Neill on Defamation*, 4th edn (London: LexisNexis Butterworths, 2015), para. 10.03; McGregor, *McGregor on Damages*, para. 5-014; D. Price, K. Duodu, N. Cain, *Defamation: Law Procedure and Practice*, 4th edn (London: Sweet & Maxwell, 2010), para. 20-03; Doley et al. (eds.), C. Doley, A. Mullis and Carter-Ruck (eds.), *Carter-Ruck on Libel and Privacy*, 6th edn (LexisNexis Butterworths, 2010), para. 15.39; M. A. Jones et al. (eds.), *Clerk & Lindsell on Torts*, 21 edn (London: Sweet & Maxwell, 2014), para. 22-221; cf A. Burrows, 'Damages and Rights' in D. Nolan and A. Robertson, *Rights and Private Law* (Oxford/Portland: Hart Publishing, 2012), p. 282. K. Oliphant, 'England and the Commonwealth' in H. Koziol (ed.), *Basic Questions of Tort Law from a Comparative Perspective* (Wien: Sramek Verlag, 2015), no. 5/82. See Chapter 8 on the position in other common law jurisdictions.

[19] [1987] Ch 38, 88 per Scott J. See also The Law Commission, *Aggravated, Exemplary and Restitutionary Damages*, Law Com 247 (1997), para. 1.9, p. 13.

£5,000 for hurt feelings and distress and no more than a nominal award to the claimant's companies.[20]

IV   The Real Object of an Aggravated Award

6/10   In recent years, a number of scholars have identified some incoherence in the cases over the function of aggravated damages. Court rulings in actions like *Shah* v. *Gale* and *Ashley* v. *Chief Constable of Sussex Police* lead one to question whether aggravated damages are truly confined to injury to feelings. The action in *Shah* was brought by the mother (and administratix) of a Naresh Shah following an attack at his residence. Having burst open the victim's front door, the perpetrators proceeded to stab him several times. Aggravated damages were awarded despite the fact that the victim was 'immediately murdered'. As Leveson J observed:

> Because he was *immediately murdered*, there is no scope for *injury to personality* but it is difficult to think of behaviour which is more serious than the attack upon Mr Shah's home.... [T]hese aggravated damages are not being awarded in respect of the murder of Mr Shah but only *for the circumstances* in which he was assaulted and no more.... Notwithstanding that this incident was *over very quickly*, having regard to all the circumstances, I award £2,000.[21]

6/11   Similarly in *Ashley* v. *Chief Constable of Sussex Police*, the House of Lords did not rule out the defendant's potential liability for aggravated damages for the death of a suspect. There, Lord Carswell in fact opined that 'it is more than a little difficult to see how such damages can be in question, when it is very questionable whether the deceased was conscious and sentient for any significant period between the shooting and his death'.[22] On the basis of the above cases, scholars like Murphy submit that, in the absence of distress suffered by the victim, aggravated damages cannot be contingent upon mental awareness although there will be many instances where this is the case. This argument does not aid the corporate claimant, however.

6/12   First, it cannot be ruled out that the victims suffered distress as a result of their brutal, albeit, swift deaths. It thus seems correct to presume some such damage. Even heightened, albeit fleeting, distress here may have been experienced, warranting additional damages.

6/13   Second, Murphy argues that while not contingent upon, or synonymous or coexistent with mental distress, aggravated damages nevertheless

---

[20] [2005] EWHC 3003, para. 162.   [21] [2005] EWHC 1087, para. 58. Emphasis added.
[22] [2008] 1 AC 962, para. 80.

seem to remedy an interest so intimately connected to the human being: dignity. Indeed, in the well-known decision of the House of Lords in *Rookes* v. *Barnard*, Lord Devlin made reference to conduct 'such as to injure the plaintiff's proper feelings of dignity and pride'.[23] That aggravated damages serve to remedy a dignitary interest denied by the defendant is increasingly shared by scholars, such as Tilbury, Beever and Berryman.[24] Murphy continues that, since dignity is 'an innate moral and human attribute, best seen as being bound with personhood',[25] it follows that aggravated damages 'could only ever meaningfully be invoked by a human claimant.'[26] He concludes that the appropriate basis for an award of aggravated damages should be undertaken from a subjective-objective perspective. While the current view remains that aggravated damages are contingent upon injury to feelings and awareness of the same, there is considerable merit in the proposition advanced earlier that in essence, the award aims to remedy an injury to dignity.

V   Legislative Reform

6/14   After some oscillation of opinion, the notion that a company cannot experience 'feelings' seemed settled by the authorities in this area of law. Under stress of convenience, however, Parliament sought to intervene. In May 2007, the Department of Constitutional Affairs, the duties of which have now been taken over by the Ministry of Justice, issued a consultation paper, the Law on Damages.[27] The paper set out for discussion the issues highlighted in a series of reports published by the Law Commission in the late 1990s including that on Aggravated, Exemplary and Restitutionary Damages.[28] Among the government's recommendations was the proposal to settle uncertainties over the use of the term 'additional damages' in the Patents Act 1977 and the Copyright Design and Patents Act 1988 by replacing it with 'aggravated damages and such amount by way

---

[23] [1964] AC 1129, 1221.

[24] M. Tilbury, *Civil Remedies* (Sydney: Butterworths, 1990), para. 3208–21; Beever, 'The Structure of Aggravated and Exemplary Damages', 89: Aggravated damages are 'an injury to the victim's moral dignity that results from the defendant's denial that the victim is entitled to respect as a moral person'; J. Berryman, 'Reconceptualizing Aggravated Damages: Recognizing the Dignitary Interest and Referential Loss', *San Diego Law Review*, 41(4) (2004), 1521–1550.

[25] J. Murphy, 'The Nature and Domain of Aggravated Damages', *Cambridge Law Journal*, 69(2) (2010), 353–377, 366.

[26] Murphy, 'The Nature and Domain of Aggravated Damages', 369, 367–368.

[27] Department for Constitutional Affairs, The Law on Damages CP 9/07, May 2007.

[28] The Law Commission, *Aggravated, Exemplary and Restitutionary Damages*.

of restitution' in line with Puffery J's ruling in *Nottinghamshire Health-care NHS Trust* v. *News Group Newspapers Ltd* (no. 5/26). However, as mental distress is an ingredient of a claim for aggravated damages – an ingredient which the court in *Collins Stewart* ruled could not be met by corporate claimants – the government sought to overcome this difficulty by clarifying that aggravated damages would be available to them. This it did in cl. 9(2) and (3) of the Draft Civil Law Reform Bill of 2009.[29]

6/15   The draft, which would have been extended across the United Kingdom, was subjected to pre-legislative scrutiny by the Justice Committee of the House of Commons, which published its report in March 2010 stating, inter alia, and in line with *Collins* that the formulation 'aggravated damages' seemed inappropriate to cases of copyright infringement that are frequently brought by companies. The Committee also highlighted the Bar Council's concern that to allow bodies corporate the privilege of damages for mental distress in these two limited fields would invite a further anomaly.[30] The question was put to rest in January 2011 when the Ministry of Justice published its response to the consultation on the Draft Civil Law Reform Bill. The Ministry noted that there was no consensus on cl. 9 and highlighted in particular the opposition of interested parties in the software industry.[31] The clause, along with other proposals, was rejected by the then coalition government in a response published in January 2011 on the grounds that the bill would not contribute to the delivery of the government's key priorities.

VI   Attributed Aggravated Damage?

6/16   While the European Court of Human Rights does not award aggravated damages *eo nomine*, the jurisprudence of English courts here could still be instructive and the reverse position is also true since some opine that there is nothing in the name 'aggravated damages'; what is being compensated is

---

[29] Clause 9(2) begins: 'In paragraph 12(4) of sch. A1 to the Patents Act 1977 (power to award additional damages for providing false information) – (a) after "sub-paragraph (3)" insert "(whether brought by an individual or a body)"' and s. 9(3) 'Section 97(2) of the Copyright, Designs and Patents Act 1988 (power to award additional damages for copyright infringement) is amended as follows – (a) after "copyright" insert "(whether brought by an individual or a body)"'.

[30] House of Commons Justice Committee, *Draft Civil Law Reform Bill: Pre–Legislative Scrutiny*, HC 300-I (2010), pp. 45–46.

[31] Ministry of Justice, *Civil Law Reform Bill: Response to Consultation*, CP(R) CP 53/09 (2011), p. 28. See also Ministry of Justice, *Civil Law Reform Bill Consultation*, CP 53/09 (2010).

grave *injury to feelings*, an element under the 'mental distress' umbrella.[32] The question then arises as to whether a company can recover damages for the injured feelings of its organs where the defendant's conduct has been particularly egregious, a view which Burrows has sympathy for.[33] While there is some merit to the attribution doctrine detailed in Chapter 7, the practice should arguably not be followed where the protection of a dignitary interest underlies the remedy.

VII   Conclusion

6/17   For now, at least, English law has thankfully escaped the statutory importation of the fiction that juristic persons can suffer injury to feelings (or indeed dignity). The decision in *Collins Stewart* is authoritative, and to seek to circumvent it via attribution would be to introduce an irregularity into what is currently a consistent area of law.

---

[32] The co-existence and availability of mental distress damages and aggravated damages led the English Law Commission to call for Parliament to sweep away the latter term. Clause 13(2) of the Commission's Draft Bill thus reads 'wherever possible the label "damages for mental distress" should be used instead of the misleading phrase "aggravated damages".' Whether a change of name is necessary remains moot. The Law Commission, *Aggravated, Exemplary and Restitutionary Damages*, p. 183. See also *Richardson* v. *Howie* [2005] PIQR Q3, para. 23 per Thomas LJ: 'It is also now clearly accepted that aggravated damages are in essence compensatory in cases of assault. Therefore we consider that a court should not characterise the award of damages for injury to feelings, including any indignity, mental suffering, distress, humiliation or anger and indignation that might be caused by such an attack, as aggravated damages; a court should bring that element of compensatory damages for injured feelings into account as part of the general damages awarded. It is, we consider, no longer appropriate to characterise the award for the damages for injury to feelings as aggravated damages, except possibly in a wholly exceptional case.'

[33] Burrows, 'Damages and Rights', pp. 282–283.

7

Attribution Theory

I Introduction

7/1   The starting point in this analysis is that once duly incorporated, a distinction exists between the legal personality, rights and liabilities of a company and of those who incorporate or control it. Difficulties therefore arise with the question of damages for non-pecuniary loss in light of their defining character, in particular when it comes to interference with bodily, mental or emotional spheres, and that of the legal person. To overcome this obstacle, a theory which we will here refer to as 'attribution' has been suggested; that is, having regard to a company's human components for the purpose of assessing the non-pecuniary loss occasioned to the company by others. Before expounding on this bold proposition (Section III), the means through which liability is imposed upon companies will be examined (Section II). In the second place, we look at the roles played by various individuals within the company to determine whose harm to impute to it (Sections IV–VI). Finally, an examination is made on the merits and shortcomings of the theory (Section VII) as well as the likelihood of its acceptance by English courts (Section VIII).

II   Corporate Liability under Tort Law

7/2   There are two bases for imposing liability upon a corporate employer in tort. In all such cases, regard is had to the actions or inactions of natural persons: (a) vicarious or indirect liability; and (b) direct liability. The distinction is relevant for our purposes.

A   Indirect Liability

7/3   The common law sees no difficulty in finding a corporation liable in tort, and in the vast majority of cases the company's liability will be vicarious. As has been observed, the 'doctrine of vicarious liability has not grown from any very clear, logical or legal principle but from social convenience and rough justice';[1] i.e. ensuring a practical remedy is obtained for victims from persons who seek to advance personal interests when the risks they take ripen into harm.[2] Deterrence is also a vital consideration. The law's position, therefore, is that a company, which achieves its objects through the instrumentality of individuals, is liable for the tortious activities of those individuals *in the same way a natural person would be for the acts of his employees.* Liability is strict and secondary; the company stands in the employee's shoes so that no blame need be established on its part.[3] A claim will lie against a company where the act complained of is one which: (a) would constitute an actionable wrong if committed by an individual; (b) is not beyond the scope of the individual's authority and is done in the course of his employment with the company; and (c) the company is or might possibly be authorised by its constitution to commit.[4] Companies can therefore be liable for a broad range of vicariously committed torts, among them negligence and nuisance.[5] Where the claimant cannot prove which employee is responsible for the breach, the company is nonetheless liable. Moreover, a company cannot generally shift this burden to the persons responsible,[6] unless a court exercises its power to apportion the overall award of damages as is just and equitable between the company and the employee, having regard to the extent of the latter's responsibility for the damage.[7]

---

[1] *Imperial Chemical Industries Ltd* v. *Shatwell* [1965] AC 656, 685 per Lord Pearce.

[2] *Various Claimants* v. *Catholic Child Welfare Society* [2012] 3 WLR 1319, para. 34 per Lord Phillips.

[3] *Lister* v. *Hesley Hall Ltd* [2002] 1 AC 215, para. 65 per Lord Millet.

[4] See B. M. Hannigan, *Halsbury's Laws Commentary on Corporations* (London: LexisNexis Butterworths, 2010), vol. 24, para. 477 and *Halsbury's Laws Commentary on Companies* (London: LexisNexis Butterworths, 2009), vol. 14, para. 296.

[5] Hannigan, *Halsbury's Laws Commentary on Corporations,* para. 477.

[6] The individual who acted on the company's behalf remains primarily liable since a duty is implied into the terms of an employment contract on the part of an employee to take reasonable care not to cause physical damage in the carrying out of his duties. However, in *Morris* v. *Ford Motor* [1973] QB 792 it was decided generally that where the risk of a servant's *negligence* is covered by insurance, it would be positively unjust for his employer to make that servant liable for it. Moreover, as explained in *Morris,* Members of the British Insurance Association adhere to a 'gentleman's agreement' preventing insurers from pursuing employees by right of subrogation to indemnify them for the sums incurred by their employer.

[7] Civil Liability (Contribution) Act 1978 , s. 2(1). By s. 2(2), it may exempt the individual from liability or order a complete indemnity by the latter.

B   *Direct Liability*

7/4   As Lord Hoffmann explained in *Meridian Global Funds Management Asia Ltd* v. *Securities Commission,* acts can be attributed to a company in several ways: first, under so-called *primary rules of attribution* which are found in its constitution, typically its articles of association[8] or implied by company law;[9] second, through *general rules of attribution,* namely, the principles of agency (i.e. through servants and agents); unlike the other two rules, this is equally applicable to natural persons. In addition to instances expressly foreseen in tailor-made corporate statutory rules, the application of both primary and secondary rules of attribution (in the latter case, where an agent has acted within the scope of their agency (actual or apparent)), may result in a company's *direct* liability.[10] In exceptional cases, however, a rule of law may require some act or state of mind on the part of that person 'himself', as opposed to his servants or agents; e.g. it may be stated in language primarily applicable to a natural person and thus excludes the application of the above rules. It is this third rule of attribution, which also results in the imposition of direct liability, that is relevant for our purposes. Rather than conclude that the law in question is not intended to apply to companies at all, the courts may fashion a *special rule of attribution* so that someone's act or knowledge or state of mind is for a given purpose said to count as that of the company.[11] The proposition has its origins in the directing mind and will theory which was coined in *Lennard's Carrying Co. Ltd* v. *Asiatic Petroleum Co. Ltd.* It is one which Burrows has seized upon

[8] Lord Hoffmann gave the following example: 'for the purpose of appointing members of the board, a majority vote of the shareholders shall be a decision of the company or the decisions of the board in managing the company's business shall be the decisions of the company': [1995] 2 AC 500, 506.

[9] Lord Hoffmann gave the following example, citing *Multinational Gas and Petrochemical Co.* v. *Multinational Gas and Petrochemical Services Ltd* [1983] Ch 258, 'the unanimous decision of all the shareholders in a solvent company about anything which the company under its memorandum of association has power to do shall be the decision of the company': [1995] 2 AC 500, 506. By virtue of the s. 28 Companies Act 2006, provisions of a companies memorandum are now treated as provisions of its articles.

[10] Section 90A and sch.10A Financial Services and Markets Act 2000 are illustrations of a statutory rule in the field of civil law and ss. 1(3) and 1(4)(c) Corporate Manslaughter and Corporate Homicide Act 2007 illustrate the position under criminal law. An example of a company incurring direct liability through agents is where the latter commits his company to a contract. The company becomes a party to the contract.

[11] *Meridian Global Funds Management Asia Ltd* v. *Securities Commission* [1995] 2 AC 500, 506–507.

(and in so doing implicitly endorses the approach of the European Court of Human Rights) in advocating the concept of identifying the 'mental distress of those individuals who constitute *the controlling mind and will of the . . . company*' or 'in some situations, the mental distress of those who the company was concerned to benefit' with the company for the purpose of computing its non-pecuniary damage. In this way a company could be entitled to damages for 'the disruption of its "peace of mind"'.[12]

7/5   While some earlier authorities sweepingly asserted that a company could not have attributed to it the mental element of its human agents[13] others took the opposite view.[14] In *Lennard's Carrying* the court was persuaded by the need to find companies liable. The case involved the loss of cargo by fire. The owners of the ship, Lennard's Carrying Company Ltd, sought to rely on s. 502 Merchant Shipping Act 1894, which excluded liability for loss or damage to goods in the absence of the owner of a British sea-going ship's 'actual fault or privity'. In particular, they averred that although Mr Lennard was the active director in a limited company, Messrs John M Lennard & Sons, which in turn managed Lennard's Carrying Company Ltd and director of the latter company, he was not aware of the unseaworthy condition of the ship. Even assuming Mr Lennard was to blame, the ship owners argued that his 'fault or privity' was not the company's 'fault or privity'. Viscount Haldane LC objected, ruling that the active and directing will of a corporation, which has no mind of its own, must be sought in the person of somebody who '*is really the directing mind and will of the corporation*'.[15] The House of Lords found that the unseaworthiness existed at the commencement of the voyage, and it was not convinced that Mr Lennard was unaware of the defects that manifested themselves in unseaworthiness. Since Mr Lennard took an active part in the management of the ship on behalf of its owners, he was the directing mind of the company and his actions were said to be the actions of the company within the meaning of s. 502. To argue otherwise would be to exempt a corporation from liability under the section altogether and it

---

[12] A. Burrows, 'Damages and Rights' in D. Nolan and A. Robertson, *Rights and Private Law* (Oxford/Portland: Hart Publishing, 2012), p. 282. See also fn 32 therein. Emphasis added.

[13] *Abrath* v. *North Eastern Railway Co.* (1886) 11 App Cas 247, 250–251 per Lord Bramwell.

[14] *Citizens' Life Assurance Co. Ltd* v. *Brown* [1904] AC 423, 426 per Lord Lindley which was decided on the basis of vicarious liability but is significant in rejecting Lord Bramwell's view above.

[15] [1915] AC 705, 713. Emphasis added.

could not be successfully contended that this was a true construction of Parliament's intentions for that provision.[16]

7/6   As Hoffman LJ (as he was then) informed us in *El-Ajou* v. *Dollar Land Holdings plc (No. 1)*, Viscount Haldane LC derived the concept of the 'directing mind' from Germanic law.[17] The underlying justification for it is, as Koziol writes, that, according to § 26 Austrian Civil Code, legal entities have to be put on the same footing as natural individuals. That section reads that 'legal persons are capable of having rights; they have the same rights and *duties* as natural persons'.[18] '[A]s corporations cannot act for themselves and, therefore, can never be liable for their own faulty behaviour, *they would fare better than individuals*. For this reason they have to be liable for officers to the same extent as individuals are liable for their own behaviour.'[19] In substance, the doctrine is a somewhat sophisticated extension of vicarious liability and agency law.[20] Like the vicarious liability doctrine and agency, the directing mind and will theory (and its subsequent context-based expansion in *Meridian*, the details of which need not detain us here) seeks to ensure a practical remedy to the injured from entities that seek to advance their interests when the risks they take ripen and deterrence of future harm. Through the theory, the company can be made directly responsible, both civilly and criminally, for the actions of individuals who can fairly be regarded as its directing mind and will. In *Tesco Supermarkets Ltd* v. *Nattrass*, the House of Lords made it clear that the board of directors or shareholders acting collectively could be treated in law as being the company for the purpose of the rule.[21] The mind and will of persons exercising senior managerial functions (i.e. non-directors) may also be relevant, as indeed that of a single director or authorised servants lower down the command hierarchy. The latter extension is rooted in *Meridian*; liability based on servants on the lower echelons of the corporate structure is likely limited to less serious statutory crimes, however.[22]

---

[16] See also *Stone & Rolls Ltd (in liquidation)* v. *Moore Stephens (a firm)* [2009] UKHL 39.

[17] [1994] 2 All ER 685, 705.

[18] E. Karner, 'Austria' in B. Winiger, H. Koziol, B. A. Koch and R. Zimmermann (eds.), *Digest of European Tort Law*, 2 vols. (Berlin/Boston: De Gruyter, 2011), vol. 2, 24/3 no. 3. Emphasis added.

[19] H. Koziol and K. Vogel, 'Austria' in J. Spier (ed.), *Liability for Damage Caused by Others* (Hague/London/New York: Kluwer International, 2003), no. 9. Emphasis added.

[20] Koziol and Vogel, 'Austria', no. 41.

[21] [1972] AC 153, 199–200 per Lord Diplock (albeit in the context of criminal law).

[22] See E. Ferran, 'Corporate Attribution and the Directing Mind and Will', *Law Quarterly Review*, 127 (2011), 239–259 who criticises the reasoning in *Meridian*.

III Attribution of Non-Pecuniary Harm

7/7   Given the extent of a company's liability for its employees, agents, etc., when they do wrong, one could legitimately argue that courts should have regard to the same persons (or some such persons), who no doubt suffer strain and anxiety, when a wrong is done to a company. To allow recourse to the non-pecuniary harm occasioned to a company's employees in calculating the company's award on the basis of a mirror application of *vicarious or indirect liability* would be wrong, however, since even a natural employer, who is 'autonomous in fact and in law', could never seek to cash in on his employees' feelings in the event of a tort against his business. This is also true as regards agents. To do so on the basis of a mirror application of *direct liability* is defensible, however, since a natural employer, who has feelings of his own, can seek compensation for injury to himself in the case of a tort against his business. As a company is 'autonomous in law but not in fact',[23] it can only be *directly liable* for wrongs through the acts or mental states of natural persons; as Fellner points out such a rule of attribution should not only apply to a company's *detriment* but should extend also in its *favour*.[24] If a natural person in the company who does have feelings were considered, this would result in full compensation, putting the company on an equal footing as a human business owner. Before evaluating the efficacy of this theory, it is useful to begin by examining whose non-pecuniary harm is best treated as the company's for the purpose of assessing the appropriate award due to it. As seen in Chapter 4 above, the EctHR does not limit its considerations to the inconveniences, anxieties and distress caused to *directors* but also has regard to a violation's impact on the *management team* and even *shareholders*.

IV Directors

A Arguments in Favour of Attributing Director's Non-Pecuniary Harm

1 A Statutory Prerequisite

7/8   The attribution theory has several attractions in the case of directors; first, because there is a statutory requirement for companies (with the

---

[23] *Bilta (UK) Ltd (In Liquidation)* v. *Nazir* [2015] 2 WLR 1168, para. 66 per Lord Sumption.
[24] M.-L. Fellner, *Persönlichkeitsschutz juristischer Personen* (Neuer Wiss Verlag, 2007). See also H. Koziol, *Basic Questions of Tort Law from a Germanic Perspective* (Wien: Sramek Verlag, 2012), no. 5/22.

exception of LLPs and EEIGs (see Table 1 in no. 2/10)) to have at least one (in the case of private companies) or two (in the case of public companies).[25] Therefore, there will always be someone at the helm who is likely to suffer strain as a result of a tort against the company.

2   Core Directors' Duties

7/9   The strain referred to earlier is real since it is directors who are charged with the supervision and control of the company's activities. The company's constitution, in particular its articles of association, regulate it.[26] Art. 3 Model Articles 2013 – which applies by default to all private and public limited companies[27] – expressly provides: 'Subject to the articles, the directors are responsible for the management of the company's business, for which purpose they may exercise all the powers of the company.' Part 10, Chapter 2 of the Companies Act 2006 sets out *general duties* of directors 'based on "certain" common law and equitable principles'[28] which under s. 170(1) are said to be owed to the company.[29] As indicated by the use of the term 'certain' above, the duties enumerated in Chapter 2 of Part 10 are of course not exhaustive. Moreover, more than one duty may apply in any given case.[30]

7/10   In earlier English cases directors' duties were 'stated in very undemanding terms.'[31] In one case it was held that 'mere imprudence or want of judgment would not in itself make a director liable'[32] and in another that a director may 'undertake the management of a ... company in complete ignorance of everything connected with [it], without incurring responsibility for the mistakes which may result from such ignorance'.[33] The cases therefore illustrate that at one point directors could take adverse effects upon their companies in their strides. The law has since evolved in response to changes, inter alia, in public attitudes to corporate

---

[25] Companies Act 2006, s. 154. Any appointment of new directors or removal of old ones must be notified to the registrar: s. 167.

[26] Companies Act 2006, s. 18.   [27] Companies Act 2006, s. 20.

[28] Companies Act 2006, s. 170(3). Thus, cases prior to the enactment of the 2006 Act remain relevant.

[29] See also *Multinational Gas & Petrochemical Co.* v. *Multinational Gas & Petrochemical Services Ltd* [1983] Ch 258, 288 per Dillon LJ: 'The directors indeed stand in a fiduciary relationship to the company, as they are appointed to manage the affairs of the company and they owe fiduciary duties to the company though not to the creditors, present or future, or to individual shareholders.' Cf fn 42 below.

[30] Companies Act 2006, s. 179.

[31] *Bishopsgate Investment Management Ltd* v. *Maxwell (No. 1)* [1993] BCC 120, 139 per Hoffmann LJ.

[32] *Lagunas Nitrate Co.* v. *Lagunas Syndicate* [1899] 2 Ch 392, 418 per Romer LJ.

[33] *Re Brazilian Rubber Plantations and Estates Ltd* [1911] 1 Ch 425, 437 per Neville J.

governance,[34] so that today the responsibilities of directors are broad and exacting. Those mentioned in s. 172 (the duty to promote the success of the company) and s. 174 (the duty to exercise reasonable care, skill and diligence in the company's affairs) exemplify the core duties involved and emphasise the law's current view on how directors ought to discharge their duties on a day-to-day basis.[35]

7/11   As to the first of these, the provision begins: 'A director of a company must act in the way he considers, in good faith, would be most likely to promote the success of the company for the benefit of its members as a whole'.[36] Although their duties are owed to the company, directors are instructed to take into account the interests of other stakeholders, including the interest of employees[37] and the need to foster the company's business relationships with suppliers, customers and others.[38] To the extent that disturbances in these and other enumerated spheres affect 'the success of the company for the benefit of its members as a whole'[39] its directors are under an obligation to consider them. In addition, the company's success may also be affected by external factors; as such one of the express considerations expected of directors is to bear 'the desirability of the company maintaining a reputation for high standards of business conduct' in mind.[40] It can thus be seen that harm to the company's reputation, unrest in matters relating to its employees or its long term planning[41] can have a distressing effect on the very persons who toil to promote the success of the company. Directors are also expected in certain circumstances to consider or act in the interests of creditors of the company[42] and failure to do so, indeed breach of any of the above duties may result in personal civil liability,[43] and liability under insolvency rules if the company is wound up.[44]

---

[34] *Bishopsgate Investment Management Ltd* v. *Maxwell (No. 1)* [1993] BCC 120, 139 per Hoffmann LJ.

[35] Other duties are: s. 171 (the duty to act within powers); s. 173 (the duty to exercise independent judgment); s. 175 (the duty to avoid conflicts of interests); s. 176 (the duty not to accept benefits from third parties); s. 177 (the duty to declare interest in proposed transaction or arrangement).

[36] Companies Act 2006, s. 172(1) refers to what 'he considers' so the test is subjective. See also *In re Smith & Fawcett* Ltd [1942] Ch 304, 306 where Lord Green MR said that directors 'must exercise their discretion bona fide in what they consider – not what a court may consider – is in the interests of the company'.

[37] Companies Act 2006, s. 172(1)(b).   [38] Companies Act 2006, s. 172(1)(c).

[39] Companies Act 2006, s. 172(1) and (2).   [40] Companies Act 2006, s. 172(1)(e).

[41] Companies Act 2006, s. 172(1)(a).   [42] Companies Act 2006, s. 172(3).

[43] Companies Act 2006, s. 178.   [44] Insolvency Act 1986, s. 212.

7/12   The duty of care, skill and diligence under s. 174 is one that is imposed
on directors individually and collectively; the obligation is a continuous
one.[45] It is plausible that having invested much care, skill and diligence
in discharging their obligations, directors may suffer inconvenience, distress or anxiety, in the event of their company being the subject of a
rights violation, and this would of course be *to the company's detriment*.
Moreover, troubles within the company impose an additional burden on
them necessitating greater care, skill and diligence.

B   Arguments Against Attributing Director's Non-Pecuniary Harm

1   Multiple Directors

7/13   The attribution theory is not without its difficulties. For one, a corporation may be run by several directors. How is the assessment of non-
pecuniary harm to be made? Aggregation would naturally lead to less
damages for non-pecuniary loss in the case of companies with a modest
number of directors than in the case of large and sophisticated companies. The existence of multiple directors also raises the question of how
fluctuations in directorships or the absence of directors at the time of a
dispute are to be assessed.

2   Various Types of Directors and the Variation of Responsibilities

7/14   It is important to also recognise that there are different types of directors. While some are directors in name, the term 'director' extends to 'any
person occupying the position of director, by whatever name called'.[46]
This thus includes shadow[47] and *de facto*[48] directors. If the argument is
that directors will invariably suffer the strain associated with harm to their
company, it seems right to take into account the mental distress of shadow
and *de facto* directors involved in a dispute as well as the fact that there are
varying degrees of responsibilities expected of persons carrying out particular directorial functions within the company. This also varies depending

---

[45]   *Re Barings plc (No. 5)* [1999] 1 BCLC 433, 489 per Jonathan Parker J.
[46]   Companies Act 2006, s. 250.
[47]   Companies Act 2006, s. 251: 'a person in accordance with whose directions or instructions
the directors of the company are accustomed to act.'
[48]   *Re Hydrodan (Corby) Ltd* [1994] BCC 161, 163 per Millett J: 'one who claims to act and
purports to act as a director, although not validly appointed as such.'

on the type and size of a company.[49] In the case of public listed companies, for example, functions undertaken by non-executive directors (NEDs) can be contrasted with those undertaken by executive directors (EDs). The duties of the former – who on average work for more than two companies (cross directorships) and commit only 2.35 days a month to the role[50] – are more supervisory and more divorced from the business of the company. Thus, they are not required to overrule specialist directors. Indeed as one judge put it: 'The duty is *not* to ensure that the company gets everything right.'[51] On the other hand full-time EDs, headed by a chief executive, are called to execute the day-to-day operational management of the company. That different standards, at least of care, skill and diligence, are expected is also illustrated by the objective and *subjective* tests under s. 174(2) Companies Act 2006.[52] By extrapolation, some directors will likely experience more strain by virtue of their office and of course the extent of the burden will also depend on the particular dispute in question.

3 Corporate Directorships

7/15 Recourse to directors in respect of the corporation's non-pecuniary claim seeks to overcome the company's non-human nature. If a director is non-human, the initial complication resurfaces. Until recently, there was nothing in the Companies Act that made it incumbent on companies to have directors who were humans. Section 155(1) Companies Act 2006 now

---

[49] As has been observed: 'The position of a director of a company carrying on a small retail business is very different from that of a director of a railway company. The duties of a bank director may differ widely from those of an insurance director, and the duties of a director of one insurance company may differ from those of a director of another'.: *In re City Equitable Fire Insurance Co. Ltd* [1925] Ch 407, 426 per Romer J. See also *Re Barings plc* [1998] BCC 583, 586 per Sir Richard Scott V-C: 'The higher the office within an organisation that is held by an individual, the greater the responsibilities that fall upon him. It is right that this should be so, because status within an organisation carries with it commensurate rewards. These rewards are matched by the weight of the responsibilities that the office carries with it'.

[50] See the Life in The Boardroom 2014: Chairman and Non-Executive Director Survey by Preng & Associates.

[51] *Singer* v. *Beckett* [2007] 2 BCLC 287, para. 399 per Park J. Emphasis added. He continued: 'The duty is to exercise reasonable care and skill up to the standard which the law expects of a director of the sort of company concerned, and also up to the standard capable of being achieved by the particular director concerned'.

[52] What is expected is the care, skill and diligence that would be exercised by a reasonably diligent person with: (a) the general knowledge, skill and experience that may reasonably be expected *of a person carrying out the functions carried out by the director* in relation to the company, and (b) the general knowledge, skill and experience that *the director has*. Subsection 2(b) applies only to the extent that it improves upon (a).

legislates that at least one director within the company must be a natural person, and companies whose structures violated that requirement had until 1 October 2010 to comply with the provision. Thus, sole corporate directorships are now illegal so that there should always be at least one human director whose mental state may be relevant to the company's claims. It is also worth noting that requirements under the UK Corporate Governance Code effectively rule out the prospect of corporate directors in the case of public companies.

4   Evaluation

7/16   The problems associated with multiple directorships, the various types of directors and the variation of responsibilities can be overcome through the use of an *objective* measure. This would also do away with the need to impute the non-pecuniary harm occasioned to natural directors behind corporate directors to the company for the purpose of augmenting the company's award (since at least one natural director will always exist). Where damages for non-pecuniary loss can reasonably be assumed in the circumstances, they are normally computed by means of *prima facie* evidence of a reasonable person in the claimant's position. There is thus a case to be made that it is not necessary to pinpoint particular directors and particular tasks executed by them in the performance of their duties. All that matters is that a company has a director capable of sentience whose non-pecuniary harm can be attributed to it. The approach is particularly justified since corporations can be directly liable for the activities of a single director. Since a company can bring a recourse action against a director in respect of damages it paid to third parties where the director in question caused such harm intentionally, the question arises as to whether a director should be entitled to recover from his company (by way of inverse recourse) for non-pecuniary harm experienced by him and awarded to the company (by way of the attribution theory) as a result of a third party's intentional wrong. The answer is simply 'no' since the tort is committed against the company and not its director. Second, a recourse action by the company seeks to teach a director who intentionally commits a wrong that the tort does not pay. Therefore, it is entirely right for the company to seek recourse from directors in such cases and yet be advantaged by any attributed damages for non-pecuniary loss as the law in the latter case seeks to teach third parties that intentional misconduct (or wrongs generally) does not pay. Indeed, a company pays its directors, inter alia, to handle wrongs, intentional or otherwise, against it by third parties. It thus seems right for the full amount of damages to rest with the company.

V Managers

7/17   Good reasons can be advanced as to why the concept premised above should not be limited to directors and indeed the Strasbourg Court at times refers to the impact of a violation upon a company's management team. Since company law allows the board to delegate its powers to managers,[53] the law may treat a company as thinking and acting through the same (no. 7/6). Where there is extensive delegation of powers to non-directors, however, the latter are analogous to shadow or *de facto* directors thus negating the need to fix the company with the distress or other non-pecuniary experiences felt by such persons, in their independent capacity as senior managers. Resort to managers is only justified where the company has no directors. This is the case with LLPs, where managers undertake personal fiduciary obligations to the legal entity in a manner similar to the way in which a director of a company undertakes such obligations,[54] and EEIGs.[55]

VI Shareholders or Members

7/18   It will be recalled that Burrows also had in mind, albeit 'in some situations', the attribution to the company of the mental distress of those whom it was concerned to benefit (no. 7/4). Although it remains unclear which situations he had in mind, such an approach is on all fours with that of the Strasbourg Court. On the one hand, the mind and will of shareholders acting collectively can be attributed to the company for the purpose of finding it directly liable since there are various instances when shareholders will be called upon to influence the company's direction. For one, shareholders have power to step in where the board is unable to act; for example, where there is a deadlock, where there are no directors or where the board is not quorate; indeed it is shareholders who appoint and remove directors.[56] There are several other instances where shareholder decisions will bind the company so long as the decision is within

---

[53] See Art. 5 Model Articles for Private Companies Limited by Shares and Model Articles for Public Companies.

[54] *F&C Alternative Investments (Holdings) Ltd* v. *Barthelemy* [2012] Ch 613, para. 205 per Sales J.

[55] See art. 20 Council Regulation (EEC) No. 2137/85 of 25 July 1985 on the European Economic Interest Grouping, OJ 1985 No. L199, 31 July 1985, p. 9, provides: 'Only the manager or, where there are two or more, each of the managers shall represent a grouping in respect of dealings with third parties. Each of the managers shall bind the grouping as regards third parties when he acts on behalf of the grouping'.

[56] Companies Act 2006, s. 168.

their general competencies. While this may well be the case, shareholders are not generally concerned in the nuts and bolts of the company. This is especially so in large companies where investors (often institutional ones[57]) tend to diversify their investment portfolios, leading to rational apathy.[58] Majority shareholders on the other hand are likely to heavily influence the direction of the company. Such persons often have large sums of wealth tied up in the business, in a market that is generally illiquid, and so are highly vulnerable where a tort to the company occurs. However, the basis of the attribution theory is that only the feelings, etc. of those persons for whose acts the company *is liable* are relevant (as there should be harmony between attributing non-pecuniary loss and attributing misbehaviour) and the company can only be liable for the actions of such persons individually where they are shadow or *de facto* directors. Since mental distress in those capacities has already been taken into consideration there is no need to have recourse to the same persons in their capacity as shareholders. In conclusion, while reference may be made to a whole host of individuals potentially affected by an infraction of a company's rights, it is the directors (and in their absence managers) who are the proper candidates under the attribution theory and the basis of such an award should be that of a reasonable person in the company's position.

VII   Evaluation of the Attribution Theory

A   The Case in Favour

7/19   At the core of the attribution theory is the valid concern that leading individuals suffer strain associated with a wrong against their company; so much is undisputed. Such persons cannot seek compensation for such damage (and rightly so) as the tort is to the company. However, companies also cannot currently seek compensation in respect of such damage (in most legal systems) as they lack sentience. The controversy is the contention that the anxiety, distress, etc., of those who head the company should be attributed to the company for the purpose of assessing the total amount of damages for non-pecuniary loss due to it. The need for equality supports that case. When it comes to imposing liability, the law casts a broad net so that, even when framed in language consistent with natural persons, a company is nonetheless responsible via a legal

---

[57] See Ownership of Quoted Shares for UK Domiciled Companies, 2014 www.ons.gov.uk/ons/dcp171778_415334.pdf.

[58] See UK Stewardship Code which seeks to discourage this. The Code came into effect on 1 October 2012 and applies to publicly listed companies on a 'comply or explain' basis.

construct which looks to the defaults of individuals behind it. When it comes to determining liability owed to it, however, the current approach is to abandon the above rules of attribution in favour of what is or is not consistent with the nature of the corporate form. Attribution should not only apply to the disservice of companies but must, as Fellner observes, 'also act in their favour when so required by the protective purpose of the norm at issue.'[59] This is the view of Germanic scholars, who it will be remembered, are credited with advancing the notion of direct liability by reference to the company's organs (no. 7/6).

7/20   'Above all, the consideration that otherwise infringing the non-pecuniary rights of legal entities would be completely sanction-free, and that the legal system therefore could not exert any deterrent effect, speaks in favour of [the attribution theory].'[60] This is a reflection of tort law's deterrent function, albeit less stigmatic than criminal law and of secondary import (no. 2/20). Since deterrence plays an especially nuanced 'role (or at least a more obvious role) in non-personal injury cases ... the damages sanction must be a serious one and not a mere token.'[61] Giving companies a right of claim would achieve this.

7/21   One might add finally that accepting the attribution theory would alleviate courts of the need to disguise awards of damages for non-pecuniary loss as pecuniary or other damages,[62] thus fostering a culture of clarity and legal certainty.

B   The Case Against

7/22   A clear tension exists between the above imperatives and the fact firstly, that the directing mind and will theory and the context-based rule in *Meridian* are only one aspect of a company's direct liability in civil law (no. 7/2) yet a company's *direct* liability always entails the attribution to it of a natural person's acts or knowledge or at times culpability.[63] That

---

[59] Fellner, *Persönlichkeitsschutz juristischer Personen*. Translated in Koziol, *Basic Questions of Tort Law from a Germanic Perspective*, no. 5/22.

[60] Fellner, *Persönlichkeitsschutz juristischer Personen*. Translated in Koziol, *Basic Questions of Tort Law from a Germanic Perspective*, no. 5/22.

[61] W. V. H. Rogers, 'Comparative Report' in W. V. Horton Rogers (ed.), *Damages for Non-Pecuniary Loss in Comparative Perspective* (Wien/New York: Springer, 2001), no. 69.

[62] Burrows, 'Damages and Rights', p. 283. A. Burrows, *Remedies for Torts and Breach of Contract* (Oxford University Press, 2004), p. 244–246 who also refers to J. Edelman, 'The Meaning of Loss and Enrichment' in R. Chambers, C. Mitchell and J. Penner (eds.) *Philosophical Foundations of the Law of Unjust Enrichment* (Oxford University Press, 2009), pp. 215–218.

[63] Koziol, *Basic Questions of Tort Law from a Germanic Perspective*, no. 5/22.

said, as non-pecuniary loss entails an interference in the bodily, mental, emotional and/or personality spheres of a person 'himself' we must adopt a mirror application of principles that allow courts to look to those behind the company where a rule requires that a state of mind should be that of the company's 'itself'. However, rather than point to a specific director that suffered stress, anxiety, etc, an objective assessment could be resorted to. Second, direct liability itself is only one aspect of the company's overall liability. To attribute to the company the feelings of its directors for all wrongs committed against it, whether directly or vicariously, seems discrepant. The fact that the scope of a company's liability for others in cases resulting in direct liability is broader than that of a natural business owner's, since it can only be directly liable through natural persons, arguably justifies the above incongruity. A further difficulty is that the authorities on the directing mind and will theory are limited to rules of law founded on culpability or wrongdoing and not mental distress or other non-pecuniary harm. Then again, to say that a company does not suffer from distress, frustration, etc., means only that there is no one whose distress, frustration, etc., could count as that of the company and it is open to the law to insist, as it does in its search for culpability, that there are such people.

7/23   That the attribution theory as postulated should be limited to corporate remedies seems anomalous. As rules of attribution trigger liability, a true mirror application of the principle would result in third-party liability to the company for torts to its directors. The fact that the latter have autonomously protected interests, however, supports the confinement of the analogy to *compensation* of violations of the company's autonomous rights. In any case, a company is not liable for all torts committed by its directors; rather, only those committed in connection with its affairs. It would therefore be wrong in the context of art. 8 ECHR, for example, to impute to a company the personal integrity of its directors with a view to granting it standing to complain about attacks upon its reputation. As stated in no. 4/30, this would not result in companies being denied protection for their reputation in light of the fact that, at the very least, corporate reputation is protected as a parasitic action under the ECHR. There would thus still be a possible claim under the Convention and the possibility of damages for non-pecuniary loss there. Where a company director is himself implicated in a statement about the company, both company and director have autonomous claims (no. 5/36).

7/24   This leaves the question of which non-pecuniary losses should or should not be attributed to companies. The exclusion of damages for non-pecuniary loss: (a) that would not ordinarily be available to natural persons (i.e. because the action does not admit such claims); and (b) those where the protection of a dignitary interest underlies the remedy (e.g. aggravated damages (no. 6/13) or the injury to feelings aspect of damages in defamation (no. 5/48)) seems a compelling starting point. An example under (a) is damages for mental distress following a breach of contract where recovery is barred for *primarily commercial contracts*, whether pursued by an individual or company (no. 5/66). The reason behind this rule is, as McGregor points out, that 'mental suffering on breach is not in the contemplation of the parties as part of the business risk of the transaction',[64] although it may well be foreseeable. Moreover, by their nature companies cannot take advantage of the exception to the rule that such damages are available where one of the substantial objects of a contract is to provide 'pleasure, relaxation, peace of mind or freedom from molestation'.[65] While companies, like natural persons, are entitled to the quiet 'enjoyment' of their property, the Court of Appeal has already ruled that a covenant for quiet enjoyment is not within the exception to the rule relating to contracts to provide peace of mind or freedom from distress since in that connection the word 'enjoyment' has a technical meaning: 'and refers to the exercise and use of the right and having the full benefit of it, rather than to deriving pleasure from it.'[66] Since by far the most likely legal wrong which will cause trouble to a company is breach of a commercial contract against it, the law post-attribution would remain that such a wrong could not produce any damages for the company for mental distress to its directors. That said, a company could pursue attributed damages under the head of inconvenience and discomfort to its directors as a result of a breach of contract and of course a broader range of damages for non-pecuniary loss following breaches of other causes of actions.

7/25   While it may at first blush appear unfair to accept attribution when a natural person who cannot experience injured feelings (e.g. comatose patients) is denied subjective damages for non-pecuniary loss, this difficulty is countered by the fact that such persons are not denied a remedy altogether. They are entitled to loss of amenity (an objective head of

---

[64] H. McGregor, *McGregor on Damages*, 19th edn (London: Sweet & Maxwell, 2014), para. 5–024.

[65] *Watts* v. *Morrow* [1991] 1 WLR 1421, 1445 per Bingham LJ.

[66] Per Balcombe LJ in *Branchett* v. *Beaney* [1992] 24 HLR 348, 355 quoting Pearson LJ in *Kenny* v. *Preen* [1963] 1 QB 499, 511.

non-pecuniary loss). In any case, there are no individuals behind such persons for the purpose of attributing acts, knowledge, etc. where a rule requires that a state of mind should be that of the individual's 'himself' as natural persons are autonomous in fact and in law. This in turn leads to the enquiry of the propriety of extending such a theory to entities such as public authorities, as Burrows suggests, and States.[67] The ECHR recently answered this question (at least in so far as States are concerned) when it upheld a claim for damages for non-pecuniary loss for the first time in the context of an inter-State application. Having confirmed that art. 41 of the Convention applies in such cases, the Court went on to award the Cypriot government € 90 million in damages for non-pecuniary loss stressing, however, that 'it is the individual, and not the State, who is directly or indirectly harmed and primarily "injured" by a violation of one or several Convention rights. Therefore, if just satisfaction is afforded in an inter-State case, it should always be done for the benefit of individual victims.' The Court reiterated that the aforementioned sum was to be distributed by the applicant government to the individual victims of the violations found in the principal judgment.[68] The reasoning on the facts is sound.

7/26   Ultimately, attribution for the sake of liability is a means to an end. As Lord Hoffmann explained in *Meridian*, reference to anthropomorphism and the likening of a company to a human body 'distracts attention' from the purpose for which the rule of attribution is used.[69] 'The question in each case' is, as Dyson J observed, 'whether attribution is required to promote the policy of the substantive rule, or (to put it negatively) whether, if attribution is denied, that policy will be frustrated.'[70] This is the question before us, namely whether 'public policy – or common sense, rationality and justice'[71] is frustrated by a denial of a broader range of awards of damages for non-pecuniary loss to companies. This question is answered positively in the context of the Human Rights Court, where it will be remembered that extensive remedial powers were denied by the Convention drafters, leaving the judges there to expand their limited competence under the then art. 50 ECHR as broadly as possible. The fact is that pecuniary loss is difficult to prove, especially in the case of the

---

[67] Burrows, 'Damages and Rights', pp. 282–283. See also fn 32 therein.

[68] *Cyprus* v. *Turkey* [GC], 12.05.2014, no. 25781/94, §§ 46, 58.   [69] [1995] 2 AC 500, 509.

[70] *McNicholas Construction Co. Ltd* v. *Customs and Excise Commissioners* [2000] STC 553, para. 44

[71] *Bilta (UK) Ltd (In Liquidation)* v. *Nazir* [2015] 2 WLR 1168, para. 9 per Lord Neuberger.

frequently invoked art. 6 ECHR (on length). Indeed, in the vast majority of cases analysed, either no damages for pecuniary loss were sought or none were awarded to the corporate victim. Similarly, it is difficult for companies in particular to pin real and substantial non-pecuniary loss. The need for the Convention to be interpreted and applied in such a way as to guarantee rights that are practical and effective thus seems to be the actual motive behind the Court's affinity with attribution; after all, corporations are the social projection of the natural persons so that to deny them remedies is to deny those behind them remedies. Ultimately, attribution for the sake of assessing non-pecuniary loss does not perfectly mirror attribution for the sake of liability, nor need it arguably. What the analysis reveals, however, is that there are some merits to the practice.

VIII The Importation of the Attribution Theory

7/27   The question then arises as to whether attribution would be accepted by English courts. The issue was touted in a 2012 case before the Court of Final Appeal of the Hong Kong Special Administration Region in which the claimant company argued, for our purposes, that the feelings of the corporate victim's agents should be attributed to it for the purpose of awarding aggravated damages.[72] Counsel for the claimant in *Oriental Daily Publisher Ltd* v. *Ming Pao Holdings Ltd* sought support for imputation from Lord Hoffmann's judgment on the rules of attribution in *Meridian*. The court rejected the contention on the basis that 'the law of libel which provides for aggravated damages as compensation for increased injury to a person's feelings'[73] excludes attribution on the basis of the general principles of agency or vicarious liability. Ribeiro PJ continued that aggravated damages are in principle only available as an increased award of compensatory damages in favour of a claimant who has a good cause of action. If a company director has an own cause of action, no problem arises. But if the cause of action lies in the company

---

[72] *Oriental Daily Publisher Ltd* v. *Ming Pao Holdings Ltd* [2013] EMLR 7, para. 120: 'A company can only act through its agents, normally its board of directors. A corporate victim of a libel can only react to a libel through its agents. One or more of the directors will suffer the usual responsibility and consequent strain that goes with initiating and conducting litigation for the company and suffering the consequences of the Defendants' conduct. There is simply no reason why the feelings and forbearance of the corporate victim's directors and responsible agents in reaction to the Defendants' intransigence (which will be the same as for an individual Plaintiff) cannot be attributed to the company.'

[73] [2013] EMLR 7, para. 123 per Ribeiro PJ.

and not in the director, the latter's hurt feelings have no bearing on the damages recoverable by the company. He added that a 'company without a soul, whose reputation is merely a commercial asset, is hardly likely to be regarded as having feelings capable of being injured, whether borrowed from its officers or employees or otherwise.'[74] Lord Neuberger, currently President of the Supreme Court of the United Kingdom, also sat in *Oriental Daily* and said he entirely agreed with Ribeiro PJ's judgment. This gives some indication of how English courts would respond if a similar argument were to be advanced before them.

7/28   Indeed, a number of arguments against any direct transplantation of the Strasbourg Court's approach into English law exist. One must remember first that that Court's approach is of course limited to entities which do not exercise public functions. Then again, this does not detract from the merits of the theory. Second, the Court's jurisprudence is reserved for breaches of fundamental rights. Then again, for the most part fundamental rights protect interests that are also protected domestically under private law, so this is no real argument against the attribution theory. Finally, it is noteworthy that the decision in *Comingersoll* was not reached unanimously (Sir Nicolas Bratza, an English High Court judge was among those who dissented). To date, only two English cases have referred to *Comingersoll*. In *Jameel* the case was merely cited before the Court of Appeal and the House of Lords.[75] In the Court of Appeal case of *Hone* v. *Abbey Forwarding Ltd (In Liquidation)*, Arden LJ went further when she ruled that the defendants (all natural persons) were each entitled to recover, inter alia, damages for mental distress, to compensate them for those consequences of a freezing order, reference being made to the fact that:

> The Strasbourg case law awarding just satisfaction to companies for non-pecuniary loss where the state had wrongly searched their premises and stopped them carrying on business (see Société Colas Est v France (2002) 39 EHRR 373) provides support: the Strasbourg court cited Comingersoll SA v Portugal (2000) 31 EHRR 772, where the non-pecuniary loss included damage to reputation and uncertainty in decision-planning. There cannot be any logical difference here between a person who trades in his own name and a person who trades through a company.[76]

---

[74] [2013] EMLR 7, para. 124.

[75] *Jameel* v. *Wall Street Journal Europe SPRL* [2005] QB 904 and *Jameel* v. *Wall Street Journal* [2007] 1 AC 359 respectively.

[76] See *Hone* v. *Abbey Forwarding Ltd (In Liquidation)* [2014] 3 WLR 1676, para. 156 per Arden LJ.

7/29   In so doing, she implicitly endorsed the *Comingersoll* decision, and this was despite the fact that no reference was made to art. 8 of the Human Rights Convention 'even though the freezing injunction could without doubt engage the [claimants] article 8 rights'. Arden LJ concluded that the court was 'entitled to take the Strasbourg case law into account in this case just as it can take any other comparative law into account where it provides inspiration for a point on which there is no direct authority in our own law.' She then went on to quote von Jhering who wrote that 'no-one would bother to fetch a thing from afar when he has good or better at home, but only a fool would refuse quinine because it didn't grow in his own garden.'[77] Whether and the extent to which other English judges will be as keen on the Strasbourg Court's 'quinine' remains to be seen. In parenthesis, neither McCombe LJ (who delivered the main judgment in *Hone*) nor Vos LJ brought the Convention into their reasoning. In any case, with respect to actions under the Human Rights Act 1998, it is evident that English courts would be bound to consider the Strasbourg approach since s. 8(4) provides that: 'In determining (a) whether to award damages, or (b) the amount of an award, the court must take into account the principles applied by the European Court of Human Rights in relation to the award of compensation under Article 41 of the Convention.' A corporate claimant denied the generous treatment of damages for non-pecuniary loss available there could bring an action before that Court under art. 13 ECHR (on the right to an effective remedy; that is if Britain does not withdraw from the ECHR).

7/30   One reason that makes it more than unlikely that an English court would accept attribution on domestic matters is that in almost any conceivable case a company can recover damages for pecuniary loss and things like loss of reputation, which straddle the boundaries (consider, e.g. the *ReachLocal* case in nos. 5/39–5/43 where the total damages were over £400,000). The question arises as to whether there is a real need to add something for the vexation of directors. As mentioned, in no. 7/26, before the Strasbourg Court damages for pecuniary loss are notoriously difficult to prove, especially as respects art. 6 ECHR, the most widely pursued infraction and this perhaps explains the need to resort to directors. Further, English courts can also award exemplary damages should deterrence be warranted, although the available categories are rather limited.

---

[77] See *Hone* v. *Abbey Forwarding Ltd (In Liquidation)* [2014] 3 WLR 1676, para. 156 per Arden LJ.

While there is less need for attribution under English law, this does not detract from the merits of the theory.

IX Conclusion

7/31   Undoubtedly, it is shareholders or members that are most desirous of the company's success. However, only the non-pecuniary harm of those persons for whose acts the company is liable should be relevant (as there should be harmony between attributing non-pecuniary loss and attributing misbehaviour). As such, one is obliged to concede that it is the directors or in their absence managers whose harm is relevant both for the above reason and the fact that they are most closely concerned with the day-to-day running of the company. In this respect, the ingenuity of the rulings of the European Court of Human Rights is to be commended. Arguably, attribution is more called for in the case of EctHR with its limited scope of redress options. Whether the proposition should be implemented outside the human rights arena, however, is another question altogether. The author shares the view put forward in *Oriental Daily* that attribution is not appropriate, inter alia, in the context of aggravated damages; not for want of merit of the attribution theory itself but because of the nature of the interest such damages in essence seek to remedy, dignity.

PART IV

Comparative Analysis and Conclusion

8

Comparative Analysis

I Introduction

8/1   As an entity overseeing the conduct of governments in forty-seven Contracting States, the Strasbourg Court has to contend with many national rules, traditions and foundations. In developing its jurisprudence, the Court periodically seeks to ascertain the state of law and practice in Member States through the help of its Research Division (no. 3/8). The examination of comparative materials, Judge Bratza observed extra-judicially, demonstrates the Court's reluctance to readily interfere 'with established laws and practices in its search to impose uniform standards on Member States.'[1] As mentioned earlier, the ruling in *Comingersoll SA* v. *Portugal* was, in part, driven by the fact that damages for non-pecuniary loss had in the past been awarded to juristic persons by the Member States of the Council of Europe.[2] That the detailed results of such research are closed to the public is, however, regrettable since it leaves one with the task of conducting an independent comparative exercise on the topic.

II   The Nature of Damages for Non-Pecuniary Loss

8/2   Although there are considerable differences in the range of situations in which damages for non-pecuniary loss are recoverable, a survey of major Council of Europe jurisdictions reveals that almost all such legal systems allow such compensation in the case of personal injury, including mental injury going beyond a merely emotional response, and loss of liberty, hence the conclusion that damages for non-pecuniary loss entail interference in the bodily, mental or emotional spheres. Damage to personality rights also attracts such damages almost everywhere. In other non-personal injury cases, the law is more diverse. A careful categorisation

---

[1] N. Bratza, 'The Relationship between the UK Courts and Strasbourg', *European Human Rights Law Review*, 5 (2011), 505–512, 509.
[2] 06.04.2000, no. 35382/97, § 34.

of the jurisprudence on this topic shows that, despite the nature of the interest harmed, e.g. a proprietary or contractual interest, if damages for non-pecuniary loss are to be awarded, the underlying interference must touch at least one of the above spheres.[3]

III   Corporations and Damages for Non-Pecuniary Loss

A   Interference with the Bodily, Mental or Emotional Spheres

8/3   Koziol speaks for most Council of Europe systems in observing that 'legal entities by nature cannot have negative emotions.'[4] This is a reflection of § 26(2) of the *Austrian* Civil Code which reads that 'legal persons... have the same rights and duties as natural persons, insofar as the law concerned does not require a natural person due to its intrinsic nature.'[5] Numerous provisions across Europe, among them § 19(3) of the *German* Basic Law[6] and § 19(3) *Croatian* Civil Obligations Act,[7] restate this in one way or the other as do scholars (in *Hungary*[8] and *Poland*,[9] for

---

[3]   W. V. H. Rogers, 'Comparative Report' in W. V. Horton Rogers (ed.), *Damages for Non-Pecuniary Loss in Comparative Perspective* (Wien/New York: Springer, 2001), no. 1–48. See also C. von Bar and E. Clive (eds.), *Principles, Definitions and Model Rules of European Private Law: Draft Common Frame of Reference*, 6 vols. (Munich: Sellier, 2009), vol. 4, p. 3172–3173. Note that Malta, exceptionally, does not 'openly' admit claims for such damages: see G. C. Demajo, L. Quintano and D. Zammit, 'Malta', in: E. Karner and B. C. Steininger (eds.), *European Tort Law 2014* (Berlin/Boston: De Gruyter, 2015) nos. 98–106.

[4]   H. Koziol, *Basic Questions of Tort Law from a Germanic Perspective* (Wien: Sramek Verlag, 2012), no. 5/21.

[5]   See E. Karner, 'Austria' in B. Winiger, H. Koziol, B. A. Koch and R. Zimmermann (eds.), *Digest of European Tort Law*, 2 vols. (Berlin/Boston: De Gruyter, 2011), vol. 2, 24/3 no. 3.

[6]   The *Grundgesetz für die Bundesrepublik Deutschland* 1949 reads: 'The basic rights shall also apply to domestic artificial persons to the extent that the nature of such rights permits'; thus, in 'Germany § 253(2) BGB [which refers to an 'injury to body, health, freedom or sexual self-determination'] cannot serve as a basis for the compensation of non-pecuniary harm to legal entities because only natural persons can be entitled to the legal goods listed in this provision.' Koziol, *Basic Questions of Tort Law from a Germanic Perspective*, no. 5/21.

[7]   'A legal entity shall have all the above-mentioned rights of personality' – defined as 'the right to life, to physical and mental health, reputation, honour, dignity, name, privacy of personal and family life, liberty, etc' under § 19(2) – 'apart from those related to the biological character of a natural person': Official Gazette, nos. 35/2005 and 41/2008, which entered into force on 1 January 2006 and abrogated the former Obligations Act 1978.

[8]   See See A. Menyhard, 'Hungary' in H. Koziol (ed.), *Basic Questions of Tort Law from a Comparative Perspective* (Wien: Sramek Verlag, 2015), no. 4/81.

[9]   K. Ludwichowska-Redo, 'Poland' in H. Koziol (ed.), *Basic Questions of Tort Law from a Comparative Perspective* (Wien: Sramek Verlag, 2015), no. 3/66. See also H. Koziol, 'Comparative Conclusions' in H. Koziol (ed.) *Basic Questions of Tort Law from a Comparative Perspective* (Wien: Sramek Verlag, 2015), no. 8/201.

example) and courts. As regards case law, the *Belgian Cour de cassation* has ruled that 'the particular interest of a legal person only comprises that which concerns the existence of the legal person as well as the goods and moral rights of this person'.[10]

8/4   The duality of the nature of the corporation and the protective purpose of the norm is thus a decisive criterion that leads to a limited recognition of their non-pecuniary aspects. Where there is coincidence of the above two fields, however, companies can sue, and the nature of the remedy we are concerned with here poses no conceptual difficulties. Courts and scholars in *Portugal*, for example, support corporate actions for non-pecuniary loss on the basis of the distinction between *danos morais* (injury to the mind, body or emotions; injuries exclusive to natural persons) and the residual *danos não patrimoniais* (so-called 'non-patrimonial' or 'non-pecuniary loss'). In *Italy* too, judges differentiate between 'non-pecuniary loss' and 'moral damage', concluding that 'the former includes any prejudicial consequence of an unlawful act that, since it does not lend itself to a monetary market evaluation, can be remedied but not compensated, whereas the latter consists of what is known as *pecunia doloris*',[11] a head of damages exclusive to human beings.[12] Consequentially, there and in *Greece*, while entitled to the protection of their non-material assets, such entities are denied the presumption of damage which concerns 'internal feelings' which are 'judged with the perceptions of human logic'.[13]

8/5   At least one *Swiss* author has reported that the 'courts recognise that [legal entities] enjoy a right of protection, going so far as to award them an indemnity to compensate their "suffering".'[14] Given the above criteria,

[10] B. Dubuisson, I.C. Durant and N. Schmitz, 'Belgium' in B. Winiger, H. Koziol, B. A. Koch and R. Zimmermann (eds.), *Digest of European Tort Law*, 2 vols. (Berlin/Boston: De Gruyter, 2011), vol. 2, 24/7, no. 2.

[11] For Portugal see A. Pereira and M. Manuel Veloso, 24/11, no. 8; for Italy see N. Coggiola, B. Gardella Tedeschi and M. Graziadei, 24/9, no. 2, both in B. Winiger, H. Koziol, B. A. Koch and R. Zimmermann (eds.), *Digest of European Tort Law*, 2 vols. (Berlin/Boston: De Gruyter, 2011), vol. 2.

[12] F. D. Busnelli and G. Comandé, 'Italy' in W. V. Horton Rogers (ed.), *Damages for Non-Pecuniary Loss in Comparative Perspective* (Wien/New York: Springer, 2001), no. 12.

[13] E. Dacoronia, 'Greece' in B. Winiger, H. Koziol, B. A. Koch and R. Zimmermann (eds.), *Digest of European Tort Law*, 2 vols. (Berlin/Boston: De Gruyter, 2011), vol. 2, 24/5, no. 2.

[14] P. Tercier, 'Short Comments Concerning Non-Pecuniary Loss under Swiss Law' in W. V. Horton Rogers (ed.), *Damages for Non-Pecuniary Loss in Comparative Perspective* (Wien/New York: Springer, 2001), no. 25.

however, there is understandably much suspicion when one seeks to advocate this or the recognition of 'moral integrity, particularly dignity' of companies, albeit in the case of serious fault, like art. 68 Terré *French* draft on the reform of French tort law does.[15] That corporations can suffer harm in their 'essence',[16] has pushed French scholars like Moréteau to question some purported awards of damages for non-pecuniary loss to companies, rationalising that such awards can only be in respect of economic loss: i.e. 'pecuniary damage that [courts] are unable to assess'.[17] Moréteau argues alternatively that what the courts are doing in awarding companies damages for non-pecuniary loss is imposing 'a non-criminal penalty, camouflaged under the name of compensation of non-pecuniary damage';[18] i.e. punitive damages.

8/6   In conclusion, despite pockets of dissent, the overwhelming consensus is in Moréteau's words that 'one cannot hurt the feelings of non-profit organisations or business entities since only natural persons (one should add: the living in general) may have feelings and experience suffering.'[19] Other jurisdictions in the UK also share this view,[20] as does *Ireland*,[21] and indeed the common law world generally,[22] with the consequence that aggravated damages are ruled out for companies.

[15] O. Moréteau, 'French Tort Law in the Light of European Harmonisation', *Journal of Civil Law Studies*, 6(2) (2013), 759–801, 783.

[16] O. Moréteau, 'France' in H. Koziol (ed.), *Basic Questions of Tort Law from a Comparative Perspective* (Wien: Sramek Verlag, 2015), no. 1/66.

[17] See also O. Moréteau and A.-D. On, 'France' in K. Oliphant and B. C. Steininger (eds.), *European Tort Law 2012* (Berlin/Boston: De Gruyter, 2013), no. 45. See also S. Galand-Carval's report, 'France' in W. V. Horton Rogers (ed.), *Damages for Non-Pecuniary Loss in Comparative Perspective* (Wien/New York: Springer, 2001), no. 74.

[18] See also Moréteau and A.-D. On, 'France'. Moréteau, 'France' no. 45.

[19] Moréteau and A.-D. On, 'France', no. 45.

[20] *Scotland*: W. J. Stewart, *Reparation* (W Green/Sweet & Maxwell, 2000), para. 2–34.

[21] J. Healy, *Principles of Irish Torts* (Dublin: Clarus Press, 2009), para. 13–38.

[22] *Australia* adopts the same position as English law: see D. Rolph, 'A Critique of the National, Uniform Defamation Laws', *Torts Law Journal*, 16 (2008), 207–248. In *Canada* it is settled law that corporations are incapable of suffering personal distress: *WeGo Kayaking Ltd* v. *Sewid* 2007 BCSC 49, para. 88 per Macaulay J. For *Hong Kong* see *Oriental Daily Publisher Ltd* v. *Ming Pao Holdings Ltd* [2013] EMLR 7, para. 123 per Ribeiro PJ. For *New Zealand* see S. Todd (ed.), *The Law of Torts in New Zealand*, 5th edn (Wellington: Brookers Ltd, 2009), para. 23.4. In the *USA*, Green and Cardi state, '[a] corporation or other legal entity may not recover non-pecuniary damages because, at least in this sense, a corporation is not human.': M. D. Green and W. J. Cardi, 'USA' in H. Koziol (ed.), *Basic Questions of Tort Law from a Comparative Perspective* (Wien: Sramek Verlag, 2015), no. 6/75. For the mixed system of *South Africa*: *Media 24 Ltd* v. *SA Taxi Securitisation (Pty) Ltd* 2011 5 SA 329 (SCA), para. 52 per Brand JA (Maya, Snyders and Theron JJA concurring).

B Interference with the Personality Sphere

8/7 Of the nineteen European jurisdictions (including the European Union)[23] that reported on the issue, Koch concludes that there was unanimous acceptance that 'legal persons... can be the subject of... *immaterial rights* and can claim compensation in tort if these have been violated.'[24] This is especially the case with personality rights, and in particular where injury to reputation is concerned.[25]

8/8 As the *Polish* Supreme Court has said, the 'essence of a legal person lies in its own separate legal existence' and with that comes a right to '*its* reputation', distinct from that of its organs or that of the natural persons that created it.[26] Injury to reputation may thus be remedied under art. 448 Polish Civil Code 1964, inter alia, by 'an appropriate sum as compensation for non-material harm'.[27] *Denmark*,[28] *Norway*,[29] *Russia*[30] and *Spain*[31] also

---

[23] Germany, Austria, Greece, France, Belgium, the Netherlands, Italy, Spain, Portugal, England and Wales, Scotland, Ireland, Denmark, Norway, Sweden, Poland, Czech Republic and Romania.

[24] B. A. Koch, 'Comparative Report' in B. Winiger, H. Koziol, B. A. Koch and R. Zimmermann (eds.), *Digest of European Tort Law*, 2 vols. (Berlin/Boston: De Gruyter, 2011), vol. 2, 24/30 no. 1. Emphasis added.

[25] Koch, 'Comparative Report' no. 3.

[26] E. Bagińska, 'Poland' in B. Winiger, H. Koziol, B. A. Koch and R. Zimmermann (eds.), *Digest of European Tort Law*, 2 vols. (Berlin/Boston: De Gruyter, 2011), vol. 2, 24/22, no. 8. Emphasis added.

[27] E. Bagińska, 'Poland' in K. Oliphant and B. C. Steininger (eds.), *European Tort Law: Basic Texts* (Wien: Sramek Verlag 2011), p. 199.

[28] V. Ulfbeck and C. Siig, 'Denmark' in B. Winiger, H. Koziol, B. A. Koch and R. Zimmermann (eds.), *Digest of European Tort Law*, 2 vols. (De Gruyter, 2011), vol. 2, 24/15, no. 2. See also V. Ulfbeck, 'Denmark' in K. Oliphant and B. C. Steininger (eds.), *European Tort Law: Basic Texts* (Wien: Sramek Verlag 2011), p. 42.

[29] B. Askeland, 'Norway' in B. Winiger, H. Koziol, B. A. Koch and R. Zimmermann (eds.), *Digest of European Tort Law*, 2 vols. (Berlin/Boston: De Gruyter, 2011), vol. 2, 24/16, no. 3.

[30] See Decree of the Constitutional Court of 4 December 2003, No 508-O where the court recognised that legal persons are entitled to damages for non-pecuniary loss under art. 151 Civil Code 1994 ruling that the provision was broader than the concept of moral damage as narrowly defined. It is notable that the Constitutional Court reached its above decision having had regard to the EctHR's judgment in *Comingersoll SA* v. *Portugal* [GC], 06.04.2000, no. 35382/97. See V. Wilcox, 'Recent Trends in European Tort Law', in M. A. Rozhkova (ed.), *Non-Contractual Obligations* (Moscow: Statut, 2015), pp. 62–79.

[31] See also M. Martín-Casals, J. Ribot and J. Solé, 'Spain' in W. V. Horton Rogers (ed.), *Damages for Non-Pecuniary Loss in Comparative Perspective* (Springer, Wien/New York, 2001), no. 119; M. P. García Rubio and J. Lete, 'Spain' in H. Koziol and B. C. Steininger (eds.), *European Tort Law 2002* (Wien/New York: Springer, 2003), nos. 30 and 32.

interpret general provisions to arrive at the same conclusion. In other legal systems, such as *Slovenia*[32] and *Portugal*,[33] the Civil Code leaves one in no doubt that legal persons possess non-pecuniary aspects that deserve the protection afforded by damages.

8/9   Accepting this is not tantamount to acknowledging that injury to reputation *per se* is compensable. In *Italy* at least, the rule is that *danni conseguenza* (consequential damage) must and can be shown. The Italian Supreme Court has said that for a natural person, one's image consists of two aspects: the opinion of oneself and one's reputation. The same two-fold standard applies in the case of corporations with some adjustments. A company's reputation may be reduced in the eyes of its employees and the public, and such damage is purely non-pecuniary and independent of any economic effects of the violation.[34]

8/10   Indeed, a legal person's personality sphere is not limited to reputation but includes honour in jurisdictions such as *Belgium*,[35] *Norway*[36] and *Croatia*.[37] The parliamentary history of art. 6:106 Dutch Civil Code 1990 also broadly recognises 'the intentional frustration of a legal entity in its non-pecuniary goals.'[38] In *France*, the failure of courts to elaborate on precisely which aspect of a legal entity's personality sphere is being protected leaves the precise ambit of this area unclear.[39] What is evident,

[32] Art. 183 Obligations Code reads: 'The court shall award a legal person just monetary compensation for the defamation of reputation or good name, independent of the reimbursement of material damage, if it finds that the circumstances so justify, even if there is no material damage.': L. Koman Perenič, 'Slovenia' in K. Oliphant and B. C. Steininger (eds.), *European Tort Law: Basic Texts* (Wien: Sramek Verlag 2011), p. 241.

[33] Art. 484 Civil Code provides that: 'Any person who makes or disseminates a statement liable to harm the personal standing or good name of any natural or legal person shall be liable for the damage caused.': A. Pereira, 'Portugal' in K. Oliphant and B. C. Steininger (eds.), *European Tort Law: Basic Texts* (Wien: Sramek Verlag 2011), p. 202.

[34] E. Navarretta and E. Bargelli, 'Italy' in H. Koziol and B. C. Steininger, *European Tort Law 2007* (Wien/New York: Springer, 2008), no. 29–31.

[35] Dubuisson, Durant and Schmitz, 'Belgium', 24/7, no. 2.

[36] B. Askeland, 'Norway' in B. Winiger, H. Koziol, B. A. Koch and R. Zimmermann (eds.), *Digest of European Tort Law*, 2 vols. (Berlin/Boston: De Gruyter, 2011), vol. 2, 24/16, no. 2.

[37] § 19(3) Civil Obligations Act 2005, which deals with legal entities, refers to 'the right to a reputation and good name, honour, name or company name, business secrecy, entrepreneurial freedom, etc'.

[38] S. Lindenbergh and H. T. Vos, 'The Netherlands' in B. Winiger, H. Koziol, B. A. Koch and R. Zimmermann (eds.), *Digest of European Tort Law*, 2 vols. (Berlin/Boston: De Gruyter, 2011), vol. 2, 24/8, no. 3.

[39] See also Moréteau and A.-D. On, 'France', nos. 43–47. See J. S. Borghetti, 'France' in B. Winiger, H. Koziol, B. A. Koch and R. Zimmermann (eds.), *Digest of European Tort*

however, is that French scholars do not consider dignity as part of the corporate personality sphere since companies are 'not conscious beings' and dignity 'deals with self-esteem and intimate feelings connecting with what makes us human beings.'[40]

8/11   Beyond this, Koziol rightly concludes that insofar as a legal entity's personality right infringement is objectively evaluated, it is 'likely to meet with a favourable response at present in the majority of the legal systems'.[41] Even *EU* law recognises this to be the case.[42] The conclusion is supported firstly by the fact that legal persons are endowed with legal personalities; second because such a violation also sounds in non-pecuniary injuries which, when objectively assessed and remedied, are not incompatible with the corporate form and finally because 'corporations are the social projection of the natural persons acting by means of them'.[43] It would thus be contradictory to remedy such damage via damages for non-pecuniary loss in the case of natural persons while denying them in the case of a violation of corporations' personality rights. Despite mounting criticism, courts in *Germany* are unreceptive of this view since 'even within the framework of the protection of personality rights based on the *Grundgesetz* (Basic Law) going beyond [§ 253(2) BGB], no compensation of non-pecuniary harm is granted to legal entities.'[44] The opinions are mixed in other common law jurisdictions.[45]

Law, 2 vols. (Berlin/Boston: De Gruyter, 2011), vol. 2, 24/6, nos. 1–5. See also J. S. Borghetti, La réparation des atteintes à l'image de marque et à la réputation des collectivités locales: Réflexions à partir de l'affaire de l'Erika, RDA n 1, Jan 2010, 53–60.

[40] Moréteau, 'France', no. 1/103. Moréteau and A.-D. On, 'France' no. 45. For the position in England see no. 6/13.

[41] Koziol, 'Comparative Conclusions', no. 8/201.

[42] B. A. Koch, 'European Union' in B. Winiger, H. Koziol, B. A. Koch and R. Zimmermann (eds.), *Digest of European Tort Law*, 2 vols. (Berlin/Boston: De Gruyter, 2011), vol. 2, 24/28, no. 1.

[43] Navarretta and Bargelli, 'Italy', no. 29.

[44] Koziol, *Basic Questions of Tort Law from a Germanic Perspective*, no. 5/21.

[45] For example, Ireland, Canada and South Africa allow corporations to sue for damages for non-pecuniary loss (without proof of damage). In *Ireland*, s. 12 Defamation Act 2009 reads: 'The provisions of this Act apply to a body corporate as they apply to a natural person, and a body corporate may bring a defamation action under this Act in respect of a statement concerning it that it claims is defamatory *whether or not it has incurred or is likely to incur financial loss* as a result of the publication of that statement.' Emphasis added. In *Walker* v. *CFTO Ltd*, CanLII 126 (ON CA), (1987), 59 OR (2d) 104, the leading case on corporate libel damages in *Canada*, Robins JA held at 113 that: 'A company whose business character or reputation (as distinct from the character or reputation of the persons who compose it) is injuriously affected by a defamatory publication is entitled, without proof of damage, to a compensatory award representing the sum necessary to publicly vindicate

C   Attribution Theory

8/12   The literature on entitling companies to sue for non-pecuniary harm to their organs in the case of a tort committed against them is thin. At the time of writing their contribution, Cousy and Droshout pointed to the fact that 'a number of problems remain unclear under *Belgian* law, with regard to the claim of a legal person for the compensation of non-pecuniary loss caused by the infringement of moral values of its members'.[46] While, the *Italian* Supreme Court rejected the opinion that a violation of a corporation's personality rights may cause pain and suffering (*pretium doloris*) to its management in one case,[47] this must be read in light of a subsequent case, Cass 337/2008, in which the court ruled:

> Even for legal entities and partnerships, non-pecuniary damage, in the sense of subjective moral damage associated with anxiety of a psychological nature, in accordance with European Court of Human Rights case law, is

the company's business reputation.' In *South Africa*, the Supreme Court of Appeal ruled in *Media 24 Ltd and Others* v. *SA Taxi Securitisation (Pty) Ltd* 2011 5 SA 329 (SCA), following a review of the cases, that corporations, whether trading or non-trading, had a right to their good name and reputation which is protected, inter alia, by a claim for damages. The court thus refused to deviate from the rule endorsed by courts for nearly a century that a corporation can claim for 'general damages' in defamation. Cf J. Neethling and J. Potgieter, 'Defamation of a Corporation: Aquilian Action for Patrimonial (Special) Damages and Actio Iniuriarum for Non-Patrimonial (General) Damages: Media 24 Ltd v SA Taxi Securitisation and Amici Curiae 2011 5 SA 329 (SCA)', *Journal of Contemporary Roman-Dutch Law*, 75 (2012), 304-312. In line with the minority judgment, Neethling and Potgieter argue that an action for general damages is not the only remedy available to protect the reputation of a corporation. This they say provides good reasons to change the status quo by discarding the *actio iniuriarum* in respect of juristic persons. Neethling and Potgieter argue that as it stands the principle function of the *actio iniuriarum* in the case of juristic persons is not the salving of injured feelings but to punish the defendant, which is not a function of the law of delict. For the position in *New Zealand* see no. 5/39 above. In *Australia*, the national uniform defamation laws prevent certain corporate bodies from bringing actions in defamation *altogether* (i.e., whether in respect of damages for pecuniary or non-pecuniary loss): see s. 9 Defamation Act 2005. A corporation is excluded from this rule if: (a) its objects do not include obtaining financial gain; or (a) it employs fewer than 10 employees at the time of publication, is not related to another corporation and is not a public body. Finally, the position in the *US* is that 'it is only in a business way, resulting in pecuniary loss, that a corporation can be damaged by an alleged libellous publication.': *Axton Fisher Tobacco Co. v. Evening Post Co.*, 169 Ky 64; 183 SW 269.

[46]   H. Cousy and D. Droshout, 'Belgium' in W. V. Horton Rogers (ed.), *Damages for Non-Pecuniary Loss in Comparative Perspective* (Wien/New York: Springer, 2001), no. 71. Emphasis added.

[47]   Navarretta and Bargelli, 'Italy', no. 36.

to be regarded as a normal consequence of the breach of the right stated in art 6 of the European Convention on Human Rights, *by reason of the mental anguish and psychological problems caused by that breach to persons appointed to the management of the entity or to its members*, with the consequence that the judge must hold that damage exist[s], save in special circumstances that exclude such damage.[48]

8/13 Unlike in Italy where the case was in respect of a Convention provision, a decision of the Federal Supreme Court of *Switzerland* seems to have adopted attribution outside that context and in so doing, undermines earlier jurisprudence which recognised legal persons as capable of mortal suffering. In a 2012 case, a company was awarded CHF 10,000 in damages for the severe impairment of its personality, in particular its *reputation*, and its right to free economic development was also said to have been gravely attacked. While acknowledging that companies have personality rights which have evolved considerably, the Swiss Federal Court was still faced with the practical difficulty in awarding the company damages for non-pecuniary loss for emotional distress. To overcome this, the court concluded that legal persons can only act through natural persons and:

> the actions of an executive body are normally equated with the actions of the legal entity itself, so that in principle there is a unity in action in the sense that the executive body and the legal entity are regarded as identical. In analogy to the commitment of the legal entity by the actions of its executive bodies, the legal entity is authorized to claim redress in its own name for moral tort ('*tort moral*') its executive bodies suffer as a consequence of a violation of their personal rights.[49]

8/14 A Swiss commentator puts the decision down to a leaning towards the Real Entity Theory (*Realitätstheorie*) as opposed to the Fiction Theory (*Fiktionstheorie*) of corporate personalities (see nos. 5/4–5/10). Corporations are real entities consisting of members. They act through human individuals as executive bodies, and so ascription should not only occur in one direction, that is, only in the case of liabilities, 'but also in that the subjective experience of such bodies may give rise to liability claims in favour of the legal entity.'[50] The amount awarded in the

---

[48] Resp Civ Prev 9 (2008) 1916. See Coggiola et al., 'Italy', no. 5. Emphasis added.
[49] Schweizerisches Bundesgericht, 11 April 2012, BGE 138/2012 III 337. See P. Loser, 'Switzerland' in K. Oliphant and B. C. Steininger (eds.), *European Tort Law 2012* (2013), nos. 42–57, in particular no. 50.
[50] Loser, 'Switzerland', no. 56.

case appears to have been on the low side, however, and oddly enough one of the reasons was that the claimant was a non-natural person (see no. 7/16 on the objective approach and no. 7/24 on attribution in the context of defamation).

8/15   If Council of Europe Member States' courts are slow in taking up the Strasbourg Court's approach, other legal bodies are not. The International Centre for Settlement of Investment Disputes (ICSID) tribunals' jurisprudence is a case in point. The precise facts of *SARL Benvenuti & Bonfant* v. *People's Republic of the Congo*[51] need not detain us save that a company, which sought to invest in Congo, pursued damages for non-pecuniary loss against Congo for injury to its reputation. In the absence of a choice of law clause in the arbitration agreement, the tribunal looked to French law (as the People's Republic of the Congo was a French colony) and upheld the company's claim, stating specifically that the government's actions had 'certainly disturbed' the company's activities. As seen in no. 4/32, the Human Rights Court awards damages for non-pecuniary loss for disruption to a company's management team. In *Desert Line* v. *Yemen*, a construction company (registered in Oman) issued proceedings against Yemen for the violation of a fair and equitable treatment clause under the Yemen-Oman Bilateral Investment Treaty. That the Yemen government had refused to settle its accrued debts with the company and that militants harassed its employees were among the company's grievances. The latter sought compensation, including moral damages, inter alia, for the stress, anxiety, harassment and intimidation experienced by its executives, in addition to unjust harm to reputation. Interestingly, the State counterargued that its President had been subject to abusive and threatening letters from the claimant company's chairman and that if anyone, it had suffered moral damage. As with the Strasbourg Court, the tribunal concluded that the respondent State did not challenge the possibility of the claimant company to be capable of moral damage. While noting that investment treaties primarily protect property and economic interests, and that it is difficult, if not impossible to substantiate such prejudice, it went on to grant the company the remedy sought. In so doing, the tribunal emphasised the impact of Yemen's actions on the

---

[51] ICSID Case No. ARB/77/2 (1980). See M. T. Parish, A. K. Newlson and C. B. Rosenberg, 'Awarding Moral Damages to Respondent States in Investment Arbitration', *Berkeley Journal of International Law*, 29 (2011), 225–245. See also I. Schwenzer and P. Hachem, 'Moral Damages in International Investment Arbitration' in S. Kröll, L. A. Mistelis, P. Perales Viscasillas and V. Rogers (eds.), *International Arbitration and International Commercial Law: Synergy Convergence and Evolution* (Hague/London/New York: Kluwer Law International, 2011).

executives of the claimant company (in particular, their physical health) and found that it was liable to reparation 'for the injury suffered by the Claimant, whether it be bodily, moral or material in nature'.[52]

IV   Conclusion

8/16   The Strasbourg Court's attention is drawn to the almost unanimous acceptance that companies are only capable of direct non-pecuniary loss to their personality sphere. English courts should also take comfort from this in their continued resolve not to limit corporate protection in defamation cases to proprietary losses. That courts are increasingly persuaded by the attribution theory, which is gaining slow but firm ground both in and outside the human rights arena, is testament to the strength of reasoning, particularly the consideration of equality, which underlies the theory. That said, the precise scope of its application would benefit from continued discussion and refinement.

---

[52] ICSID Case No ARB/OS/17 (2008), § 289.

9

Conclusion

I Introduction

9/1   It has been shown above that businesses are formed for a variety of reasons, and various structures are employed for these purposes. The advantages attending the corporate form mean that it is companies that dominate economic activities in England, countries subject to the jurisdiction of the European Court of Human Rights and indeed, activities across most global economies. Yet it remains a challenge for legal systems to carve out – with as much consistency and as little consternation as possible – the appropriate application of rules in respect of these subjects as evidenced by the state of the European Court of Human Rights' jurisprudence and the discourse at domestic level. This book set out to explore the theoretical and legal foundations of a practice that is in part troubling, corporate awards of damages for non-pecuniary loss. It opened with four premises that: (a) damages for non-pecuniary loss should be available only for interference in the bodily, mental or emotional sphere on the one hand and/or interference with the personality sphere on the other; (b) a corporation, not being a physical person, cannot suffer interferences in the bodily, mental or emotional sphere; (c) notwithstanding the foregoing, a principle of 'equality' demands that, since a company can be directly liable for the acts of its organs, it should in principle also be entitled to sue for damages for *some* non-pecuniary harm experienced by them; (d) a company has a 'personality' which is not merely an interest of a proprietary character (e.g. the property a company has in its 'goodwill') and should therefore be entitled to damages for non-pecuniary loss for interference with the non-proprietary aspects of its personality. What follows is a brief summary of the reasoning underpinning these findings.

II   Theoretical and Legal Foundations of the Four Premises

A   *Non-Pecuniary Spheres*

9/2   Non-pecuniary loss is an everyday feature of life that the law has been aware of from a very early stage. The concept is one that is adaptable to changing societal values, morals and ethics so that from time to time new heads of non-pecuniary loss are recognised and remedied. Nonetheless, a common thread runs through such damage which can be categorised into harm that entails personal injury (caused by physical or non-physical impact) and those that do not (resulting in inconvenience and discomfort, mental distress, social discredit and bereavement). The essence of such damage is interference in one's bodily, mental, emotional and/or personality spheres which results in harm other than to money, property or wealth. By its very nature, non-pecuniary harm is incommensurable. Coherency, consistency and ultimately justice are compelling reasons why any expansion of the heads of non-pecuniary loss must remain true to the description of its essential characteristics. These must also inform a particular subject's entitlement to damages for non-pecuniary loss. In the case of companies, whose attributes are conferred upon them by law, care must therefore be taken to uphold the mentioned correlation.

B   *The Nature and Attributes of Corporations*

9/3   Terminological references to companies as 'persons' and as having 'personalities' may well be distractive, but such metaphysical labels should not detract from the true nature of corporations. A company is an entity that is distinct from the natural persons that form and are duly authorised to act on its behalf. Separate legal personality is *the* fundamental attribute that stands companies apart from other business entities and from which all other attributes flow. Attaching to corporate personality is a name and with it the capacity to enter into contracts, sue and be sued, purchase, possess and dispose of property and accomplish other legal acts *in that name*. Separate legal personality therefore brings with it autonomy, and with autonomy comes accountability and exposure to criticism, which if unjustly earned may harm the very name through which a company conducts its affairs; hence the need to recognise corporate reputation. A company also has the unique potential to exist in perpetuity as without this feature it would cease to exist upon the death or change of any member or shareholder. What can therefore be derived from the above is first that a 'person' is a subject capable of rights and duties and second that the law confers legal persons with only those qualities that are reasonably necessary and proper for them to possess to enable them to carry into effect their existing inherent or express powers. As such English courts, at least, and indeed a preponderance of the Council of Europe courts examined above, have not seen fit to conclude that a company has a body, mind or emotions. This has implications for what rights and remedies the latter can pursue.

C   Corporate Rights

9/4   The European Court of Human Rights has never sat down to enumerate the key characteristics of the legal person; however, deductions can be drawn from its approach to them. Insofar as the *merits* of a case are concerned (corporate rights), the EctHR is consistent in its recognition of the limitations inherent in the corporate form. In particular, the Court has ruled that certain Convention rights including those enshrined in arts. 2 (right to life), 3 (prohibition of torture) and 5 ECHR (right to liberty and security) are simply ones that cannot be guaranteed in respect of corporations. These provisions contemplate the protection of life, physical and mental integrity, inalienable attributes of human beings. As such, the Court has concluded that they are by their very nature not susceptible of being exercised by a legal person. Others, among them, arts. 10 (freedom of expression), 11 (freedom of assembly and association), 13 (right to an effective remedy) ECHR, and of course art. 1, Protocol No. 1 (protection of property), are sufficiently broad in their essence and/or drafting to accommodate companies. In England, the approach is summed up by the notion that a company can bring an action in respect of a tort in the same way as an individual, save for torts of a purely personal nature. Courts in both jurisdictions are thus governed by the inherent nature of the Convention article or nominate tort in question and more specifically the interests it seeks to protect on the one hand and the nature of the victim that seeks to rely upon it on the other. As to the latter, one is left to conclude that the EctHR draws a parallel with English courts in characterising companies as lacking physical, mental and emotional qualities. On the other hand, both English and Strasbourg judges alike accept, in light of the overlap between corporate personality and personality rights, that a good name is an aspect of the personality sphere deserving of respect. Legal persons can thus seek to vindicate their reputations under any tort actionable by them so long as reputation is central to the tort in question. Theoretically, a company can claim damages where any

Convention provision applicable to it results in collateral damage to its reputation.

9/5 These conclusions enable one to speculate on the outcome of the Strasbourg Court's likely ruling on rights that it is yet to decide upon. This is the case for example with respect to the stand-alone right to reputation under the private life aspect of art. 8 ECHR. Such a right has only relatively recently been extended to natural persons. While inconsistent on the issue, the Court's case law appears to limit an action to those instances where the injury to reputation interfered with 'personal integrity', an interest which it considers inalienable. Such a restriction accords with the fact that reputation is only mentioned as a ground of permissible restriction of the right to freedom of expression under art. 10(1) ECHR and consequentially should be selectively protected. Should the Court authoritatively establish this to be the case, one is led to conclude that legal persons cannot engage the right. Indeed, while on the one hand stating that private life includes activities of a professional or business nature, the Court has so far preferred to protect companies under other aspects of art. 8 ECHR, namely home and correspondence. One could of course argue that the personal integrity of the leading persons within the company could be attributed to it for the purpose of enabling it to sue under art. 8 ECHR. As will be seen below, however, the proper approach to attribution is to confine it to remedies, a topic we will now turn to.

D Corporate Remedies

1 Direct Non-Pecuniary Loss

9/6 Whereas English courts invoke the same considerations at the *remedies* stage, namely, the protective scope of the remedial tool and the nature of the wronged, this is not the case with Strasbourg courts, the result being that companies are deemed to be capable of stress, frustration and other forms of non-pecuniary loss peculiar to natural persons. Parliament in England at one point also sought to presume that companies had feelings (so as to award them aggravated damages). However, it was forced to make a hasty retreat and rightly so. First, the approach offends the primary proposition that corporations lack real anthropomorphic features. The law has not furnished them with a body, mind or emotions not only because they are beyond the basic requirements necessary and proper for a company to possess to enable it to carry into effect its goals but also because such an application would require an undue stretch of the imagination. Second, it is inconsistent with the EctHR's own case law (at the merits stage) of denying companies rights under certain provisions on the basis of incompatibility of the right and subject and with its practice of attributing to the company the non-pecuniary harm experienced by its human components for the purpose of awarding it damages for non-pecuniary loss (nos. 9/12–9/15).

9/7   An identification of non-pecuniary loss as requiring interference in the bodily, mental, emotional and/or personality spheres leads one to question other aspects of the Court's approach: in particular, that of awarding such damages for the inordinate length of proceedings under art. 6 ECHR and its resort to a mere finding of a violation as just satisfaction for the non-pecuniary loss suffered by a corporate applicant. As to the former, in no legal system are such delays traditionally remedied by damages for non-pecuniary loss, even in the case of natural persons. One's suspicions are roused further by the fact that the tabular assessment is based on elements such as the duration of the trial, the number of tiers of proceedings and the complexity of the case, before being adjusted in light of the local economic circumstances in the respondent State. Of course, protracted proceedings may result in injury to reputation, or distress in the case of natural persons, but where the award is purely for the excessivity of the length of the proceedings alone it is difficult to see what aspect of the assessment corresponds to non-pecuniary loss.

9/8   As for a finding of a violation as just satisfaction this appears to be a form of restitution in kind, an institution that is accepted as an alternative to damages in some Continental legal systems and indeed, one that takes precedence over damages. Bydlinski's conclusion that a finding as just satisfaction seeks to grant emotional satisfaction for the vexation caused by the denial of rights is sustainable in the case of natural victims. It also accords with the Commission's stance that corporate applicants are capable of injury to feelings and with the Court's rulings in like direction, but such conclusions lead to an absurdity. Given the absence of interference in the bodily, mental or emotional spheres, there is no difficulty in theory in accepting that the Court is in fact compensating injury to personality. The problem one encounters with that proposition, however, is that not all violations impact upon personality rights, especially in the case of legal persons, unless one takes the route that violations of all Convention rights are an affront to personality in a loose sense. That, however, fails to take into account that a violation does not always result in the Court stating that its finding constitutes just satisfaction as regards the non-pecuniary loss found (or in an award of damages for non-pecuniary loss).

9/9   It may well be that the Court is compensating unquantifiable pecuniary loss. While such losses are also difficult to calculate, they are not 'non-pecuniary' in the absence of interference in at least one of the above spheres. An alternative view, in so far as art. 6 ECHR is concerned, is that such so-called 'damages for non-pecuniary loss' are in fact punitive – a conclusion consistent with the fact that length of judicial proceedings has most occupied the Strasbourg Court in quantitative terms and could well benefit from deterrence: the primary goal of punitive damages. If this is indeed the case, there is nothing conceptually wrong with corporations receiving pecuniary or punitive damages except that a change in terminology would be conducive to consistency and clarity. Continental lawyers may, however, feel distinctly uneasy about the apparent importation of punitive damages into their legal systems by the back door.

9/10   It may well be the company's human components the Court has regard to in ensuring satisfaction via its judgment. One cannot simply disregard the fact, however, that the attribution doctrine of *Comingersoll,* which we will return to shortly (nos. 9/12–9/15), was conceived long *after* the Court devised this non-intrusive remedy. Then again, it takes time before inchoate legal concepts and propositions are expounded and labelled. That minor 'subjective' damages for non-pecuniary loss experienced by the company's components is the underlying, albeit unarticulated, rationale behind the judges' approach cannot be ruled out, therefore. A particularly convincing justification is that the EctHR is seeking to give tangible recognition – via its transcript – of the value and importance of the complainant's fundamental rights by issuing such a judgment. Even if that is the case, since specific reference is made to damages for non-pecuniary loss, the Court should at least be able to point to non-pecuniary interference. Several rationales, some more convincing than others, may therefore motivate the EctHR's approaches.

9/11   While it is self-evidently impossible for companies to suffer interference in the bodily, mental or emotional spheres, they have separate legal personality and a vested interest in protecting aspects of such personality. There is therefore no reason why companies should be denied protection of their reputation to the extent that the compensation awarded does not conflict with the internal logic of personality rights on the one hand and the *legal person* on the other. Since defamation is not *primarily* concerned with 'subjective' consequences of a statement, injury to feelings is *only parasitic* upon the action. The main point of such proceedings is vindication of injured reputation, i.e. a threat to one's position in society; such a threat can affect both natural and legal persons. In any case this aspect of the injury is remedied through *objective* damages for non-pecuniary loss. Only natural persons are entitled to damages for injury to feelings occasioned by the defamation; i.e. *subjective* damages for non-pecuniary loss. English judges are thus to be fully supported for recognising that corporate reputation is not merely an interest of a proprietary character (cf goodwill), despite the potential implications of s. 1(2) Defamation Act 2013, and that a company should therefore be entitled to damages for non-pecuniary loss for interference with the non-proprietary aspects of its personality.

2   Indirect Non-Pecuniary Loss

9/12   Perhaps the most dynamic development of the Strasbourg Court's case law in this field is its practice of imputing to companies forms of suffering, e.g. uncertainty, disruption, anxiety and frustration, experienced by the individuals within them with an eye to assessing the company's damages for non-pecuniary loss. The attribution doctrine is garnering support from various courts (in Italy and Switzerland), international tribunals and academics (among them Burrows, Fellner and Koziol). It is an approach that is characteristic of the Court's firmness in its attempt to produce practical and effective outcomes. Though counter-intuitive, attribution has it merits. First, it is inescapable that a wrongdoer's actions impose additional responsibilities and cause consequent strain on individuals within the company. Second, the principle promotes the legitimate objective of equality. If logically worked out, the incorporeal nature of the corporation would abolish its liability. To overcome this, the law adopts the position that a company, which achieves its objects through natural persons, is liable for the tortious activities of those individuals in the same way a natural person would be for the acts of his agents or employees. In the case of such vicarious liability, no blame or culpability for an act or omission on the part of the employer is required. Liability is strict in the sense that the latter stands in its employee's shoes. Some rules, however, may be premised on culpability, thus requiring personal fault or stated in other language primarily applicable to a natural person. To exempt a company from liability would mean they would 'fare better' than their human counterparts (no. 7/6). Rather than conclude that such rules are not intended to apply them, the law sees no difficulty in attributing the required element from natural persons within the company so as to hold it *liable*. When it comes to the *capacity to be the subject of a legal right and remedy*, while the law could have again looked to such natural persons and conferred upon it as broad a right and remedy base as it does a liability base, it has not gone so far. Rather, a company's rights and remedies are determined by attributes appropriate to its form. As Fellner notes, parity would be upheld if attribution did not only apply to a company's *detriment* but also in its *favour* (no. 7/7).

9/13   Since it is a company's directors that are responsible for its day-to-day running, it is normally they who are equated with the actions of the company whenever the company's personal culpability is at issue. The weight of this very responsibility means it is invariably they who suffer the brunt of a wrong against the company, especially in light of the increasingly demanding duties that they owe to their company. Given the need for harmony between the attribution of misbehaviour to the company and the mirror rule of attributing non-pecuniary loss, it is the non-pecuniary disturbances to directors (and in their absence managers) that should be relevant for the purpose of assessing the company's compensation. An *objective* assessment by means of *prima facie* evidence of a reasonable person in the company's position would avoid difficulties associated with multiple directorships, the various types of directors and the varying degrees of responsibilities expected of persons carrying out particular directorial functions within the company. As the violation is against the company, such damages for attributed non-pecuniary harm cannot be claimed by its directors way of internal recourse against the company.

9/14   A further limitation arising from the fact that the violation is against the company is that directors also do not have standing to sue for damages for distress, frustration, etc., resulting from a third-party's violation of their company's rights. As such, such losses currently lie where they fall in most jurisdictions. Just like attribution for the purpose of establishing personal culpability seeks to protect victims, attributed non-pecuniary harm also aims at a practical remedy for the injured company and crucially it seeks to deter those who might otherwise be prepared to provoke corporate breaches. A further compelling case is the desirability of promoting clear and consistent legal reasoning. Acknowledging attribution alleviates courts of the need to hide behind their true motives, thus distorting the law. It is true of course that attribution for the sake of establishing personal culpability is not a true mirror application of that for the purpose of redress. However, any perceived bias in favour of companies caused by the application of the theory is outweighed on careful inspection (nos. 7/22–7/26). Ultimately, attribution is always driven by considerations of 'context' and 'purpose'. Would rationality and justice be frustrated if denied (no. 7/26)? The question can only properly be addressed having weighed all relevant considerations and by reference to the fundamental principles governing the legal system in question. In the case of the EctHR, with limited remedial powers, the context and purpose in and for which attribution is invoked is justifiable. The need for the Convention to be interpreted and applied in such a way as to guarantee rights that are practical and effective is clearly an overriding consideration.

9/15   While attribution for the purpose of establishing personal culpability results in the company's liability, limiting its mirror application to remedies and not rights seems proper: first, since directors have autonomously protected rights and second, since the company is only liable for torts committed by them in connection with its affairs. As mentioned earlier (nos. 7/24 and 9/5), it would therefore be wrong in the context of art. 8 ECHR to impute to a company the personal integrity of its directors with a view to granting it standing to complain about attacks upon its reputation. Also where a breach is not generally compensated by non-pecuniary remedies in the case of natural persons (e.g. in the case of economic torts), it would be wrong to compensate companies.

Finally, where the damages in question aim to remedy an affront to dignity – aggravated damages, for example – it would not be appropriate for the court to accede to a company's request. This is because dignity is too autonomous an interest to attribute.

III   Conclusion

9/16   Decision-makers are faced with various competing considerations and it is to be expected that having weighed all material considerations, different judges may legitimately arrive at different answers. The conclusion reached here is that there is still much to work out in so far as the scope and application of the attribution theory is concerned. What is clear, however, is that legal systems stand to learn from one another, and in the words of the one-time President of the European Court of Human Rights 'such dialogue can only serve to cement a relationship between'[1] national and EctHR courts.

---

[1] N. Bratza, 'The Relationship between the UK Courts and Strasbourg', *European Human Rights Law Review*, 5 (2011), 505–512, 512.

CPSIA information can be obtained
at www.ICGtesting.com
Printed in the USA
LVHW050008080119
603029LV00023B/384/P